The Two Pragmatisms

The Pragmatist tradition in philosophy has, through the work of Richard Rorty, recently achieved a status until now has not been accorded to its founder, Charles Sanders Peirce. Much of Peirce's work and his life has remained hidden and little explored, status instead lying with William James, who is known to have misinterpreted Peirce's work.

The Two Pragmatisms: From Peirce to Rorty maps out the changing status and key ideas of the Pragmatist movement explaining the diverging paths of the 'Two Pragmatisms' from Peirce's pioneering work on the theory of signs, to Rorty's seminal writings on the 'mirror of nature'. The Realism of Peirce is contrasted with the anti-Realism that characterises much of the contemporary writing on Pragmatism. The work of Rorty in particular is used to explain the importance of Pragmatism today, in particular through his debt to Dewey, whom he has described as one of the three most important philosophers of the century.

The Two Pragmatisms: From Peirce to Rorty is a clear account of a philosophical movement that cannot be ignored, and should be read by anyone with an interest in contemporary philosophy.

H. O. Mounce lectures in philosophy at the University of Wales, Swansea. He is the author of *Wittgenstein's Tractatus: An Introduction*.

The Two Pragmatisms

From Peirce to Rorty

H. O. Mounce

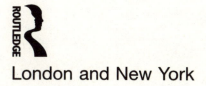

London and New York

First published 1997
by Routledge
11 New Fetter Lane, London EC4P 4EE

Simultaneously published in the USA and Canada
by Routledge
29 West 35th Street, New York, NY 10001

Typeset in Baskerville by Routledge
Printed and bound in Great Britain by
T J Press (Padstow) Ltd, Padstow, Cornwall

British Library Cataloguing in Publication Data
A catalogue record for this book is available from the British Library

Library of Congress Cataloguing in Publication Data
Mounce, H. O.
The two pragmatisms: from Peirce to Rorty / H. O. Mounce.
Includes bibliographical references and index.
1. Pragmatism – History. 2. Pragmatism. 3. Peirce, Charles S. (Charles
Sanders), 1839–1914. 4. Rorty, Richard. I. Title. B832.M686 1996
144'.3–dc2096–21878
CIP

ISBN 0–415–15282–8 (hbk)
ISBN 0–415–15283–6 (pbk)

To the memory of Gwyneth and Joseph Mounce

Contents

Acknowledgements

I should like to express my gratitude to Ian Tipton and Helen Baldwin, the former for the care with which he read this work in manuscript, the latter for the skill with which she prepared it for publication. My greatest debt is to my wife who was a continual source of strength during the time when the work was written.

Introduction

Pragmatism is the distinctively American philosophy. The history of philosophy in America, before the end of the nineteenth century, is usually divided into three periods. The first is dominated by Christianity in its Calvinist form. The main figure here is Jonathan Edwards, who wrote a masterly work on the freedom of the will. Edwards is one of the greatest American philosophers, but the problems he tackled had their origin in European thought. In theology he was a follower of Calvin. Calvin's scientific views belonged to the medieval period. Edwards was familiar with the scientific and philosophical views which arose out of the Newtonian system. One of his main aims was to show that the truth of Calvinism remained unaffected by this great revolution in European thought. The second period is dominated by the Transcendentalists, who may be roughly characterised by saying that they attempted to preserve the spiritual and moral values of the Calvinists whilst rejecting their dogmas. Here again there is a strong European influence. The thought of Emerson, for example, though distinctive in expression, derives its substance from German Idealism and from the Romantic movement more generally. The third period is dominated by Pragmatism. Here, for the first time, the direction of influence is reversed. Pragmatism is not a body of thought which arose in Europe and then was extended to America; it is one which arose in America and then was extended to Europe.

The classic works of Pragmatism were written by C. S. Peirce, William James and John Dewey. But it was James who made Pragmatism famous. He was a philosopher who had exceptional powers of expression and, in the early years of the century, he was widely read in Europe. In this way, Pragmatism became a leading topic of discussion. In Britain, it had an advocate in F. C. S. Schiller; in France, it was developed in an original way by G. Sorel. After James's death, it continued to be a leading doctrine, largely through the influence of John Dewey and his colleague G. H. Mead, who applied it, in a powerful way, in social psychology. It lost influence during the middle decades of the century with many philosophers, first in Europe, then America, turning towards Logical Positivism, but it never entirely lost its hold on American philosophy. It began to revive in the 1950s, when Quine advanced a view which was in some respects akin to it. In our own day, it may be said to flourish, being defended by such leading American philosophers as Hilary Putnam and Richard Rorty.

Now one of the main aims of this study is to show that if we reflect on its development we shall find that Pragmatism has not had a single form. As we have seen, it was James who made Pragmatism famous, but the doctrine has its origin in the work of C. S. Peirce. Both men were opposed to those forms of scientism which arose in the nineteenth century and were variously known as Scientific Rationalism or Materialism or Positivism. As I hope to show, however, Pragmatism was transformed during the present century into a version of that scientism to which both men were opposed. This was possible because, in important respects, James misunderstood Peirce's views so that the Pragmatism he developed was not the one developed by Peirce himself. In effect, there were two Pragmatisms. Moreover the Pragmatism adopted by James lent itself easily to that transformation which it is an aim of this study to describe. In describing it, we may hope to distinguish what is of permanent value in Pragmatism and also to throw light on some of the most important developments in twentieth-century philosophy.

Chapter 1

Peirce: his background and his account of inquiry

Charles Sanders Peirce was born in 1839 in Cambridge, Massachusetts. His father, Benjamin Peirce, taught at Harvard, being professor there of mathematics and astronomy. At this time, Harvard was already one of the world's leading centres of learning and Benjamin Peirce, one of its most prominent figures, exerted a great influence in America on the development of mathematics, and of science more generally. Charles was a favourite with his father, who developed his ability in mathematics and fostered in him a love of science and philosophy. Given the brilliance of his gifts, and his father's influence, Charles Peirce might have been expected within his lifetime to become famous and influential himself. In fact, when judged by that standard, his life was a signal failure. He held only one academic post, being appointed in 1876 as a lecturer in logic at the John Hopkins University. As a teacher, he was a success, but after about five years he was dismissed from his post in circumstances which were never disclosed to the public. For some thirty years, he worked for the United States Coast and Geodetic Survey, where he made some important contributions to the science of measurement. However, his work seems not to have been fully appreciated and in 1891 he was forced to resign. By this time he had written a number of philosophical articles, some of great brilliance, although they had not been appreciated outside a small circle. In 1891, he retired to Milford, Pennsylvania, where he continued to work at his philosophy, being supported by a dwindling inheritance, occasional lectures and writings, and eventually the charity of his friends. His writings during this period were voluminous but he never succeeded in working them into a book. He died in poverty in 1914.

Peirce exhibited in his life the sort of disorder which one associates more readily with an artist of the Romantic or Bohemian period than with a philosopher and scientist. It was only very recently, some eighty years after his death, that he received a full biography (see Brent 1993). This is not an accident. Some of the most important aspects of his life were not easily accessible to a biographer, for they had been judged too scandalous to disclose. It was clear, however, that many of the difficulties in his life were due to faults in his own character. Many thought him arrogant and contentious, he had difficulty in submitting to authority, his lifestyle was thought extravagant or unconventional, and there were rumours of drug addiction and alcoholism. He had no head for practical affairs – for example, for many years he believed that he could remove his financial difficulties by speculating in business ventures. His belief was that a man of his intelligence could easily make a fortune in business, should he put his mind to it. Repeated failure did not cure him of this delusion.

It is possible, however, that much of the instability in his life had medical causes. Joseph Brent has revealed that Peirce inherited from his father a form of nervous disease known as trigeminal neuralgia. This disorder, known in the nineteenth century as facial neuralgia, is marked by acute pain affecting one or more of the three branches of the fifth cranial nerve on either side of the face. The pain may be triggered by a variety of causes, such as stress, a cold wind or a touch on the face, and may occur every few minutes for several days or even weeks. It is said that there are few ailments which give rise to greater suffering. There was no treatment for this disease in the nineteenth century. To relieve their suffering both Charles and his father resorted to the use of ether and opium. It is likely that in this way Charles became addicted to drugs, resorting later to the use of morphia and cocaine. Instability in temperament is not difficult to understand in someone who suffers from such a disease. Peirce's friends and colleagues noted that he was subject to startling changes of mood. Sometimes he would be charming company, cheerful, pleasant, considerate; at other times he would be cold, suspicious, impatient of the slightest crossing and given to violent outbursts of temper. It is difficult to believe that this instability was not caused in large part by his nervous disorder.

Peirce's work stands to his life in poignant and mysterious contrast. There was no instability in his love of inquiry which, through the disorder of his life, he pursued with unremitting tenacity of purpose. In his writing there is nothing of violence or contentiousness. Rather, he appears as his friends and colleagues remembered him when he was at his best. He lacks the instinctive grip on the reader's attention which one finds in his great contemporary William James. But that is often because of the purity of his interest. He loses the reader because he has become absorbed in his subject and forgets his audience. Moreover, the sense of order, which was lacking in his life, is everywhere expressed and celebrated in his work. He held that the truth is what remains when one eliminates from one's work everything that is merely personal, arbitrary or individual. He found an ideal of inquiry in the work of the medieval scholastics and he thought that the best of modern science was conducted in the same spirit. This was a view which divided him sharply from his contemporaries and from the later Pragmatists, who tended to think that serious inquiry had begun only at the Renaissance. But in Peirce's love of the scholastics there was no trace of sentimentality or nostalgia. He loved them not because they were medieval but because they expressed values that are permanent. These values he describes in prose of remarkable purity.

> The men of that time did fully believe and did think that, for the sake of giving themselves up absolutely to the great task of building or writing, it was well worth while to resign all the joys of life. Think of the spirit in which Duns Scotus must have worked, who wrote his thirteen volumes in folio, in a style as condensed as the most condensed parts of Aristotle, before the age of thirty-four. Nothing is more striking in either of the great intellectual products of that age, than the complete absence of self-conceit on the part of the artist or philosopher. That anything of value can be added to his sacred and catholic work by its having the smack of individuality about it, is what he has never conceived. His work is not designed to embody *his* ideas, but the universal truth; there will not be one thing in it however minute, for which you will not find that he has his authority; and whatever originality emerges is of that inborn kind which so saturates a man that he cannot himself perceive it. The individual feels his own worthlessness in comparison with his task, and does not dare to introduce his vanity into the doing of it. Then there is no machine-work, no unthinking repetition about the thing. Every part is worked out for itself as a separate problem, no matter how analogous it may be in general to another part. And no matter how small and hidden a detail may be, it has been conscientiously studied, as though it were intended for the eye of God.[1]

In tracing the influences on Peirce's philosophy, it will be important to begin with the views of his father. Benjamin Peirce was a Unitarian, but in his views of philosophy and religion he had certain assumptions in common with thinkers in the Calvinist tradition. The greatest figure in this tradition was Jonathan Edwards, who developed a form of

Absolute Idealism, superficially similar to the Idealism of Berkeley, but developed independently and based on different considerations. The Idealism of Edwards arose from his reflection on the Newtonian system which he accepted, indeed admired, but which in one important respect seemed in conflict with the Calvinist view of the world – namely, that God is the omnipotent power who governs the world in all its details. On the Newtonian system, or so it seemed, the world originated in God but thereafter proceeded independently, being governed in its workings by its inherent laws. Edwards became convinced that this conflict between the two systems was merely apparent and that it would disappear once it was realised that the validity of the Newtonian system was not absolute, as was commonly thought, but merely approximate or relative. He was led to this conclusion by his noting that the central ideas in the system could be defined only in relative terms. The notion of mass, for example, is indistinguishable from what attracts or resists. But these are relations. What is the substance which supports those relations? The world as it appears in the Newtonian system is relative to a substance which never appears in the system itself. For Edwards, that substance is God. In many passages, often of haunting beauty, Edwards portrays the objects of the physical universe as shadows of divine reality. They are shadows because they lack substance when taken in themselves, and yet, when properly understood, they can disclose what makes them real. In this they are like signs or symbols. Thus Edwards portrays the world, also, as a network of signs, which mediate between God and ourselves and are therefore, when properly understood, a revelation of God himself. For Edwards, the Newtonian system, when taken as absolute, gives to the universe a false appearance of substance. It then appears as opaque and meaningless. But our signs and symbols are likewise mere matter, opaque and meaningless, unless taken in their workings. Now consider, not the objects in themselves but their workings within the Newtonian system and at once there appears law or order, which is nowhere explicable within the system itself. The objects themselves are real only within the order of the world which is itself a reflection of the divine order. And science, for Edwards, is valuable as a study of that order. Thus taken, it is valuable, not primarily for its practical utility, but as a source of religious contemplation.

This last view is one that was shared by Benjamin Peirce. 'There is but one God', he said, 'and science is the knowledge of Him' (see Murphey 1993: 13). God he spoke of as the 'Divine Geometer'; nature was the expression of his wisdom and science, the means by which that wisdom might be understood. Benjamin Peirce, however, was not an

Idealist. He held that mind and matter were sharply to be distinguished. The harmony between them he took to be pre-established by the will of God. The harmony was such, however, that it guaranteed a correspondence between our ideas and reality. He believed that every theorem in mathematics was realised somewhere in nature and that nature as a whole was but the realisation of mathematical ideas. Consequently, the discovery of reality in scientific investigation was not simply a possibility; it was a religious duty. This he supported by a view which had an influence on his son. Since the harmony between mind and matter was pre-ordained, all investigators, given adequate time, must come to the same conclusion. 'The conclusion in every department of science is essentially the same. Whatever may have been the play of fancy, or the delusion of superstition, or the allurement of profit, at the outset, the end has ever been a congregation of facts, organised under law, and disciplined by geometry' (ibid.: 15).

C. S. Peirce's thought cannot be properly understood unless it is appreciated that it belongs to the family of ideas which has just been sketched. It belongs, in short, to the tradition of American thought which flourished until the end of the nineteenth century and which had its origin in European traditions that extend back to the Greeks. Peirce's work, and indeed that of James, can in fact be seen as an attempt to preserve that tradition, by discriminating what is sound in science whilst rejecting its sceptical implications. In one important respect, however, Peirce differed from his father. He rejected his radical dualism and came, like Jonathan Edwards, to accept a form of Objective Idealism. Jonathan Edwards and C. S. Peirce, the two greatest American philosophers, are therefore akin, not simply in power of intellect but also in their fundamental views.[2]

It was Kant, however, who first stimulated Peirce to philosophical work. He said that when he was in his twenties he was one of Kant's devotees. What is of central importance in Kant's thought is the idea that sensory experience is permeated with order. This order cannot be grasped independently of sense experience but neither can it be derived from sense experience itself. For example, our idea of existence involves the concepts of space and time, for every object exists in some spatial and temporal relation to some other. The concepts of space and time are empty unless grasped as relations among the objects which appear in sense-experience. Concepts without sense intuitions are empty. But the concepts of space and time cannot be derived from our sense experiences themselves. For example, unless we could already distinguish one sensation as earlier or later than another, we could grasp no order amongst them and then we would lack any conception not simply of the world but even of our own sensations. Sensory intuitions without concepts are blind.

'Produce an after-image of the sun', says William James, 'and look at your finger tip; it will be smaller than your nail. Project it on the table, and it will be as big as a strawberry; on the wall, as large as a plate; on yonder mountain, bigger than a house. And yet it is an unchanged retinal impression' (see Kemp Smith 1924: 116).

The image of the sun varies according to its surrounding field. This is not done by conscious reasoning. The moon at the horizon, against a background which includes trees and houses, appears larger than it does at the zenith. Most people know it is not in fact larger but they still see it as such. Nor can this be explained by the stimulation of the retina. 'When we look at the moon through a telescope, the moon stimulates an extent of retina many times larger than when we look at it with the naked eye, and yet it is a smaller, not a larger, moon that is then apprehended' (ibid.: 116). The world in sense experience appears already interpreted as though by signs or symbols. It is not that we receive sense experience and then interpret what is given. Press your hand against a table and you are immediately aware of the object which resists it. You could not feel the table without the sensations in your hand but you do not first receive the sensations and then infer the existence of the table. Rather, indeed, it is the other way around. For you almost certainly cannot tell what sensations occurred in your hand, so that to find out you would have to repeat the process and note what sensations occur in your hand when you are aware of the table. The sensations call attention not to themselves but to what they signify. Thus, in the given context, their function may be likened to that of signs or symbols. As we shall see, Peirce became convinced that it is through signs or symbols that all our knowledge of the world is mediated.

Kant's account works against those given earlier both by the Rationalists and by the Empiricists. The Rationalists, who believe that our concepts arise through the workings of pure reason, cannot explain how those concepts get back into sense experience. The Empiricists, who believe that concepts arise as the result of sense experience, cannot explain how sense experience is intelligible in the first place. Neither appreciate that sense experience is already permeated with order. It is true that Kant expresses this view in different and inconsistent ways. For example, he sometimes speaks, in the manner of the Rationalists, as though the experiences which occur to the mind have no order until the mind stamps its own order upon them. This would suggest that order is generated entirely by the human mind, independently of its relation to the world. But that is certainly not the view which appears in the most profound sections of the *Critique*. In these sections, it is evident that there is order in the mind only because it partakes of an order which is independent of it. The point may be illustrated by reference to the section on the refutation of Idealism. The Idealism to which Kant refers is *subjective*. It is of the greatest importance to distinguish this from the Idealism held by Edwards and by Peirce. Their Idealism is *objective* and is compatible with the most thoroughgoing Realism. It holds that the world is constituted by an order which is mental in character but which is quite independent of the *human* mind. Subjective Idealism, by contrast, holds that the only object of which I can be immediately certain is my *own* mind. This view leads easily into solipsism. For how can I be certain that anything exists independently of my mind? The view rests, however, on an evident presupposition. It presupposes that my conception of the world and of myself is subjective in origin. That indeed is why the only object of which I can be immediately certain is my own mind. For it is a contingent matter whether anything corresponds to my conception of the world, but it is entirely certain that I do have this conception and therefore I do exist. Now Kant denied the presupposition. In purely subjective terms, there is no concept of the world. Without an objective order, I should lack the concept not simply of what is objective but also of what is *subjective*. The subjective is distinguished only against the background of the objective. I have a concept of myself only as distinguishable from what is *not* myself. This, again, is a view which had a great influence on Peirce.

A further consequence follows from Kant's views. At a fundamental level, there is no difference between logic and phenomenology, between the forms in which we think about the world and the way the world appears. In the way the world appears to us there is already present the fundamental forms of our thought. For the forms of logic simply make explicit those forms without which there would be no world for us. Kant assumed, somewhat too readily, that logical forms were already exhaustively displayed in Aristotelian logic and on the basis of this logic he derived the fundamental forms of thought, distinguishing twelve categories, in addition to the forms of space and time. Peirce was profoundly influenced by this enterprise, but he soon decided that the twelve categories could be reduced to three, which he called First, Second and Third. As we shall see, these categories are intimately connected with his analysis of the relation between sign and signified, which, he argued, is triadic in form. Peirce retained the three categories throughout the developments in his thought but they underwent considerable changes in their contents. For this, there were various reasons. One of the most obvious was that he changed his mind about the status of Aristotelian logic. Being one of the finest logicians of his century, he was acquainted at an early stage with developments in the logic of relations, which showed that there were forms of inference that could not be reduced to those in Aristotle. This persuaded him that the Kantian system contained fundamental difficulties; the consequences of this we shall consider later.

There was, however, one important feature of Kant's system which Peirce rejected before he became acquainted with the logic of relations. Kant distinguishes between the world in its phenomenal aspect, as it appears to the human mind, and as it exists in itself, out of relation to the human mind. For Kant, the world as it exists in itself, which he called the noumenal world, is essentially unknowable. Peirce was persuaded that the idea of what is essentially unknowable is a confused one. In this, he might well have been influenced by Kant's immediate successors in the German tradition, and especially by Hegel, the most famous of these. Hegel had a celebrated argument which he directed against Kant's attempt to limit knowledge to the phenomenal. The argument is that to draw a limit, one needs to know what lies on both sides of it. It follows that to draw a limit to knowledge, one needs to know what lies on the other side of that limit. But if one knows what lies on the other side, it cannot be a limit to knowledge. In short, nothing in principle is unknowable. This argument had an immense influence, being, for example, a main support of that Positivism which itself accumulated such an immense influence in the course of the nineteenth century. Indeed its effect is to turn Kant himself into a Positivist. For his views are compatible with Positivism, once one removes from them all reference to the noumenal. Nevertheless Hegel's argument is in fact fallacious. It rests on an equivocation in the words 'drawing a limit', which are ambiguous between acknowledging a limit and bringing one into existence. One who brings about a limit, where none before existed, presumably knows what lies on either side of the limit he draws. It is evident, however, that Kant was not in that sense drawing a limit. Rather he was acknowledging one that existed in the nature of the case. To acknowledge a limit one certainly does not need to know what lies on either side of it. If my garden runs into a brick wall, I know it has its limit. I do not need to know what is on the other side of the wall. Hegel's argument has its variations. For example, it is sometimes said that in drawing a limit, Kant is implicitly claiming to know that there is something on the other side. But he cannot know this if what he draws is a limit to knowledge. This argument also is fallacious. One may have sufficient evidence on one's own side of a limit to know there is something on the other, without having sufficient evidence to know what that something is. Kant would contradict himself only if he claimed to know *what* lies on the other side. But it is evident that he claimed nothing of the sort.

In accepting Hegel's view, Peirce caused himself grave difficulties. In order to appreciate his mature thought, it will be useful to consider these difficulties and to consider also how he extricated himself from them. In accepting Hegel's view, Peirce was accepting, in effect, that nothing exists except in relation to the human mind. In this idea there is already a tendency towards Anti-Realism or Subjective Idealism. This tendency was reinforced by another in Peirce's early thought. As we have suggested, he became convinced that knowledge is mediated through signs or symbols. In a sense, to see is to interpret. At first, however, he construed all interpretation on the model of conscious inference or hypothesis. Now it seems natural to contrast inference or hypothesis with immediate perception or awareness of the world. Indeed it seems natural to suppose that inference or hypothesis requires immediate perception or awareness if it is to be checked or confirmed. But in Peirce's early work there is no such contrast. Immediate perception or awareness, on closer analysis, is itself inference or hypothesis. It follows that an inference or hypothesis can be checked only by another and that only by another, and so on *ad infinitum*. It is now difficult to see how one can have any contact with the world. The scepticism inherent in this position can be avoided, or so it seems, only by adopting some form of Anti-Realism or Subjective Idealism. One has to suppose that nothing exists independently of its being interpreted by the human mind. But that route was blocked for Peirce by his instinctive preference for Realism. In all his work, Peirce holds that Realism, in some form, is a necessity of thought. At this stage, Peirce's work is in a state of acute tension. He attempts to extricate himself from his difficulties by falling back on a view of his father's. As we have seen, his father held that all investigations have a tendency to converge on a final conclusion. Now the final conclusion is, of course, independent of what you or I happen to think here and now. On the other hand, it is not independent of human thought or experience in general. Peirce attempted to solve his difficulties by identifying the Real with the final conclusion to which all investigations converge. In that way he could hold, along with Hegel, that the Real does not transcend human thought or experience, whilst retaining a measure of Realism, in so far as the Real transcends what you or I happen to think here and now.

For reasons we shall consider later, this compromise proved unsustainable. Peirce was finally extricated from his difficulties in the 1880s,[3] when he came to see the error in his construing all interpretation on the model of conscious inference or hypothesis. He then adopted a view hardly distinguishable from that held by the Scottish philosophers of Common Sense.[4] Thomas Reid, for example, like Peirce, held that sensations may be likened to signs. Reid insisted however that the signs were *natural*. They were not set up nor were they worked by conscious reasoning. The processes involved in sensory experience are of course complex but they belong to psychology rather than to epistemology. The *knowledge* involved in sensory experience is given *immediately*, not by inference from sensory experience itself. By the 1890s, Peirce was stating similar views quite explicitly. Referring to the processes involved in sensory experience he says:

> Such inferences are beyond the jurisdiction of criticism. It is the part of psychology to explain their processes as it can; but, as long as they are out of the focal plane of consciousness, they are out of our control; and to call them good or bad were idle. The ordinary business of life is, however, best conducted without too much self-criticism. . . .
>
> (Murphey 1993: 360)

Around the same time, Peirce revised his categories, introducing as the second category what he called haecceity. This is a scholastic term signifying the experience of brute reaction to what is independent of oneself. The effect of this is to introduce into his philosophy that contact with reality which had hitherto been lacking. He retained the idea of convergence as a mark of the truth. One may take as true that opinion on which independent investigations converge. But that is because the best explanation for the convergence of investigations that are genuinely independent is that they are guided by what is independent of themselves and therefore are in contact with the real. Here it is not convergence which explains the real. Rather it is the independence of the real which explains why convergence is a mark of truth.

Moreover, as we shall see, these developments in Peirce's thinking serve to clarify elements that are essential to his Pragmatism. Thus in the above quotation, he is distinguishing, in effect, between those interpretations which are mediated through the body in its relation to the world and conscious inference or hypothesis, as it is found, for example, in science. He is implicitly distinguishing between *practical* certainty and *theoretical* inquiry and his point is that the former is more fundamental than the latter, being for the most part immune to its criticisms. Elsewhere he says that when we first come to theoretical enquiry we are 'laden with an immense mass of cognition already formed'. Theoretical inquiry may cause us to revise some of this knowledge. But it cannot eliminate it, for then it would eliminate itself. Without the certainty of practical knowledge, we should no longer know what counts as being certain in theoretical inquiry. Indeed we should lose our grasp on meaning. For meaning is essentially practical. One grasps the meaning of a concept, not by contemplating an entity, but by acquiring a *capacity* or *habit* in handling it. Any capacity or habit is essentially *general* and therefore cannot be formulated as a set of finite instances. Meaning, in short, that it cannot be grasped by theoretical formulation; it can be acquired only in practice. These are some of the points which we must consider in detail.

INQUIRY AND THE CRITIQUE OF CARTESIANISM

We have indicated the background to Peirce's thought and have indicated, also, some of its developments. We must now consider in more detail his work itself and it will be useful to begin with some of his best known writings, the group of articles which he published during the 1860s and 1870s,[5] in which through a criticism of Cartesianism, he develops his own view of inquiry.

Peirce's view is best appreciated by contrast with those which were dominant in the previous century through the work of the Empiricists and the Rationalists. The Empiricists argued that knowledge is derived from experience. John Locke, for example, argued that the child's mind at birth is like a blank sheet of paper. It is through sense experience that the mind, initially blank, has knowledge imprinted on it.[6] The Rationalists, by contrast, claimed that knowledge is based on reason, which is innate. Nevertheless, the two schools, in spite of their differences, had one feature in common. Both took for granted that knowledge ought to be absolute, in the sense of being independent of presupposition or perspective. The point will be seen clearly if we consider the work of Descartes, normally taken to be the first of the Rationalists. Descartes framed the project of submitting all his beliefs to systematic criticism with the aim of achieving absolute certainty. In his *Meditations* he noted that many of his beliefs were held simply on the basis of authority. He had accepted them as a child through the influence of parents and teachers. He believed this to be an inadequate basis for knowledge. He therefore proposed to step, as it were, outside his beliefs and to subject them to rigorous criticism. He would hold as doubtful any of his beliefs, however inclined he might be to accept them, just so long as they could be shown, under the pressure of criticism, to fall short of complete certainty. He finds, as he proceeds, that one after another of his beliefs turns out to be doubtful. Indeed he finds some reason to doubt even the simplest and apparently most obvious of his beliefs, such as that he is sitting in front of a fire in his dressing gown. Eventually, however, he arrives at the famous proposition '*Cogito ergo sum*' (I think therefore I am). In his own existence as a thinking being, Descartes believes he has found an object of indubitable truth. The truth is indubitable since it presupposes nothing. The proposition has only to be considered to reveal its own truth. On its basis, Descartes believes he can build a system in which everything is proven and therefore known with complete certainty.

Descartes' aim then was to step outside his beliefs and to examine them without presupposition. As we have said, his conception of knowledge was in a sense absolute. The view of the Empiricists was, in this respect, very similar. Thus, as we have seen, knowledge, for Locke, is acquired by a mind initially blank. The mind is not directed by prior motive, interest or belief. Knowledge is not sought for; it arrives, imprinting itself on a mind in itself passive. What is common to both schools, one might say, is that they neglected the standpoint of the observer in the acquisition of knowledge, treating him as if he viewed the world from no particular position within it. For Peirce, on the other hand, the observer is in the midst of the world and knowledge is acquired always from some point of view or perspective. Putting the point very roughly, he replaced an absolute with a relative conception of knowledge.

Scheffler, in his book on Pragmatism, gives a simple example to illustrate Peirce's view (Scheffler 1974: 43). Consider a cat placed for the first time in a closed puzzle box. The box is constructed with a latch which opens the door when struck. Not having been fed for a while, the cat is hungry and it sees the cream which has been placed outside the door. Since it is hungry, it wants the cream, but it cannot get it. Its hunger is an irritating stimulus that spreads in its effects, producing a set of movements, a kind of thrashing about, which is virtually unordered or random. This activity continues until some movement happens to strike the latch, releasing the cat from the box and enabling it to satisfy its hunger. In subsequent trials, the activity becomes shorter, the movements less random. Finally, the cat learns to manipulate the latch in a direct and economical manner when put in the same situation again.

Here we have a concrete example of a creature's acquiring knowledge. The example is very simple; even so, it is more complex than either the Rationalist or the Empiricist view would allow. For example, sense perception, as the Empiricists would claim, had an essential place in the cat's learning. It sees the cream. But why is it the cream as opposed to some other object that it notices? Obviously it notices the cream because it is hungry. In other words, it notices the cream because its attention is already directed. Perception, in short, requires a mind not passive but active. We notice not just what is there, but what we look for; and what we look for is determined by our prior interests, needs and desires. In the same situation, people with different motives will see different things.

Again, we may affirm, with the Rationalists, that the cat's acquiring knowledge involved some power of reasoning. It *worked out* how to release the catch. But the cat's reasoning, no less than its perceiving, occurs in a context. Without its hunger, it would have no problem; without its seeking to appease its hunger, there would be nothing to count as a solution. What is at work is not reason in the abstract but a living creature seeking its ends. The cat's reasoning, in short, is as much directed as its perceiving. The cat reasons in a definite situation, the problem that arises in that situation being determined by needs or desires which have occurred in its life more generally.

Now Peirce generalised these points so that they apply as much to theoretical as to practical reasoning. All reasoning is from a point of view or perspective. Inquiry arises from doubt, which is a type of irritation, a frustration in what one believes or expects, inquiry being an attempt to remove the source of frustration and achieve a state of settled belief (see Buchler 1950: 10). But inquiry presupposes that one already has some belief or expectation; otherwise, there would have been no frustration, no impetus to inquiry. Peirce is not of course denying that one might have occasion to revise one's earlier beliefs,[7] but one cannot simultaneously revise all one's beliefs, for then one would have no means of distinguishing which beliefs are true and which false. Peirce's explicit criticisms of Descartes are first, that what he contemplates is only apparently coherent. One cannot revise all one's beliefs. For then, as we have seen, one would have no means for distinguishing which beliefs are true. Second, Descartes' doubt is not a real or living one. For example, he proposes to reject even those beliefs about which he feels no doubt, just so long as a possible doubt can be brought against them. Thus he does not *feel* doubtful about whether he is sitting in front of his fire. He merely supposes it would be possible to doubt it. But a possible doubt is not a real one. Genuine inquiry arises when someone feels a real difficulty in his beliefs. No one is required to reject a belief simply because it may be doubted but only because he does in fact doubt it. Descartes' project is in fact the merest parody of genuine inquiry, for he raises doubts that he does not really feel and attempts to solve them whilst occupying no particular position.

Pragmatism, then, as an account of inquiry, elucidates doubt or belief by relating it to the one who inquires. It treats him as in the midst of the world, viewing not the whole but some aspect of it, in the light of some body of belief, from some point of view or perspective. Now that is a view which emerges from any serious reflection on modern science. What is revealed is the need to take into account the standpoint of the observer, to remind oneself that how the world appears will depend partly on how it is but partly also on the position from which one observes it. There are any number of examples which can illustrate the point. Take as an illustration the discovery that the earth is in motion around the sun. The person who simply observes the sun will take it to be moving; it is only if he takes into account his own position in observing it that a different possibility emerges, namely, that it is only because of his position that it appears to move. He may then conclude that what is moving is not the sun but his position relative to it. He arrives at this conclusion because he has widened his perspective. He is now considering not simply the sun but his own position in relation to it, a perspective which enables him the better to understand both his own position and the sun.

The same point may as easily be illustrated by referring to our knowledge of ordinary objects. Of any object, we know more than can be obtained from a single perspective; indeed we should attribute to any object features which exist independently of its being observed at all. Whether or not it is observed, it reflects light, resists other objects, and so on. It would evidently be foolish, however, to suppose that we obtain this knowledge from no perspective whatever; evidently we obtain it by adopting a variety of perspectives. For example, we walk around the object, viewing it from different angles. Our knowledge of the object is what we have compiled in noting from various perspectives how it appears. Indeed if we attribute to objects features that exist independently of its being observed, it is because, by so doing, we best explain how it appears from more than one perspective. For example, we explain how it appears differently at different times by supposing that something has occurred to it in between. In other words, scientific inquiry proceeds by moving from one perspective to another, and it gropes towards a more general view of things by adopting a perspective wider still. It does not begin with a general view of the world, with a total perspective, and then proceed to fill in the details. Rather it begins with the details, with a limited perspective, and attempts to grope outwards.

The above point may be illustrated by considering Peirce's analysis of the three fundamental forms of inference: deduction, induction and abduction. Induction is the process whereby we generalise on the basis of a number of instances. Having seen many black ravens, we conclude that all ravens are black. At the time when Peirce wrote, it was widely believed that this was the basic process in science. Peirce denied this, arguing that induction serves not to initiate theory but rather to test it. The basic process in initiating theory he called abduction or hypothetical inference. His point may be illustrated by reference to the atomic theory of matter. Scientists did not arrive at this theory by seeing in a number of cases that matter has an atomic structure and then concluding that all matter has this structure. In the ordinary sense, they never saw the atomic structure of matter. Rather, they began with a problem. For example, a solid object may be compressed. You can make it occupy less space without its losing any of its matter. There is nothing in ordinary experience which explains this. The scientist frames a theory that the matter of the object has gaps in it, though this is not detectable at the phenomenal level. In short, he frames an atomic theory of matter. Compression can now be explained. When force is exerted on the object, the atoms which comprise its matter move more closely together. It may be noted that this theory satisfies the intellect rather than the senses, being adopted for intellectual considerations rather than merely empirical ones. It is true that the senses have their part to play. For the theory must be tested at the inductive level. Thus the scientist deduces what consequences might be expected to follow in ordinary experience, were his theory true, and then tests to see whether they do follow. But the theory itself is not arrived at by induction – it is a hypothetical inference, framed to solve a problem. As such, it is not a mere extension of ordinary experience. Rather it offers a perspective quite different from the ordinary one. Indeed it offers a new conception of the matter of which an object is composed, one which, for certain purposes, will replace the ordinary conception. Moreover, the new conception is not final. Further inquiry will reveal problems that can be solved only by framing a fresh conception. The history of science, for example, reveals that the atomic theory has been preserved only by repeatedly modifying its conception of the atom.

It is worth noting that Peirce's analysis of the three forms of inference is one of remarkable brilliance. For he has shown not simply how they are to be distinguished in their function but also how they are related in practice. Thus *abduction* which initiates theory requires *induction* in order that the theory may be tested through its consequences. But these consequences can be tested only because, through the process of *deduction*, we can determine what they might be.

Now the view of science we are illustrating here has an important consequence. As we have said, scientific activity is, as it were, groping into the unknown. Since this is so, any general view of things which we develop today is liable to be replaced tomorrow by our moving into a wider perspective still. This view of science is known as *Fallibilism*. The view is that as scientific inquiry proceeds it is always liable to replace its own results. This means that the picture of the world that it develops or suggests at any given time is not absolute. Tomorrow we are likely to change. This view is not pessimistic. Quite the contrary, it presupposes that science is, or can be, progressive. Tomorrow we are liable to change our view because we are liable to be in a better position to appreciate where we stand today. That in its turn presupposes, of course, that our general view, at any stage, will contain something true. Science can progress because what is true at one stage can be taken up into the view that replaces it, so that at a later stage we are in a better position to appreciate the earlier one.

Implicit in this view is a criticism of that Scientific Positivism which acquired such prestige in Peirce's lifetime. Scientific Positivism is not of course a scientific theory. It is a world-view, or Weltanschauung, derived from science. It holds, for example, that the world has no overall meaning, all things being the product of chance and blind causation, that all things are determined, that science is the only mode of knowledge, and so on. Now the criticism of this view is that it takes as a final picture of the universe what are merely the results of science at a particular stage of development. Moreover, it is not difficult to discern the particular stage in question. What the Scientific Positivist takes as a final picture of the universe are the results science achieved around the middle of the nineteenth century. The laws of Newtonian physics, which flourished at this time, are treated as an ultimate description of how things are. In fact it was discovered, almost before the century had ended, that Newton's laws held only in an approximate form. They are reliable when applied to large-scale objects. But they will not serve in the study of matter at a more fundamental level.

Peirce did not live to examine these discoveries, but they would not have surprised him. For example, he had already argued that the laws or regularities of science depend on measurement being in some degree *imprecise*. Any regularities, he claimed, may be shown to contain irregularities, given a further precision in measurement. An example from ordinary life will illustrate what he meant. Consider any two objects supposedly of equal height. Given a more precise form of measurement, we usually find some difference between them. But that, it might be thought, is just an accident. Might there not be two objects which remain equal in height however precise we make our measurement? That cannot be so, since if we could refine our measurement indefinitely, we should find eventually that the objects dissolve into clouds of atoms in perpetual motion. At that level, the notion of equality in height cannot be applied at all. In short, there is a sense in which the notion of equality can be applied only because our measurement always contains some degree of imprecision. More strictly, the idea of precision in measurement varies according to the way in which the world appears to human beings.

It might be said, therefore, that, on the Fallibilist view, science studies the world not wholly as it is, but as it appears, relative to some human observer. Put in that way, however, the view is easily misunderstood. It needs to be distinguished carefully from another, which it superficially resembles and which has often been attributed to Kant, namely, that science never studies the world as it really is but only as it appears. The latter view rests on a confusion between different types of distinction. The point is important, so we must consider it in some detail.

What is essential to grasp is that the difference between the world as it wholly is and as it appears is *not* the same as the difference between reality and illusion. What the Fallibilist view entails is *not* that science is concerned with illusory appearances, the world as it is being wholly unknown. Quite the contrary, it entails that the world is known through the way it appears. What appears is the real world. The point is easily grasped once one sees that the way an object appears to a human being is itself a matter of objective fact. For example, it is an objective fact that the sun when viewed from the earth appears to be in motion. That really is how it appears. Indeed it would appear as such on a film taken by a movie camera. The statement may be misleading so far as it induces one to attribute more to the sun than may properly be gained from the way it appears. Taken in itself, however, it is entirely true. The point may be put another way by saying that it is only on rare occasions that appearances are entirely illusory; in most cases, we are put in touch with some feature of objective fact. For example, from the fact that the sun appears to be in motion when viewed from the earth, one may infer that one or the other is in motion and that is evidently an objective fact, something that holds true independently of human observation.

The point may be further illustrated by taking an example that Peirce used himself. It is evident that colour vision depends on a relation between object and observer and that this relation does not hold in the case of all sentient creatures. An object will appear coloured only to a creature that is receptive in certain ways to light. Not all the animals are receptive in those ways and, indeed, some are receptive in ways other than in those we are ourselves. In short, colour is a phenomenon of light and of the way that light is received. It is relative to certain conditions, being a feature of a relation. The point, however, is that a relation is not illusory; it is a matter of objective fact. It is an objective fact, for example, that a lemon in normal light will appear to most human beings as yellow. The relation has its subjective aspect since it requires a perceiving subject. But the subject is only one element in a relation which is not his own creation. Given he is in that relation, he has no choice but to see the lemon as yellow. The relation as a whole, of which he is simply one element, is itself an effect of causes which lie more deeply in nature and are independent of the subject. In short, the relation is an objective feature of nature. Peirce himself puts the point as follows.

> It is said that what is relative to thought cannot be real. But why not, exactly. *Red* is relative to sight but the fact that this or that is in that relation to vision that we call being red is not *itself* relative to sight; it is a real fact.
>
> (Peirce 1935(V) para. 430: 288)

Let us rephrase the point. It is evident that a relation requires distinct objects. A is related to B only if B is distinct from A. But if the relation between A and B holds between distinct objects, each will exist independently of that relation, having features that enter into the relation and others that do not enter into the relation at all. It follows that where the relation is between subject and object, observer and observed, the subject may detect features in the object which exist independently of his observing it. In other words, the experience of the subject, occurring within an objective relation, enables him to detect real features in the object, features themselves objective. For example, it is through perceiving its colour that I am able to locate a lemon. But a lemon's location does not depend on my perceiving it. It is easy to see, therefore, that there is no incompatibility between studying how an object appears and studying objective fact. But it is equally easy to see that the way an object appears within a given relation will not be exhaustive of that object, so that one may take a wider perspective that includes the earlier relation and enables one the better to understand it. In that way science proceeds. For example, a lemon's appearing yellow to a subject may be considered from within a wider perspective which enables one the better to understand why the lemon appears to that subject as yellow.

Peirce's Pragmatism, as an account of inquiry, can be usefully summarised by reference to the following passage:

> Philosophers of very diverse stripes propose that philosophy shall take its start from one or another state of mind in which no man, least of all a beginner in philosophy, actually is. One proposes that you shall begin by doubting everything, and says there is no one thing that you cannot doubt, as if doubting were as 'easy as lying'... But, in truth, there is but one state from which you find yourself at the time you do 'set out' – a state of mind in which you are laden with an immense mass of cognition already formed, of which you can not divert yourself if you would; and who knows whether, if you could, you would not have made all knowledge impossible to yourself? Do you call it doubting to write down on a piece of paper that you doubt? If so, doubting has nothing to do with any serious business. But do not make believe; if pedantry has not eaten all reality out of you, recognise, as you must, that there is much that you do not doubt in the least.
>
> (Peirce 1935(V) para. 416: 278)

Wherever theoretical inquiry takes its rise, it presupposes much that is already known. It is in the context of what is known, in the context of practical certainty, that it gets its point and direction. Thus whether a belief is certain or doubtful is not inherent in that belief but is relative to its context. It is this point which is neglected both by the Rationalists and the Empiricists. The Rationalist seeks to find knowledge in propositions which are inherently indubitable, which are intuited by reason;[8] the Empiricist in what is indubitable in sense experience. But no proposition or experience is inherently indubitable. Any proposition or experience *may* be doubted, given an appropriate context. Certainty depends not on a belief or an experience taken in itself but on the context into which the belief or experience enters. The context includes what I go on to do and what I did before. But the context itself does not stand in isolation. For there is the great mass of my cognitions already formed, which I bring with me into that context and which helps me to make sense of it. Thus our certainty cannot be *rationalised* in the sense of being shown to rest on self-evident truth. Moreover, though we may give reasons for our certainty, we cannot formulate the whole mass of cognition which lies behind those reasons and on which they depend. Consequently there is a limit to the giving of reasons in any activity including science. There can be no knowledge, indeed no giving of reasons, unless some things are simply taken to be so. Otherwise, we can have no ground for distinguishing one reason as better than another, and nothing can count as certain. As we shall see, for Peirce, in his mature thought, certainty cannot rest on a theoretical criterion; it is acquired in practice.

As theoretical inquiry proceeds, it will adopt perspectives wider than that of ordinary practice, which it may cause us to alter or amend. But it will never eliminate that perspective. For it will need to resort repeatedly to ordinary practice in order to test or verify its theories and the theories themselves, so far as they are successful, will preserve what is sound in ordinary practice as a condition of their success.

We have considered Pragmatism as an account of inquiry but it provides, also, an account of meaning. To appreciate this, we must next consider Peirce's view of language or theory of signs.

Chapter 2

Peirce: the theory of signs

It has been a commonplace amongst philosophers, for some two hundred years, that it is anthropomorphic to apply such terms as 'meaning' and 'purpose' to nature. These terms apply only within human life and not at all to the world which surrounds it. This view has its difficulties, especially since it holds also that there is nothing in human life which is not the product of that surrounding world. It now seems impossible to account for the existence of meaning and purpose. For that reason, materialists seek to eliminate 'meaning' and 'purpose' altogether, it being deemed anthropomorphic to apply those terms not simply to nature but even to human beings. Peirce's view is the exact opposite. Meaning and purpose are real; they are not the product of human activity for there is no activity, recognisable as human, which does not already possess them. Their source lies more deeply in nature which therefore must involve processes akin to those in human life that exhibit meaning and purpose. To assume a gulf between nature and human life leaves human life itself inexplicable; to preserve continuity by eliminating from human life all elements of meaning and purpose is in intellectual terms suicidal. Now the vehicle of meaning and purpose in human life is language. 'All thought whatsoever', says Peirce, 'is a sign, and is mostly of the nature of language.' Consequently the study of language is a study of the mind in its relation to the world and therefore a study of the world itself. It is implicitly metaphysical. For this view, Peirce is often criticised by his commentators. He is accused of attempting to derive conclusions about the world from the study of linguistic or logical forms. But that criticism is based on the very assumption of an absolute gulf between language or logic on the one hand and the world on the other, which it is precisely Peirce's intention to deny. We shall be enabled to clarify these points if we look more closely at his account of language or theory of the sign.

We have noted that there is an intimate connection between Peirce's theory of the sign and his universal categories of First, Second and Third. Thus a sign (first) always stands for an object (second) to an interpretant (third). This holds true whatever we take as our unit of meaning, whether it be a term (e.g. redness), a proposition or an argument. In fact, Peirce held that it is an argument which is the basic unit of meaning. Like Frege, he held that a term has meaning through its entering into a proposition. But he held also that a proposition has meaning in relation to those which precede or follow it, as it enters into an argument. The ultimate context of meaning is the language, a whole system of signs. But in any case, whatever we take as our unit of meaning, it is always, if only implicitly, triadic.

In order to make this clear, Peirce was at pains to show that a genuinely triadic relation, for example, A gives B to C, cannot be reduced to a dyadic or monadic form. It seems obvious that it cannot be reduced to a monadic form, such as A is red. It may not be so obvious, however, that it cannot be reduced to the dyadic. For example, why can it not be reduced to two facts each dyadic in character: A parts with B, C comes into possession of B? This may seem plausible at first sight but on reflection it will be obvious that those two facts, even when taken together, do not have the intentional character of giving. B is *given* to C only when A intends him to have it. The intentional relation is inherently triadic. Again, dyadic forms may be used to express the sign relation, for example, A means B or A signifies B. But they do so only when elliptical in form: A cannot mean B except *to* someone, who must interpret it as standing for B (see Gallie 1952: 116).

Peirce allows that one may, for certain purposes, distinguish between signs in terms of natural or dyadic relations. One may then distinguish between three classes: symbols, icons and indexes. An index is a sign which stands to the world in some purely natural relation, for example, dark clouds mean rain. An icon functions by likeness or resemblance, as a picture resembles a person. By contrast, a symbol, as in most languages, is related to the world in purely conventional terms. It is obvious, however, that icons and indexes, no less than symbols, are signs proper only when they are interpreted. Thus the purely natural relation between dark clouds and rain has no meaning at all, until someone takes the dark clouds to indicate that rain will follow. Again, if the picture resembles a person then by the same token the person resembles the picture. Which represents which? That depends on how they are taken.

Any sign, then, is triadic – the sign standing for some object to an interpretant. Now it may be natural to suppose that by an interpretant Peirce means some person or mind. In fact that is mistaken, or rather, misleading. For Peirce the interpretant of a sign is always some further *sign*. This point, which is one of Peirce's most profound, is not as difficult as at first it seems. An example will illustrate it. If I am uncertain whether you mean a particular object, I may point to that object in order to check your meaning. Here I, a person or mind, attempt to interpret what you mean. Peirce is not denying this; he is not suggesting that signs interpret one another without involving persons or minds at all. To see what he means consider the gesture by which I attempt to interpret what you say. I point to the object. But pointing simply as a movement of the body is meaningless. It counts as an interpretation only in a context where it can itself be taken in a certain way. It is itself a symbolic gesture. In short I respond to your sign by producing a sign of my own. One sign interprets another. Moreover, it is irrelevant that in certain contexts I may make no overt gesture. Some process, let us suppose, passes through my mind. Everything that has been said about the gesture applies equally to that mental process. If it interprets a sign it is itself a sign.

These points can be further clarified in a way suggested by W. B. Gallie. As he says, the sign relation may seem at first sight to be best expressed as follows:

> (i) a sign stands for (ii) an object by (iii) stimulating some organism or person to (iv) some appropriate response which is (v) itself capable of signifying the object of the original sign.

> (1952: 120)

Now it is clear that Peirce in his analysis has eliminated (iii) and (iv). He has done so because a sign cannot stimulate a person to some appropriate response unless this response is capable of signifying the object of the original sign. Consequently all we need are (i), (ii) and (v). That is what Peirce means in his own definition.

> A *Sign*... is a First which stands in some genuine triadic relation to a Second, called its *Object*, as to be capable of determining a Third, called its *Interpretant*, to assume the same triadic relation to its Object in which it stands itself to the same Object.

Pierce's view has implications that many have found puzzling. For example, it implies that there cannot have been a first sign. Nothing counts as a sign except in relation to other signs. Consequently there cannot have been a first one. This is puzzling because it is now difficult to see how the whole system of signs could have arisen in the first place – but, in fact, the point is not as puzzling as it appears. It can be understood, indeed, by reference to a common phenomenon. At what point does a child cease to imitate words and actually start to speak? Which is his first real word or sentence? The question is misguided because there is no such first word or sentence. The child's speech is continuous with the purposive behaviour he exhibits prior to speech. One may say at a certain time that he does not yet speak and at another time that he does, but there is a stretch in between where it is arbitrary what we say. As a moving object is always between points and never at a single one, so meaning never appears in a single instant but only over a stretch of time. It takes time to mean something.

These points can be revealed from another angle. Although Peirce himself did not immediately see this point, it follows from what he says that meaning cannot be identified with conscious interpretation. For a sign can be interpreted only by another. Consequently if every sign had to be consciously interpreted, we should be involved in an infinite regress. To know the meaning of one sign we should need to know a second; to know the meaning of that, a third; and so on *ad infinitum*. Meaning, therefore, must have a base below the level of conscious inference, where it is carried by the body. For example, a dog salivates when it sees food. This bodily reaction is an implied form of classification. The dog's world is divided into what is and what is not food. The reaction already has the elements characteristic of meaning – for example, it is *general*. It is adjusted not to this particular food but to the *kind* of food which nourishes the dog, of which this food is an instance. Without such forms of classification, inherent in the reactions of the body, no child would ever grasp language. Thus a child is *taught* the meaning of 'red' by being shown instances, but he *grasps* the meaning of 'red' when he goes *beyond* the instances he is shown, when he reveals an implicit understanding of the *class* into which those instances fall but which goes beyond any of its actual instances. Further, these reactions are not merely general in their implications but also teleological. Thus the dog's reactions serve the function of nourishing it, of satisfying its needs. The idea that language requires a first sign is based on the assumption that there must be a first act of meaning in order to originate it. But this is a delusion. Language flows out of the relations between creatures and the world and these relations already have the characteristics of meaning.

It follows that the study of language is a study of the relations between creatures and the world and therefore of the world itself. For example, we may already conclude, from what has been said, that the relations between creatures and the world cannot be explained in terms of mechanical causation and therefore that the world itself cannot be explained exclusively in mechanistic terms. This is evident, especially, in the reality of the general. As we have said, generality is inherent in the most primitive of a creature's reactions. The dog is not adjusted to this particular food and then to that, from which it infers the kind of food that suits it. Unless it was *already* adjusted to food of this *kind*, it would never have picked out this particular food in the first place. The sexual instinct is not adjusted to some particular member of the opposite sex but to the opposite sex in general. Disposition tells us, as it were, what *kind* of objects to pursue and leaves the selection of its instances to contingent circumstances. But then the disposition cannot be explained by its instances. Disposition or habit has real generality. Every real generality has *continuity*. By this Peirce means that it cannot be reduced to a set of its actual instances. Moreover, this is not fanciful abstraction. The reality of the general is everywhere apparent. Evolutionary biology, for example, depends directly on the reality of habit or disposition, for without it there could be no explanation of how the species are adapted to their environment. Yet there is nothing in a Positivist or Mechanistic philosophy which can explain the generality which is inherent in those habits or dispositions. As we shall see, Peirce's Realism with regard to law, habit or disposition is the most essential feature of his mature philosophy. Without it, his Pragmatism is unintelligible.

It is worth noting that there are striking resemblances between Peirce's theory of the sign and some of the views in Wittgenstein's later work. This is especially evident in the case of Wittgenstein's celebrated argument against the idea of a private language. A private language is precisely one in which there is a first sign. Thus Wittgenstein imagines that an individual gives meaning to a sign 'S' simply by associating it with one of his sensations. Thereafter he knows the correct way to take S, by recalling the original act of meaning. Here S is a first sign, since it derives its meaning simply from the relation between the individual's mind and its object, being unrelated to any other sign. Now Wittgenstein's criticism of this idea may be expressed in Peirce's terms by saying that meaning is not a dyadic but a triadic relation. On the idea of a private language, meaning is two-term. Thus the correct way of taking S is determined by a two-term relation in which the sign is related directly to an object. For Peirce and Wittgenstein meaning is essentially three-term. A term is related to an object only if there is *already* a correct way to take it. And only if there were already a correct way to take S could it be related to its object. Peirce would also have rephrased this criticism in terms of generality. Thus on the idea of a private language, the meaning of S is constituted by a relation between a mark and a particular object. From this is generated a general way of taking S. But this is a delusion. A sign is *inherently* general. Thus a particular object can never be the meaning of a sign. A sign, such as a proper name, may be used to refer to a particular object but then its meaning lies not in the object but in its use and a use is inherently general.

For Peirce, then, human beings cannot initiate meaning, except on the basis of other meanings. He expressed this point in striking fashion by saying that the intelligent mind *is* 'a sign developing in accordance with the laws of inference.' In other words, language is not the creation of the human mind; rather what is distinctive in the human mind depends on the existence of language. This means that human beings are *creatures*; so far from inhabiting a realm which is their own creation, they have no properties which are not already implicit in nature, whose creatures they are. Thus communication is already present in the lives of young children and of the animals, so that human language is only one form, though perhaps the most developed, amongst others, out of which indeed it *has* developed. Moreover, signs are not merely the outward expression of human thought. Human thought is *in* signs. It need not always be overt. A man may think to himself. But he does so in the forms by which he communicates with others. Peirce argued that inner thought is internalised dialogue, in which a person communes with himself, taking on himself the part of the other.[1] Inner thought, it is true, need not always occur in words. A remark of yours may call an image to my mind. But that image, if it has a significance, will have the character of a sign. For example, its significance will depend on what was said before and what I go on to say later. In a different context, the same image might have an entirely different significance. Peirce argued, also, that the very idea of the self presupposes signs or symbols. An animal has no *idea* of itself, because it has no sign or symbol to distinguish itself from others. This means that the self presupposes the not-self. I have an idea of myself because I have a language in which other people can be distinguished over and against myself or myself over and against other people. In the manner of Kant, therefore, Peirce argued that the self or the subject presupposes the intersubjective order of a social life and that in its turn, requires as its context, the objective order of nature.

We have now considered most of the elements which are needed to understand Peirce's Pragmatic account of meaning. But there is one essential element which we have only touched on and which we need to consider in more detail. This is his Realist view of law, habit and disposition.

LAW AND HABIT

It has been a characteristic of modern science to employ explanations which are mechanistic in form. The behaviour of a body or substance is explained by reference to an underlying mechanism or structure. There are reasons, however, to suppose that this form of explanation cannot be ultimate. A structure when static does not explain its own movements. We may seek an explanation in some further underlying structure. But then we have the same problem. If we suppose a still further underlying structure we are heading towards an infinite regress, whereby there is an infinite number of mechanisms underlying every operation. On the other hand, if we suppose an ultimate mechanism or structure we leave its own workings inexplicable.

An example will further develop the point. An acorn grows into an oak. Now if we are familiar with such a growth, we may identify the structure in the acorn which is needed for it to occur. But we must know how it grows *before* we can identify that structure, for there is nothing in the structure, when taken in itself, which would enable us to deduce it. Moreover, the same point applies to whatever structure underlies the overt one. Now if we identify the nature of the acorn with its structure, its future growth is only accidentally connected with that nature. For it is the structure which exists now, not its future growth, and that future growth cannot be deduced from the structure itself. The trouble is that in practice no one can believe this. No one believes it is an accidental fact that an acorn, in the appropriate circumstances, grows into an oak. There is a law at work, a necessity involved. In short, there is a real tendency in the acorn which belongs as much to its nature as does its structure but which cannot be explained in mechanistic terms. Now that is the Realism of Peirce. 'Realism, for Peirce', says W. B. Gallie (1952: 153), 'means the acceptance of the fact that the laws of nature are as real, and as much matters that we take account of practically as any or every particular configuration or succession of individual existents.'

In holding this view, Peirce was opposed by what he termed the 'Nominalist Weltanschauung' of his age. On the Empiricist view, for example, there is no law or tendency of the acorn which is not reducible to its being an acorn now and an oak in the future, the law existing only in the human mind as a summary of the facts mentioned. Peirce agreed that a law or tendency has characteristics of the mental but he denied that it exists only in the *human* mind. The human mind, as we shall see, is in part *constituted* by laws or tendencies, which therefore could not conceivably be its own creation. For Peirce, law or tendency bespeaks living intelligence objective in the world. Against Nominalism, he argued as follows.

> Five minutes of our waking life will hardly pass without our making some kind of prediction; and in the majority of cases these predictions are fulfilled in the event. Yet a prediction is essentially of a general nature, and cannot ever be completely fulfilled. To say that a prediction has a tendency to be fulfilled, is to say that the future events are in a measure really governed by a law. If a pair of dice turns up sixes five times running, that is mere uniformity. The dice might happen fortuitously to turn up sixes a thousand times running. But that would not afford the slightest security for a prediction that they would turn up sixes the next time. If the prediction has a tendency to be fulfilled, it must be that future events have a tendency to conform to a general rule. 'Oh' but say the Nominalists, 'this general rule is nothing but a mere word or couple of words!' I reply, 'Nobody ever dreamed of denying that what is general is of the nature of a general sign; but the question is whether future events will conform to it or not. If they will, your adjective 'mere' seems to be ill-placed. A rule to which future events have a tendency to conform is *ipso facto* an important thing, an important element in the happening of those events.
>
> (Gallie 1952: 152)

We may elaborate on these points. No scientific law is specifiable purely in terms of empirical content. The law that arsenic poisons, for example, mentions no arsenic in particular, nor any actual case of poisoning. It is entirely general in form. *If* there were arsenic it *would* poison. From this, it is true, we may deduce in an actual instance that *this* arsenic will poison. But we could have deduced the same conclusion *whatever* the instance of arsenic. The law, as Peirce says, is in the nature of a general sign. It indicates an intelligibility in the behaviour of arsenic. This is the *way* that the behaviour of arsenic is to be understood. It is an error therefore to suppose, with the Empiricists, that it is by an induction from particular instances that one arrives at the existence of law. Every law transcends its actual instances.

Consequently, law is prior to induction which serves merely as a selective procedure. Thus, what induction shows is not that there is law in the behaviour of arsenic; it merely helps you to select which law that might be. The *existence* of law could never be a discovery; for it could be a discovery only amongst creatures who previously had no knowledge of it. But without the knowledge, however implicit, of law or habit, there would be no such creatures; there could be no life. The dog, as we said, does not conclude by induction from particular foods that there is a kind of food which nourishes it. It is already adjusted to a kind of food and is thereby enabled to select particular instances. The child who has been burned does not arrive by induction at the generality 'fire burns' and then deduce that this will burn since it is fire. His experience of being burned is implicitly general, so that he immediately sees the next fire as what will burn him. Generality is inherent in his behaviour. Now, similarly, we implicitly take an instance of arsenic in a general way. We do not look to see whether there is a law involved in its behaviour but only what that law might be. It is here that induction has its part to play. In supposing, however, that law is *based* on induction, the Empiricist mistakes a selective and therefore subordinate procedure for the prime reality. The prime reality is the existence of law, for without it there would be nothing to select.

It is important to note however that Peirce's Realism is distinguishable in important respects from that of the Medieval Realists, whom he so greatly admired. The Medievals, for the most part, construed the general or the universal on the model of the term: redness, hardness, justice, etc. It is fatally easy, on this view, to treat the general as though it were a peculiar kind of particular or at any rate, to treat apprehending the general on the model of apprehending a particular thing. This is assisted by a tendency, which seems natural to the human mind, to construe the real as physical substance, to suppose nothing is real unless it can be seen or grasped. When this tendency is dominant, it destroys the very reality of order. For order consists essentially in relationships and is not itself an object. Now Peirce's treatment of the general is essentially *relational*. Thus the necessity of a law, as we have seen, is conditional. *If* you have so-and-so *then* you will get such-and-such. Peirce was influenced in this view by his studies in the logic of relations. But he was influenced also by the considerations that moved Jonathan Edwards. Modern science has made progress precisely by overcoming the tendency to think of reality in terms of physical substances.[2] It has discovered that the nature of an object is best revealed by considering it not in its substance but in its relations. Indeed, in the Newtonian system, as we have seen, substance in the ordinary sense entirely dissolves. An object is a collection of attractions and repulsions. The qualities of an object are revealed by the operations one can perform on it. The hardness of an object, for example, is revealed by the number of objects it will resist if it is scratched.

'The existence of things', says Peirce, 'consists in their regular behaviour. If an atom has no regular attractions and repulsions, if its mass was at one instant nothing, at another, a ton, at another a negative quality, or its motion, instead of being continuous, consisted in a series of leaps from one plane to another without passing through any intervening places, and if there were no definite relations between its different positions, velocities and directions of displacement... such a disjoined plurality of phenomena would not make up any existing thing. Not only substances, but events too, are constituted by regularities' (Gallie 1952: 155).

Thus it is not simply the behaviour of an object which is best revealed in its relations. One cannot that easily distinguish between the behaviour of an object and its nature. Its nature is best revealed in its behaviour. The nature of an object is revealed not at an instant but in its behaviour over time. Peirce's Pragmatic account of meaning can be seen as a reflection of this view. Just as the hardness of an object is revealed in the operations one performs on it, so the sign 'hardness' is grasped in operations – in grasping, for example, the operations involved in revealing that an object is hard. It is because objects have real habits or dispositions, constitutive of their nature, that we grasp them in signs through grasping habits or dispositions and this involves our acquiring habits or dispositions ourselves. Thus meaning is not an entity. To grasp meaning is to acquire a capacity. Peirce's Pragmatism rests on his Realism.

These points will be further apparent if we return to the study of language. As we have said, a child will acquire the capacity to use a word on the basis of being instructed by reference to a handful of instances. This capacity, like any other, is indefinite or unlimited in its scope. It has real continuity or generality; in short, it cannot be reduced to an actual set of instances. Thus it is impossible to formulate the instances to which a child, having acquired a word, will go on and apply it. Attempts have been made to explain this by reference to mechanisms in a child's brain, it being assumed that these encode a set of rules which govern the whole of his future usage. There are, perhaps, many problems about language which can be solved by reference to the brain. But this is certainly not one of them. For any mechanism in the brain will itself be limited in structure. Consequently we have what in effect is the same problem. How can a limited structure give rise to an unlimited ability? And if we suppose an underlying mechanism, we are heading, as we have said, towards an infinite regress. Moreover, it is evident that no set of rules can explain the usage of a word. The point has been well expressed by Wittgenstein in his discussion of following a rule. Any set of rules or criteria may be interpreted, theoretically, in an infinite number of ways. Consequently the rules or criteria, when taken in themselves, cannot explain how they are to be followed in practice. It is not through rules or criteria that we can explain the capacity to use words; without that capacity the rules or criteria would be useless. It is the practical capacity which is important, not the rules or criteria. This indeed is merely a variation on Peirce's point. Capacities or habits cannot be formulated as a set of actual instances. They possess real generality or continuity.

It follows that meaning can be grasped *only* in practice, through acquiring habits or capacities in handling signs or symbols. No one can acquire the meaning of a sign through a formulation unless he can apply it to future cases and that capacity cannot be explained by reference to that formulation taken in itself. This is identical with Peirce's Pragmatic Maxim. It will be useful to state it in what I think is the best form.

> For the maxim of Pragmatism is that a conception can have no logical effect or import differing from that of a second conception except so far as, taken in connection with other conceptions and intentions, it might conceivably modify our practical conduct differently from that second conception.[3]

Meaning, in short, is determined by practice and if two different formulations nevertheless have the same use, they have the same meaning.

It is important to see that this view is identical with the view that a sign or symbol can be interpreted only by another. Suppose, for example, that the *meaning* of 'red' is indicated by reference to a particular red object. It is evident that *this* relation to an object is quite different from any relation to an object in the normal use of the word. This remains true even if it happens to be the same object that is referred to in a normal use. That is because when an object is used to indicate the meaning of a word, it really serves as an alternative symbol for the word, whereas in the normal use that is not true of the object referred to. But it serves as a symbol only because it indicates the habitual use of the word, for it is in this use that the meaning of the word lies. Moreover, that is the only way habitual usage can be indicated: in symbolic form. That is because, as we have seen, habit or disposition cannot be formulated as a set of actual instances. It can only be symbolised. Consequently a sign or symbol can be interpreted only by a sign or symbol.

These points will enable us to clarify an aspect of Peirce's thought which many have found puzzling. Peirce held that every sign is endlessly capable of evoking an endless series of further interpretant signs. This can easily be seen to follow from what has been said. No habit or disposition can be formulated as a set of instances. Consequently we cannot formulate all that we are committed to in our use of words. There is always more in what we mean than we can consciously know. This point is of great importance. It has been a disastrous error in the philosophy of language, during the present century, to identify meaning with formulable criteria or rules.[4] Meaning can never be fixed in that way. It should indeed be evident on reflection that the uses of words are continually being transformed in ways which seem continuous from a later point but which could not have been anticipated from an earlier one. Moreover, as usage is transformed so are transformed the rules or criteria involved in that usage. For example, the original criterion for 'motion' lay in a contrast between moving and stationary objects on the surface of the earth. The ball is moving by contact with the tree which it bounces past. Through the influence of the Copernican theory, we have accepted that the earth as a whole is in motion, which means that the tree is moving as well as the ball that bounces past it. So now we have nothing in absolute terms with which to contrast motion. Yet no one feels he is using the word in a peculiar sense when he refers to the motion of the earth.

The feature to which we refer is a feature of every purpose or intention. Every purpose or intention commits a person to more than he consciously formulates. An example may illustrate the point. Suppose on Monday I resolve to give up chocolate. Then on Thursday I am offered a chocolate, am tempted and fall. Why should we say I am tempted, which implies a conflict? Why not say I have one desire on Monday and another on Thursday, which implies no inconsistency at any specific time? Perhaps it will be said that on Thursday I still feel Monday's desire, so that I both do and do not desire the chocolate. But that need not be true. On Thursday my only desire may be for the chocolate. Yet I may still feel inconsistent when I satisfy it. The answer is that purpose or intention is not an occurrent state but is continuous. I am already committed on Thursday, for that was implicit in Monday's resolve. Consequently I am committed on Thursday whatever I feel. Note, however, that on Monday I was not consciously thinking of Thursday. Indeed I am no more committed on Thursday than an any other day; and no less. It takes time to reveal what is involved in any intention or purpose. We may vary the example. It may be that on Thursday I *find myself* refusing a chocolate which I plainly desire. And for a moment I might be unable to formulate why I do so.

It is worth noting that these phenomena are akin to implication in logic or mathematics. 'I certainly think', says Peirce, 'that the certainty of pure mathematics and of all necessary reasoning is due to the circumstances that it relates its objects which are the creations of our own minds, and that mathematical knowledge is to be classed along with knowledge of our own purposes. When we meet with a surprising result in pure mathematics, as we so often do, because a loose reasoning had led us to suppose it impossible, this is essentially the same sort of phenomenon as when in pursuing a purpose we are led to do something that we are quite surprised to find ourselves doing, as being contrary, or apparently contrary, to some weaker purpose' (see Peirce 1935(V) para. 166: 102). This, again, shows that logical and mathematical forms have their roots in the fundamental operations by which the mind makes sense of the world.

In this chapter, we have considered Peirce's Pragmatism as it appears in his mature thought. In the next, we shall consider it in an earlier version. Without doing so, we cannot properly understand the history of Pragmatism.

Chapter 3

Peirce: Pragmatism and William James

We have been considering Peirce's Pragmatism as it appears in his mature thought. It exerted its greatest influence, however, not in that form but as it appeared in 1878 in his paper, 'How To Make Our Ideas Clear' (see Hauser and Keleusal 1992(I): 124–41). We must consider that paper in some detail.

Peirce begins by criticising the view, which he attributes to Descartes, that our terms are made clear by precise definition, in the abstract. Against this, he argues that we understand a term when we know how to handle it in practice. Thus our understanding of 'hardness' is acquired not by abstract definition but by our knowing what in experience would count as hard. For example, a hard thing is one that will not be scratched by many other substances, will make a noise when struck, will offer resistance if pushed, and so on. Now it is irrelevant whether a person can define hardness; he knows what it means just so long as he recognises in practice that something having these sensible effects will count as hard. So far, his argument differs little from what may be found in his mature thought. But he then proceeds to the following formulation of his Pragmatic Maxim.

> Consider what effects, which might conceivably have practical bearings, we conceive the object of our conception to have. Then, our conception of these effects is the whole of our conception of the object.
>
> (Hauser and Keleusal 1992(I): 132)

It will be useful to contrast this with a later formulation:

> The entire intellectual purport of any symbol consists in the total of all general modes of rational conduct which, conditionally upon all

the possible different circumstances and desires, would ensue upon the acceptance of the symbol.

(Peirce 1935(V): 293)

These formulations are strikingly different. In its first formulation, the maxim is hardly distinguishable from the verification principle of the Logical Positivists: the meaning of a proposition is determined by the method for verifying it in sense experience. This is especially obvious when the first formulation is taken in its original context, for in this context it seems evident that what Peirce means by 'effects' is '*sensible* effects'. For example, he argues as follows against the Catholic doctrine of the Eucharist:

> Thus our action has exclusive reference to what effects the senses, our habit has the same bearing as our action, and our belief the same as our habit, our conception the same as our belief: and we can consequently mean nothing by wine but what has certain effects, direct or indirect, upon our senses; and to talk of something as having all the sensible characters of wine, yet being in reality blood, is senseless jargon.

(Peirce 1935(V): 131)

Now in the later formulation, the elements which suggest the verification principle have been removed. We must note in particular the following alterations. Peirce has removed the words 'practical bearings'. This is almost certainly because William James, in the meantime, had extended the Pragmatic Maxim to cover not simply meaning but also truth. According to James, it was the truth and not simply the meaning of a conception which was determined by its practical bearings and this appeared to mean that there is no difference between whether a conception corresponds to the facts and whether it is useful to hold it.[1] Peirce removed the words because he wished to dissociate himself from any such interpretation. The point is emphasised also at the beginning of the formulation where Peirce states that he is concerned with the 'intellectual purport of any symbol'. In other words, he is primarily concerned to elucidate meaning for intellectual purposes, not for practical ones. We may note further that the word 'effect' has disappeared. The meaning of a symbol is now determined by the *general* mode of *rational* conduct which would follow in appropriate circumstances from accepting it. There is no implication that those modes of conduct are exhausted in their dealings with the sensible effects of objects.

Now it is important to see that these are not simply reformulations designed to avoid misunderstanding. They represent substantial changes of view. When Peirce wrote 'How To Make Our Ideas Clear', there were still deep confusions in his philosophy and, in that paper, he committed himself to views which are in conflict with his best thought. It is one of the many poignant facts about Peirce, that what recognition he received during his lifetime was based on views that he no longer held, that were indeed in direct conflict with those he did hold. It will be important to illustrate these points in detail.

As we have noted, Peirce suggests that the sensible effects of a substance exhaust what we mean by it. What we mean by 'wine', for example, is exhausted by its look, taste, smell, etc. Now, for scientific purposes, it seems evident that no substance can be so defined. For example, it sometimes happens, as the result of scientific inquiry, that a substance is separated, or defined independently, from those sensible effects by which it was originally picked out. This could hardly occur if its sensible effects exhausted its meaning. Where a substance is picked out by its sensible effects, this is only *relative to certain circumstances*. The sensible effects, picked out relative to those circumstances, are not taken as exhaustive of the substance. For example, 'gold' was originally defined by its phenomenal qualities, as yellow and metallic. Later it was defined by a chemical process, as soluble in aqua regia. Nowadays it is defined by its atomic structure. It is one and the same substance which is being referred to throughout these changes. This could hardly occur if the meaning of 'gold' were exhausted by its being picked out as yellow and metallic. In short, it cannot be, as Peirce implies, that our conception of those sensible effects is 'the *whole* of our conception of the object' (my italics).

The confusion in Peirce's view may be illustrated by referring to what he says about the Catholic doctrine of the Eucharist. According to Peirce, that doctrine is not so much false as meaningless. That is because those who hold the doctrine identify flesh and blood with the elements of the eucharist whilst accepting that those elements do not have the sensible qualities of flesh and blood. Now I should not deny that this doctrine has its difficulties but the difficulties are not those mentioned by Peirce. There is, for example, no incoherence in supposing that flesh and blood, on a given occasion, may possess none of their normal sensible effects. In a chemical analysis of those substances, none of their normal effects need appear. Yet no one denies that the chemist is analysing what would normally be taken as flesh and blood. The difficulty with the Catholic doctrine is not that the flesh and blood have none of their sensible effects, nor yet that they have the sensible effects of bread and wine but that it is unclear how substances which have effects of the second kind are to be identified with substances which in other circumstances have sensible effects of the first. Here there is a contrast with the analysis of the chemist, since in chemical analysis there is an evident link with the normal effects of the substances being analysed. The link is evident because the chemical analysis will help explain why those substances do normally have those effects.

Now it is not simply that Peirce is mistaken in these views. What is important is that the views are in conflict with the whole drift of his Pragmatic account of inquiry. For the effects of supposing that natural objects are exhausted by their sensible effects is to render absolute our normal view of the world. It is to say, in effect, that there is nothing to objects other than the way they ordinarily appear. It is of the essence of Peirce's account of science, the account often termed Fallibilism, that no such view is absolute. Indeed, as we have seen, science, properly speaking, takes its start from the move beyond that ordinary view of the world. So far from confining itself to objects as defined by their sensible effects, it seeks for a deeper explanation which will enable it to explain, amongst other things, why objects have those sensible effects.

But it is clear that the views in this paper undermine not simply Peirce's Pragmatic account of inquiry. They undermine also his Pragmatic account of meaning. The point may be illustrated by referring to a problem that arises for him in the course of the paper. At a certain point, he asks whether *whilst* we are *not* testing a substance for hardness, we can call it hard. The problem is evident, given his view of meaning. Thus if 'hardness' just means certain sensible effects, how can we call an object hard at the time it is exhibiting no such effects? The difficulty is not one that arises in ordinary speech. Thus if an object resists scratching, we call it hard, meaning it was hard all the time and not just when we were attempting to scratch it. The problem arises only given Peirce's view of meaning. Moreover, what is especially significant is that, given this view, the problem cannot be avoided by offering a conditional analysis. In other words, it is idle to argue that the object was hard all the time, since what is meant by 'hard all the time' is that it *would* have resisted scratching *had* one put it to the test. For if nothing has meaning except in terms of sensible effects, it is only in terms of sensible effects that a conditional has meaning. But then in order to have meaning it must cease to be conditional. To say at five o'clock that an object *would* resist scratching is only to say that it *has* resisted scratching at some time before five o'clock or *will* do so at some time later. But at five o'clock precisely, the object neither does nor does not resist scratching. Therefore it neither is nor is not hard. Peirce is in effect denying what lies at the centre of his philosophy, the reality of continuity. The essence of what is continuous is that it cannot be reduced to its actual instances and it is in their continuity that one finds the reality of conditionals, laws and habits. But in 'How To Make Our Ideas Clear' he offers a view according to which they can have no meaning except as an arrangement of sensible instances:

> There is absolutely no difference between a hard thing and a soft thing so long as they are not brought to the test. Suppose, then, that a diamond could be crystallised in the midst of a cushion of soft cotton, and should remain there until it was finally burned up. Would it be false to say that that diamond was soft? ... We may, in the present case, modify our question, and ask what prevents us from saying that all hard bodies remain perfectly soft until they are touched, when their hardness increases with the pressure until they are scratched. Reflection will show that the reply is this: there would be no *falsity* in such modes of speech. They would involve a modification of our present usage of speech with regard to the words hard and soft, but not of their meanings. For they represent no fact to be different from what it is; only they involve arrangements of facts which would be exceedingly maladroit. This leads us to remark that the question of what would occur under circumstances which do not actually arise is not a question of fact, but only of the most perspicuous arrangement of them.
>
> (Peirce 1935(V): 132).

Peirce's solution, in short, is that the issue is merely verbal. If one wishes, one may say that objects are soft whilst they are not being tested. But one's statement, so far as the facts are concerned, will not differ from saying they are hard. That is because the only facts are those revealed in testing. Consequently what one says in between can be determined by convenience. By 'the facts' Peirce means, of course, 'sensible effects'. Now the trouble with this is that it is circular. If one defines 'the facts' as 'sensible effects', it is tautologous to assert that where there are no sensible effects there are no facts. The problem which Peirce does not address is why anyone should so arbitrarily define what counts as a fact. In ordinary discourse, if a question were raised at five o'clock about an object's hardness and five minutes later, when tested, it resisted scratching, we should take it as a fact that the object was hard, not just at five minutes past the hour, but five minutes earlier when we raised the question. Indeed the question we should take ourselves to be addressing would be the one raised at five o'clock, not a separate one, raised five minutes later.

In his later work, it was this section in the paper that Peirce was especially concerned to repudiate:

> Let us now take up the case of the diamond which, having been crystallised upon a cushion of jeweller's cotton, was accidentally consumed by fire before the crystal of corundum that had been sent for had had time to arrive.... The question is, was that diamond *really* hard?... To say, as the article of January 1878 seems to intend, that it is just as an arbitrary 'usage of speech' chooses to arrange its thoughts, is as much as to decide against the reality of the property, since the real is that which is such as it is regardless of how it is, at any time, thought to be.

Peirce proceeds to give a chemical analysis of a diamond and then concludes. 'But however this may be, how can the hardness of all other diamonds fail to bespeak *some* real relation among the diamonds without which a piece of carbon would not be a diamond? Is it not a monstrous perversion of the word and concept *real* to say that the accident of the non-arrival of the corundum prevented the hardness of the diamond from having the *reality* which it otherwise, with little doubt, would have had' (Peirce 1935(V) para. 457: 310).

Peirce writes to the same effect in other passages:

> I myself went too far in the direction of nominalism when I said that it was a mere question of the convenience of speech whether we say that a diamond is hard when it is not pressed upon. I now say that experiment will prove that the diamond is hard, as a positive fact. That is, it is a real fact that it *would* resist pressure....
>
> (Peirce 1935(VIII) para. 208: 166)

It is not surprising that Peirce should want to repudiate that section in his 1878 paper. The interesting question is why he should have written it in the first place. To answer this, we must return to issues that we mentioned in our first chapter, when we were indicating the development of Peirce's thought. When he wrote his 1878 paper, Peirce had accepted the view that there can be no reality which transcends experience. As we said, there is already in this view a tendency towards Subjective Idealism. If, for example, there is nothing to this stone other than appears in my experience, how do I distinguish between my experience and the stone? The stone becomes, or so it seems, just a set of my experiences. That, of course, was not a conclusion which Peirce was ever inclined to accept. To avoid it, the natural move is to resort to the conditional. There is more to this stone than appears in my experience because it *would* appear in your experience also. The reality of things lies in their offering permanent possibilities of sensation. But what is a possibility? If there is nothing that transcends experience, there can be nothing to a conditional other than appears in experience. Every possibility, in other words, must at some stage be actualised.

Now when he wrote his 1878 paper, Peirce believed he could show how every possibility will be actualised. To show this, he resorted to the view, held by his father, that inquiries converge on a final conclusion. What at the moment appears as a possibility will, if it is true, appear as actual in the final view of the universe towards which all inquiries converge. And this is the view he offers in the last section of his 1878 paper:

> The opinion which is fated to be ultimately agreed to by all who investigate is what we mean by truth, and the object represented in that opinion is the real. That is the way I would explain reality.
>
> (Peirce 1935(VIII): 139)

The difficulties in this view are evident. On the face of it, it is quite implausible to suppose that on every genuine issue there will eventually be an agreement or a convergence towards such an agreement. It seems more plausible to hold that the true opinion is that on which inquiry *would* converge, given ideal conditions. The trouble is that this claim is conditional and, for Peirce, every conditional has to be actualised. Consequently he is committed to the view that on every genuine issue there *will* in fact be a convergence towards a final opinion. That, however, is not the fundamental difficulty. The fundamental difficulty lies in his view that a conditional must be equivalent to the set of its actual instances. Thus suppose there is a convergence to the final opinion. Still, there are no real unactualised possibilities in the present. For example, there is no real possibility here and now that this stone is hard, for whatever is actualised in the final opinion, no such possibility is actualised here and now. The most that can be actualised is some similar but different possibility in the future. Peirce is caught in a dilemma because he is attempting to assimilate Realism with Phenomenalism or Subjective Idealism and the views are incompatible with one another. The Phenomenalist element requires that a conditional be equivalent to the set of its actual instances; the Realist demands just the opposite. His assumptions require conditionals in order to preserve some measure of Realism whilst simultaneously undermining the reality of those very conditionals. These points are well expressed by Murray G. Murphey:

> It seems quite clear that Peirce was not aware of these difficulties when he wrote the paper 'How To Make Our Ideas Clear' in 1878, from which the passage about the diamond is quoted. And this statement helps explain why his statement of the pragmatic maxim in that same paper implies that the concept of the object is definitionally equivalent to a conjunction of phenomenal experiences. Other passages in this article show very clearly that Peirce thought the meaning was the set of habits which the object is conceived to involve. But it is nevertheless true that the maxim itself states that the concept of the effects is equivalent to the object. The point is that Peirce himself at this point did not clearly distinguish the law from the set of all instances of the law, and the reason he did not is that to make such a distinction would have required admitting possible instances which are never actualised. It was just because Peirce was trying to merge phenomenalism and realism that he confused the difference between the two (Flower and Murphey 1977(II): 593).

WILLIAM JAMES

Pragmatism, as we have said, became famous in the work of William James. In his lectures on Pragmatism, James attributed his central ideas to Peirce. This was an act of characteristic generosity. Peirce at the time was poor and neglected. James was hoping to gain for him some of the attention he deserved. Unfortunately the views he attributed to Peirce were drawn exclusively from the paper written in 1878, some thirty years previously. Moreover, the aspects of the paper which James emphasised were those that Peirce had abandoned. As we have seen, the paper is a mixture of Realism and Phenomenalism and, in its handling of conditionals, it embraces a Nominalism which is in direct conflict with Peirce's mature thought. It was precisely the elements, in the paper, of Nominalism and Phenomenalism that James emphasised. As a result, Pragmatism is turned into a form of extreme Empiricism. Peirce's attempts to avert the misunderstanding proved unavailing. He was in any case in a difficult position. For he greatly admired James and appreciated his generosity. In consequence, it is

Pragmatism in James's version which has become dominant. At this stage, it will be useful, therefore, if we consider in some detail the differences between James's version and Peirce's. This will in no way exhaust what is of interest in the work of James himself. Later, we shall turn to his work as a whole and attempt to distinguish in it what is of permanent value.

It was commonly assumed in the nineteenth century that science had serious implications for one's view of the world and, in particular, that it had undermined religious belief and established materialism and determinism. James and Peirce were akin in rejecting that view. Both in their work attempted to reject the apparent implications of science whilst discriminating what was sound in science itself. Both attempted, in short, to accept science without accepting scientism. James's work in pure philosophy, as distinct from philosophical psychology, was largely confined to the last ten or fifteen years of his life. In this work, he adopts a strategy which may be described as taking the weapons of one's enemy and turning them against him. Thus he takes Empiricism, commonly thought to form the basis of science, develops it to an extreme point, in the form of a metaphysic which he terms Radical Empiricism, and then attempts to show that this entails not determinism but the possibility of free choice, not scepticism but the possibility of religious belief.

The strategy is at once at work in the first of his lectures on Pragmatism. He there makes his famous distinction, amongst philosophers, between the tough and the tender-minded. The tough are Empiricist, trusting in hard facts and sense experience, tending to be irreligious, determinist, materialist and sceptical. The tender, by contrast, are Rationalist, trusting in principles and the intellect, tending to be religious, free-willist, idealist and optimistic. What James offers is a philosophy in which tough-minded methods will be used in defence of tender-minded beliefs. The values of the Rationalist will be defended by the methods of the Empiricist. He then proceeds, at the beginning of the next lecture, to introduce Peirce's Pragmatic Maxim:

> To obtain perfect clearness in our thoughts of an object . . . we need only consider what conceivable effects of a practical kind the object may involve – what sensations we are to expect from it, and what reactions we must prepare. Our conceptions of these effects, whether immediate or remote, is then for us the whole of our conception of the object, so far as that conception has positive significance at all.
>
> (James 1992: 39)

From this point, James's thought develops in two related but different ways. We can see it at work in one way where he is dealing with religious and metaphysical disputes. He argues that such disputes, intractable on the intellectual level, become transformed once one takes into account their practical bearings on life, once one approaches them in Pragmatic terms:

> Free-will is... a general cosmological theory of *promise*, just like the Absolute, God, Spirit or Design. Taken abstractly, no one of these terms has any inner content, none of them gives us any picture... Our interest in religious metaphysics arises in the fact that our empirical future feels unsafe, and needs some higher guarantee.
>
> (James 1992: 68)

Again, in the last lecture he says:

> Well, the use of the Absolute is proved by the whole course of men's religious history. The eternal arms are then beneath. Remember Vivekanda's use of the Atman: it is indeed not a scientific use, for we can make no particular deductions from it. It is emotional and spiritual altogether.
>
> (ibid.: 130)

James is arguing that religious and metaphysical beliefs come alive, really mean something, when one takes into account their practical bearings. This is sufficiently Empiricist, for by 'practical bearings' James means their empirical consequences for life. Yet when we consider them in these terms, we may well find that we have good reason to adopt religious or metaphysical beliefs that the tough-minded Empiricist thinks us bound to reject. The Pragmatic Maxim, in short, can work in defence of metaphysical and religious belief.

Now, as A. O. Lovejoy showed at the time, James is here running together two quite different views. For in his use of 'practical bearings' he has failed to distinguish between the effects of a proposition and the effects of believing it. The two are plainly different. Thus, for example, whether it is satisfactory to believe that it is raining is evidently distinct from what effects have to be satisfied in order to affirm that it is raining in the first place. The Pragmatic maxim, as framed by Peirce, was exclusively concerned with the latter. It was intended to elucidate what effects were involved in the meaning of a proposition, not what effects would follow from believing it.

Moreover, once this distinction is made clear, it becomes evident that

James is involved in a contradiction. He says that religious and metaphysical beliefs have no content until one takes into account the effects of believing them. For example, he says of Vivekanda's use of the Atman that its significance is *entirely* emotional and spiritual; taken in itself, it has no empirical consequences. But if these beliefs, when taken in themselves, have no empirical consequences then, when taken in themselves, they fail the Pragmatic Test. In short, they are meaningless. But if they are meaningless, how can they be believed? How, except through delusion, can one achieve spiritual and emotional satisfaction from what is meaningless?

In fact, James can be extricated from this dilemma. The effect of extricating him, however, is to show that his view has nothing to do with Peirce's Pragmatism. Thus he would have to return to views for which he argued, some years earlier, in his famous paper 'The Will to Believe' (1918). He there argued that one sometimes has the right to put one's faith in beliefs that cannot be conclusively established on the theoretical level. R. B. Perry calls this the principle of 'fideism'. It seems clear that it is this principle James needs in his lectures on Pragmatism. Instead of saying that religious and metaphysical beliefs have no empirical content, he should have said that in terms of their empirical content they cannot be conclusively established on theoretical ground. It would then have been open to him to argue that we may nevertheless put our faith in them. As we shall see, there is something to be said for the principle of fideism. The point for the moment, however, is that it derives no support, as James supposes, from Peirce's Pragmatic Maxim. 'Pragmatism' says Perry 'is the application of practical principles to the theoretic process itself; fideism is the justification on practical ground, of overbelief – that is, of belief which lacks conclusive theoretic support' (Perry 1958: 71).

In one way, then, the lectures work, though confusedly, towards a defence of faith. But they work also towards establishing a metaphysic of reality and truth. In this respect, James is only too faithful to certain aspects of Peirce's 1878 paper. As we have seen, Peirce in that paper was pushed towards Nominalism and Phenomenalism because he held as a basic assumption that there can be nothing in reality which transcends experience. Now that basic assumption is one which James is entirely ready to embrace:

> Pragmatism unstiffens all our theories, limbers them up and sets each one at work. Being essentially new, it harmonises with many ancient philosophical tendencies. It agrees with nominalism, for instance, in

always appealing to particulars; with utilitarianism in emphasising practical aspects; with positivism in its disdain for verbal solutions, useless questions and metaphysical abstractions.

(Perry 1958: 42)

The principles of Nominalism and Positivism or Phenomenalism are dominant throughout the lectures, so that Pragmatism, in James's handling, is transformed into an extreme version of Empiricism. For example, as an instance of Pragmatism at work James refers to Berkeley's analysis of 'matter':

> Berkeley's criticism of 'matter' was . . . absolutely pragmatic. Matter is known as our sensations of colour, figure, hardness and the like. They are the cash-value of the term. The difference matter makes to us by truly being is that we then get such sensations; by not being, is that we lack them. The sensations then are its sole meaning. Berkeley doesn't deny matter, then; he simply tells us what it consists of. It is a true name for just so much in the way of sensations.
>
> (Perry 1958: 56)

James mentions also Utilitarianism. This element becomes prominent when, going beyond Peirce, he advances a theory of truth:

> Our account of truth is an account of truths in the plural, of processes of leading, realised *in rebus*, and having only this quality in common, that they *pay*. . . . Truth for us is simply a collective name for verification processes, just as health, wealth, strength, etc. are names for other processes connected with life, and also pursued because it pays to pursue them. Truth is *made*, just as health, wealth and strength are made, in the course of experience . . . .
>
> (Perry 1958: 107)

Elsewhere he says:

> Everywhere . . . 'truth' in our ideas and beliefs means the same thing that it means in science. It means . . . nothing but this, *that ideas (which themselves are but parts of our experience) become true just in so far as they help us to get into satisfactory relations with other parts of our experience* . . . .
>
> (Perry 1958: 44)

Again, he says:

> *'The true', to put it very briefly, is only the expedient in the way of our thinking, just as 'the right' is only the expedient in the way of our behaving.* Expedient in

almost any fashion; and expedient in the long run and on the whole of course.

(Perry 1958: 109)

Now it would be difficult to imagine a set of doctrines more evidently in conflict with Peirce's mature thought. On Peirce's view, there can be meaning in our terms only because we can acquire habits or dispositions in applying them to the world and this can be acquired only because there are real habits or dispositions in the world itself. So far from habits or dispositions depending on any process of verification there is no process of verification that does not require the existence of real habits or dispositions. Moreover, neither in the world nor in ourselves can any habit or disposition be reduced to an actual set of experiences or instances. On Peirce's account of inquiry, it is true, our theories are always partial or approximate, relative to the human, but that is because there is more to reality than we can experience. It is just because reality is incommensurable with any of our actual standards or criteria that so much effort is needed to determinate it and that the results obtained are never more than approximations, fallible and imperfect (Boutroux 1912: 301). That the world transcends our experience is the very condition of Realism and thereby, also, of Peirce's mature Pragmatism.

These points will be further elucidated if we consider for a moment a classic paper written by James's contemporary J. B. Pratt (James 1992: 156–60). Pratt notes that Pragmatists, influenced by James, sometimes identify the truth of a belief not with its being verified but with its verifiability. For example, on page 103 of his lectures, James himself says that 'Verifi*ability*' in certain circumstances 'is as good as verification.' Those who sympathise with James's views often insist that this represents his considered position. He identifies the truth of a belief not with its actual verification but with the *possibility* of its being verified. One suspects, however, that they say this simply because they think it the more sensible view to hold. In fact, in a number of places James says the exact opposite. For example, on page 100, he says 'Truth *happens* to an idea. It *becomes* true, is *made* true by events. Its verity *is* in fact an event, a process: the process namely of its verifying itself, its veri-*fication*.'

But what Pratt notes is not simply that such passages occur but that they represent the only view which is consistent with James's metaphysic. For the lectures are soaked throughout in Nominalism and Phenomenalism. In innumerable passages, James has insisted that modality is simply a shorthand device for referring to the actual and that the abstract really exists only in particulars. Consequently, the view that truth is equivalent to verifiability can be held consistently only by those whom James calls intellectualists and takes as his opponents. Pratt says:

> For verifiability is not a process, it is not included within anyone's experience, but is a general condition or set of conditions which transcends every single finite experience. It is not a felt 'leading', it is not a 'form of the good' nor a 'satisfactory working', nor any other kind of experience or experience-process. It is a totality of relations which are not within any finite experience.... Verifiability is transcendent of experience in exactly the same sense in which the intellectualist makes truth transcendent. The intellectualist, indeed, might not be willing to accept it as a complete account of truth.... Still the identification of truth with verifiability comes immeasurably nearer to the intellectualist's view of truth than to the ordinary pragmatic view.... *Truth for the pragmatist does not mean verifiability*; it means the process of verification. It is wholly within experience.
>
> (James 1992: 156–7)

But given that truth appears *within* the verification process, Pratt continues, how does it *actually* appear? How does a belief become an actual truth? What, in short, is the cash-value of 'verification'? This is a question that James raises himself and answers as follows:

> But what do the words verification and validation themselves pragmatically mean? They again signify certain practical consequences of the verified and validated idea.

He explains this further by saying that the verified ideas lead us:

> through the acts and other ideas which they instigate, into or up to, or towards, other parts of experience with which we feel all the while ... that the original ideas remain in agreement. The connexions and transitions come to us from point to point as being progressive, harmonious, satisfactory. This function of agreeable leading is what we mean by an idea's verification.
>
> (James 1992: 100–1)

But is this agreeable leading, Pratt asks, itself wholly *within* experience? For example, is it subjective in the sense that a person is agreeably led just so far as he *feels* satisfied with his leading? In that case, as Pratt shows, two incompatible beliefs can both turn out to be true (ibid.: 159). On the other hand, by agreeable leading James may mean objective utility. Thus he explicitly compares his view with utilitarianism and in a number of passages suggests that a belief is true when in the long run it proves expedient or useful. In that case, however, James is again caught in a contradiction. For utility, whether in the long run or the short, presupposes independent fact. A simple example will illustrate the point. Suppose I claim that it is raining. Suppose, also, that the truth of that remark depends on its expediency or usefulness. For example, if I believe it is raining, I shall take precautions to keep dry. Someone who believes it is not raining will not take these precautions. He gets wet; I remain dry. That shows my belief is true, i.e., it has proved useful. But surely my belief has proved useful only if I have in fact remained dry. How is that to be established? Surely not by the usefulness of believing it, for then we are on an infinite regress. Unless we can take it as a fact that I have remained dry, we have not proved the usefulness of my believing it is raining. But if we can take it as a fact that I have remained dry, why can we not, at least in some circumstances, take it as a fact that it is raining? In short, utility can be a test of truth only if truth is independent of utility.

On reflection, it will be clear, as Pratt suggests, that what *makes* a claim true is simply the occurrence of what is claimed. 'It is raining' is true when it is raining. It may be said that we have not specified in that sentence what counts as an occurrence of rain. But that is something one learns in learning the meaning of 'It is raining'. In short, it is learned in practice. Criteria, otherwise, would be useless; for any criterion is useless unless it can be applied and it can be applied only where there is already an ability to grasp what occurs.

We may grant, of course, that the occurrence of what is claimed need not be evident; often it has to be *found out*. One may find out that it is raining by looking; one may rely on testimony; one may also detect the truth by its fruits; in short, by its usefulness. For example, most people trust a weather report not because they have that mastery of meteorology which would enable them to check it against the facts but simply because such reports tend to work. Here utility certainly plays its part. The weather report, when received, is not checked against the facts; we accept it because we have found that such reports enable us to cope with our experience. Here we have the model for James's theory of truth, at least in one of its versions. Note, however, two points. First, not every test of truth is like this; second, not even this is as James supposes. Thus, on closer inspection, we shall find in such cases that the utility of a belief is a sign of truth not because the two are equivalent but because it is the truth which provides the best explanation of its utility. Consider, by contrast, the following case. Suppose that someone, by employing a particular method of gambling, had succeeded on four nights in succession in winning large sums of money at a local casino. Have we sound reason to employ his method in that casino this evening? Not if we believe he simply had a run of luck. In other words, we should not accept the method as sound simply because it has worked: we should accept it only where its having worked is best explained by its soundness, that is, by its corresponding, as Peirce would insist, to objective tendencies or dispositions in the facts.

Moreover, we must emphasise a point already mentioned. None of these methods is infallible, and at some stage in all of them one is thrown back on one's own judgement. One may look and still not see correctly; witnesses may lie; circumstantial evidence may be deceptive; utility may be the product of chance. In each case, subsidiary rules may help to prevent error in applying the primary ones. But in applying the subsidiary rules error is still possible and one cannot go on applying rules for ever. If truth is ever known, someone has been convinced, has made a judgement, has taken something to be so. That is the fundamental act, presupposed in all our knowledge. What makes a claim true is the occurrence of what is claimed. What makes it known is that someone has taken the occurrence as such. How do we know he is correct in so taking it? Only by considering the matter for ourselves and by arriving, or not, at the same judgement.

In spite of their confusions, James's lectures are a remarkable achievement. They were delivered in Boston in 1906 and were addressed not to philosophers but to the educated public at large. The aim was to convey to that public, through some of the leading ideas in philosophy, a sense of what is important about philosophy itself. One could not imagine the aim being better achieved. The style is extraordinary, modulating from the vernacular to the abstract, and back again, with effortless virtuosity. Every lecture pulsates with life. Moreover, as one moves through its pages, one will come across many of the philosophical ideas which were to flourish in the present century. Students of Quine, for example, will find that he was anticipated in criticising certain dogmas of Empiricism. Thus his criticism of the second dogma is anticipated in the following passage, where James is explaining how we came to form new opinions.

The process here is always the same. The individual has a stock of old opinions already; but he meets a new experience that puts them to a strain. Somebody contradicts them; or in a reflective moment he discovers that they contradict each other; or he hears of facts with which they are incompatible; or desires arise in him which they cease to satisfy. The result is an inward trouble... from which he seeks to escape by modifying his previous mass of opinions. He saves as much of it as he can, for in this matter of belief we are all extreme conservatives. So he tries to change first this opinion, and then that... until at last some new idea comes up which he can graft upon the ancient stock with a minimum of disturbance of the latter....

(James 1992: 45)

Quine's criticism of the first dogma is anticipated in the following:

But how plastic even the oldest truths nevertheless really are has been vividly shown in our day by the transformation of logical and mathematical ideas, a transformation which seems even to be invading physics.

(ibid.: 47)

Nevertheless in their philosophical aim, the lectures are a failure. For their leading ideas, so far from serving to undermine scientism, serve only to perpetuate it. In that aim, as we shall see, James was more nearly successful not in his metaphysics but in the area where he was a master, philosophical psychology.

Chapter 4

Peirce: metaphysics and cosmology

We have still to consider in detail Peirce's explicit metaphysical and cosmological views. It will be useful to do so because they take us to the heart of his philosophy and because it seems to me that even the best of Peirce's commentators, in some important respects, have misunderstood them. An exception is Joseph Brent. As he implies in his biography, one cannot properly understand Peirce's central views unless one appreciates that they belong to what Leibniz called the Perennial Philosophy. This is a set of ideas which around 500 BC were found throughout the main civilisations of the world, which had an immense influence on Greek culture and, through it, on European culture in general. One finds these ideas expressed, for example, in the opening lines of Lao Tzu's *Tao Te Ching.*

> The Tao that can be expressed
> is not the eternal Tao.
> The name that can be named
> is not the eternal name.
> 'non-existence' I call the beginning of Heaven and Earth.
> 'Existence' I call the mother of individual beings.
> Therefore does the direction towards non-existence
> lead to the sight of the miraculous essence,
> the direction towards existence
> to the sight of spatial limitations.
>
> (Lao Tzu 1985: 27)

'Existence' is the world of spatial limitation, in short, the physical universe. It has emerged from a 'miraculous essence' which is described as 'non-existence' for that is how it appears from within the physical universe itself. In other words, the physical universe is a fragment of transcendental reality. From this reality, it has been, as it were, extruded.

Hence it is marked by what is brute, non-rational, by contingency and chance. These are what Peirce in his universal or metaphysical categories calls Firsts and Seconds. But the universe is real; consequently it cannot consist wholly of Firsts and Seconds; Firsts and Seconds cannot constitute a universe. The universe is real because it is suffused by transcendent reality in the form of law, generality, the relationships into which objects enter. These are what Peirce calls Thirds. In this, however, there is a paradox. The palpable is real only through the impalpable, through what least appears as real. Thus law is not an object. It appears in the necessity by which objects are related; it therefore *shows itself* in the way objects behave but it is not itself a behaving object. For that reason, the *Tao Te Ching* is pervaded by symbols of indirection. The 'female' is one; 'water' is another. Water is the weakest and most yielding of substances. It serves as a symbol of the Tao because it also prevails. Nothing is weaker than water yet in the end it wears away even the hardest rock. What 'exists' then is not law; yet law shows itself in what 'exists'. The relation is akin to that of sign and signified. Every sign, it may be noted, has its arbitrary element. 'It is red' when taken as a set of marks is arbitrary, so that what it means could be meant by some other set, which itself would be no less arbitrary. Yet those marks, in use, take on meaning, and signify what is other than themselves. So, also, the arbitrary element in the world, its empirical residue or brute matter, in itself unassimilable to law, reveals in movement a reality that transcends it. The world is then itself revealed as the very word of God. It is the matter in which that word is embodied, so that there is a triadic relation between God, the world and ourselves, in which through the mediation of the world, which is God's word, we are related to God himself. We shall see, as we proceed, that Peirce's metaphysics is properly understood only when seen against this background.

For Peirce, metaphysics is a form of reflection. This has as its object what he describes, on some occasions, as the fundamental forms of logic and, on others, as the fundamental features of the mind in its relations to the world. These descriptions are thought by some of his commentators to be inconsistent. They criticise him for confusing a logical with a factual inquiry. But this criticism, as we have said, is based on the assumption that one may distinguish at every level between logic and fact. This was not an assumption that Peirce shared. For him, there was no absolute gulf between logic and language on the one hand and the world on the other. Indeed he held, as we have just implied, that the triadic relation of the sign expresses the fundamental relations between the mind, the world and God. He did hold that a logical inquiry is distinguishable at every level from a *psychological* one. Psychology is a science which studies, for example, the special conditions under which a certain mental process would or would not occur. But the features that are fundamental to the mind are not those which occur only under special conditions; they are features of the mind in all its workings. Moreover psychology, like any science, conducts its inquiries from an impersonal or third person point of view. But in this, again like any science, it depends for its material on knowledge which is gained, not in that way, but through personal engagement with the world, through knowledge obtained in practice. This knowledge for the most part is beyond the criticism of science. It is elucidated not by a special science but through personal reflection. This reflection, when it takes a fundamental form, is precisely metaphysics.

We must now consider in some detail the fundamental categories which Peirce thinks will be elicited by such reflection. Roughly, these are feeling (First); reaction (Second) and law or habit (Third). We must emphasise that these categories are isolated in analysis; they are not isolated in fact. Quite the contrary, there can be no intelligible experience which does not involve all three. It will be obvious that these categories correspond to what, in his theory of the sign, Peirce takes as the fundamental forms of logical relation: monadic (feeling); dyadic (reaction); triadic (law).

To explain his category of First, Peirce imagines a person who is sensitive only to the green element in light (Peirce 1935(VI) para. 2: 150). Then everything he sees will be green. Peirce remarks that this will not attract his attention; he will not know that he sees everything as green. In short, knowledge requires contrast, which implies generality. For example, how does one see the greenness of an object as distinct from its roundness, its colour as distinct from its shape? The two are distinguishable, but how are they distinguished? One needs further experience, for example, the experience of green objects that are not round and round objects that are not green. Consequently to know one is seeing green is to know one is seeing *an instance* of what can appear in objects of a different shape and may not appear in objects of the same shape. In short, there is generality involved. Knowledge of the singular presupposes the general. One does not approach the general having discerned the sharply singular. Knowledge begins in what is vague and general and only later becomes particularised. As William Hamilton used to say, one can distinguish a close acquaintance from a stranger who looks almost exactly like him, but one would have great difficulty in stating what details in particular enable one to do so. The child begins by calling every man of the appropriate size and shape his father and only later fastens on one man in particular.

But although the general, says Peirce, enters into the knowledge of sensation, it does not explain its felt quality or *quale*. 'Quale' is a Latin word which means 'particular suchness'. An example will enable us to see what Peirce means. Someone who uses a stick to probe a dark hole is not aware of the vibrations transmitted from the stick to his hand. What he feels seems to be located not in his hand but at the tip of his stick. One may be inclined to say that the sensations he feels are not really in the stick; they are in the hand. In fact, however, they are only located in his hand relative to his attention being focused there. Typically, indeed, such sensations perform the function of focusing attention. That is precisely why what a person feels seem to be at the tip of his stick. It is to the tip of his stick that his attention is directed. The point is especially evident in the case of malfunctioning. Someone whose hand has been amputated may nevertheless feel sensations in the hand which no longer exists. In this case, the sensations are located at a point entirely disconnected with his body. In fact there is nothing at this point. What is true is that it is towards this point that his attention is directed. Sensations then have a role or function within the economy of the body. Moreover a function is general. *The important point, however, is that the function into which a sensation enters does not explain its felt quality or quale.* Its 'suchness' is not exhausted by its general role. This is especially evident where sensations with entirely different qualia have exactly the same function. Thus for most purposes, a colour-blind person can identify objects as readily as a sighted one. Cournot remarked that a race of colour-blind creatures would not thereby be prevented from developing a physics almost exactly the same as our own. (By contrast, physics would be radically different amongst a race of creatures who were less than a millionth of a millimetre in height.) The reason for this is that the visual sensations of the colour blind and the sighted differ simply in their qualia and not in their relations or in the patterns they form. But the role of visual sensations, in identifying objects, is determined by their relations, by the patterns they form, not by their qualia. In short, the visual sensations of the colour blind and the sighted have the same function. Nevertheless they differ in their *qualia*.

Qualia enter into law but they cannot be assimilated to it. By law they can neither be explained nor limited. They are an element in the world of *spontaneous variety*. Within the Perennial Philosophy, they constitute part of the empirical residue or arbitrary element. They are a phenomenon of chance. It is Peirce's intention, as we shall see, to show that chance is not a product of our ignorance but a real element in the universe. Moreover he will argue that the present law-like state of the universe has evolved from a more primitive state which, relative to the present, may be characterised as one of chance or spontaneity.

Now Peirce says that in qualia one does not find existence, but only its possibility. He is referring to qualia as isolated in analysis. One may have an idea of what he means if one reflects on the experience of an abrupt intrusion of excruciating pain. Such pain fills the consciousness, so that one loses all sense of what or when or where. This is pure quale. Moreover, it is important to note that one loses the sense of oneself no less than that of an objective world. In pure quale one loses the sense of existence. What then is the source of this sense? It cannot be derived from law. All law is conditional. It appears only when something is given. Thus from a law one cannot derive any actual existent, except on the basis of some other actual existent, which is itself not derived from law. Existence is given in Second, which is an immediate awareness of something over and against oneself. It seems evident, as we have said, that in this Peirce was decisively influenced by Reid, Hamilton and the Scottish philosophers. Bump into an object in the dark and one is immediately aware of something not oneself. This is the primitive sense of existence, the source of one's idea no less of the self than of the not-self. In short, the sense of reality is given in the awareness of reaction, of contingency, in what is simply so, whatever our thoughts about it. If the world conformed exactly to our thoughts there would be no difference for us between our thoughts and the world. We should then lose our sense of the objective world and thereby of the subjective also. Reality enters through what is arbitrary in relation to our thought, in the awareness of what is just brutely so. We must note again, however, that we are here dealing with the categories as isolated in analysis. Peirce is *not* suggesting that Second, the awareness of reaction, occurs without context and independently of sensation and law. There can be no such awareness. Every intelligible experience, as we have said, involves all three categories. Indeed it may already be apparent that the categories are interrelated. Thus law (First) presupposes actual existents, the sense of which is given in reaction (Second). But the sense of reaction requires some element of sensation (First). Moreover sensation is intelligible only given reaction and Law (Second and Third). Nevertheless, the sense of reaction can be isolated in analysis because although it presupposes sensation and law, it cannot be *assimilated* to them. Thus, as we have seen, there is nothing in sensation and law to provide a *conception* of an objective existent. Consequently, no objective existent can be *inferred* from sensation and law. That, again, is not to deny that underlying our immediate awareness of objective existents there are processes, physiological or psychological, which are akin to inference. But the effect of these processes in the conscious mind is not itself an inference; rather it is an immediate awareness of real existents. Without that contact with reality, there would be no sense of a reality even to infer.

First and Second represent the elements in the world of spontaneity, chance and contingency. These elements are real but if they alone were real we should not *know* that they were. Hence the reality of law or habit, Third. Peirce uses 'law' and 'habit' more or less interchangeably. At first, there seems to be an obvious contrast. Law, in the physical world, is fixed, unchanging, but habits develop or grow. A habit develops, for example, as it is exercised or indulged. In fact, Peirce denies this contrast, at least in an absolute sense. He argues that laws, even in the physical world, are of the nature of habits and that they too have developed and grown. It may be noted that whereas mechanical processes never turn purposive, there is a tendency for purposive activities to turn mechanical. For example, one does not learn to ride a bicycle without conscious attention, but thereafter the activity becomes habitual, turns mechanical, and one no longer has to think about it. Peirce argues that physical law is of the nature of habit which has hardened and become mechanical. It has done so in the development from a more primitive state which, relative to the present, may be characterised as one of spontaneity and chance. The real significance of this view, however, will become apparent only as we proceed.

Peirce's metaphysical views have as their main concern the problem of continuity and discontinuity. The view which affirms the reality of continuity, law, generality, Peirce calls *Synechism*. The view which affirms the reality of discontinuity, chance, contingency, he calls *Tychism*. Most philosophies suppress or minimise the reality of one of these elements. Peirce affirms the reality of both. Thus his categories of First and Second represent those elements in the world of real chance and contingency; his category Third, those elements of real law and generality. He made use of these categories to provide an illuminating classification of the various philosophies which have appeared throughout history. For example, Hobbes's philosophy is pure Tychism. He attempts to characterise the world almost exclusively in terms of the category of Second, contingency, interaction. Hence his philosophy is Nominalist and Materialist. Berkeley altogether omits the category Second. There is nothing in his world except sensation and human or divine purpose. His philosophy is based exclusively on the categories of First and Third. It is evident that Peirce's own philosophy before the 1880s belongs in this respect with Berkeley's. He had ignored the reality of Second. Positivism takes this process further omitting also the category of Third and dissolving the world into pure sensation. Hegel's philosophy, by contrast, is pure synechism. He attempts to make the world entirely rational, admitting as real only those aspects which fall under law or Third. Peirce mentions three philosophers who have done justice to all the categories: Plato, Kant and Reid.

COSMOLOGY

We may now turn to Peirce's cosmology, the elements of which have already been indicated. Peirce argues that existing regularities are contingent and not ultimate. They have developed from a more primitive state of spontaneity through the play of continuity and discontinuity, generality and chance. There is therefore a tendency in the universe to take on regularity, to move from a less to a more ordered state. But there is equally a *tension* between regularity or order on the one hand and spontaneity or chance on the other. Thus order is very imperfectly achieved. The universe is in a state of *becoming*. Everywhere it exhibits 'the brute reactions and mutual interferences of things and systems of things which have so far failed to come into conditions of equilibrium one with another' (Gallie 1952: 221). There is here an obvious analogy with human conduct. The generality of intention only imperfectly realises itself in actual regularity of conduct because it is in constant tension with those contingencies of occurrent desire which work against it. For Peirce the processes at work in human conduct are aspects of the processes at work in the universe at large.

Now in order to appreciate Peirce's cosmology, it is important to grasp that it is essentially directed against that Positivism or Materialism which was dominant in his age and which, implicitly or explicitly, embraced the mechanist philosophy. Like Edwards, Peirce believed that this philosophy was based on a failure to understand the limitations of the Newtonian system. Peirce, indeed, was almost alone amongst philosophers and scientists of the nineteenth century in appreciating those limitations. For example, he was one of the first to see that there is an important difference between those processes in nature which are reversible and those which are not. A dynamic or mechanical process is reversible. The process by which the first ball moves the second would, if reversed, make the second ball move the first. But most of the processes in ordinary life are irreversible. The process by which you melt an ice cube will not flow back once again into an ice cube. Peirce remarks that substantially everything in ordinary experience is of this kind, except the motion of the stars. Now if we look at irreversible processes we shall find that they have chance as an essential element. For example why does heat flow in one direction? If a hot body touches an ice cube, the ice cube melts. Why does the cool body not become a little hotter and the hot body a little cooler? That is theoretically possible. For example, if the particles of the respective bodies met, as it were, head on, they would repulse one another; this would leave the particles of the cool body moving a little more quickly so that it would be a little hotter and those of the hot body moving a little less quickly so that it would be a little cooler. But the chances of this occurring are hardly to be considered. It is enormously likely that particles will interpenetrate and that the particles of the hot body being quicker will disperse themselves the more rapidly. So the ice cube melts. This of course is a law: heat melts ice. But it rests on a mass of contingencies and is, in a manner, statistical. Heat melts ice because of all the possibilities of trajectory amongst the particles in the bodies involved, the overwhelming majority will lead to its doing so. Here we have law based on a set of chances amongst contingencies. It is not based on that alone. For there is also the generality involved in the movement of the particles. Without knowing what *kind* of movements are involved we could not determine which configurations are and which are not probable. These points have become more evident, since Peirce's time, through the development of quantum mechanics. In quantum mechanics, the laws for determining the behaviour of particles are explicitly statistical. Moreover, since an object is a collection of particles, this means that the laws for determining their behaviour, even in reversible processes, are also in a sense statistical. They may be treated as certainties for practical purposes, because at this level the possibility of error is negligible. Here we have an idea of scientific law strikingly different from the one which was common in the nineteenth century. But it conforms exactly to the one that Peirce employs in his cosmology.

Now it must be noted that the play of generality over contingency leads not simply to order but to order of different kinds, some weaker, others stronger than the one we have considered. An example of a weaker form may be found in the throw of a die. One may calculate the possibilities of a die's falling on one side. For example, the chances of throwing a six are 1:6. Moreover, in throwing a die over a reasonably long period the six does in fact fall roughly in that proportion. There will be runs which vary from that proportion but they will not vary in any systematic way. Consequently, the probability of throwing a six has a kind of order and can be stated as a law. Why is that so? The answer once again lies in the relation between generality and chance. The die is so constructed that it will always fall on one of its sides, intermediate positions being excluded. That is a general tendency in the die. Given that tendency and given that the causes operating on the die are distributed by chance so that they do not favour any of the sides in particular, one may expect over a long run that the sides will come down in roughly equal proportion, 1:6.

Moreover, there are forms of order which are stronger than those we have considered, in the sense that they have the tendency to become more orderly or to develop into more complicated forms of order. An obvious example is the evolution of the species. Given a tendency to adaptation in the species and given also a tendency of variation in its forms, neither of which can be explained by chance, or not exclusively so, then the play of chance in the environment will tend to the survival of the better adapted and that, in its turn, to better or more complicated forms of adaptation, and so on. That again is precisely one of the ideas that Peirce adopts in his cosmology.

It is clear that the *elements* of Peirce's cosmology are not speculative but may be exhibited in the world about us. Moreover, their implications are of the first importance. We may distinguish three such implications. The first is that mechanical phenomena are not fundamental in nature; the second, that the regularities of physics are contingent and are not ultimate; the third, that since the processes of nature are not fundamentally mechanical, there need be no gulf between those processes and the processes of mind.

We shall return to these points. But first let us consider Peirce's cosmology as a *historical* account. In this respect, it has attracted numerous criticisms. As I have implied, however, most of these criticisms seem to me confused. Let me therefore try to illustrate my point. A number of commentators suggest, or make it easy to assume, that when Peirce describes how the law-like state of the universe has developed from a more primitive one, he is attempting to explain law or continuity itself. But what he is attempting to explain is the present law-like state of the universe, those regularities which exist at present. His point is that these are not ultimate, as was commonly assumed in his own day, but have developed from prior conditions. Law or continuity itself he does not attempt to explain but rather presupposes in his explanation. As we shall see in a moment, law or continuity can be explained only on the basis of a higher law or continuity. Law or continuity itself is transcendent. It is the form that transcendent reality takes in the universe.

A failure to appreciate that point is at the basis of a number of other criticisms. For example, Murray Murphey argues that Peirce's evolutionary account of the universe is incoherent because every evolutionary process requires an environment but there is no environment for the universe itself. Gallie says that Peirce has described the original state of the universe exclusively in terms of his category First (chance or spontaneity) and that this is inconsistent with what he says elsewhere, namely, that every occurrence involves all three of his categories. Both these criticisms presuppose that for Peirce the physical universe is ultimate. But that is not at all what he believed; he believed rather that the physical universe is a fragment of transcendent reality. As such, it must in some sense have environment. Nor, as Gallie supposes, is the universe ever devoid of law or continuity. Law or continuity is always present, however implicitly, for it is constitutive of the very reality of the universe.

That law or continuity, however, cannot be exhaustively grasped. As we have seen, no continuum can be reduced to a set of actual instances. Nor can it be reduced to a set of actual regularities. Thus an actual regularity (heat melts ice) presupposes generality (for example, in the motion of the particles) which cannot be reduced to it. The reality of law or continuity is shown in that actual instances or actual regularities are unintelligible without it. Consequently those instances or regularities are themselves symbolic of what transcends them. We may rephrase the point. Peirce's metaphysics is essentially concerned with the reality of both continuity and discontinuity. Now granting their reality, how are they related? This problem cannot be resolved unless we see discontinuous phenomena as the material in which continuity embodies itself. But if it had embodied itself completely the material would not be discontinuous. Consequently that material must be the partial embodiment of continuity, that in which continuity is still working itself out. Now that is the essence of Peirce's cosmology.

These points may be clarified if we consider in some detail one of the papers in which Peirce expounds his cosmology. For our purpose, the most useful is the one entitled, *The Logic of the Universe* (Peirce 1935(VI):134–41). As we might expect, the problem at its centre is that of continuity (para. 191): 'How then can a continuum have been derived? Has it for example been put together? Have the separated points become welded, or what?'

Peirce implies that this is an impossible supposition. A continuum cannot be pieced together out of its instances. The general precedes the particular. The line in all evolution is from the more general to the less, from the vague to the definite.

> In Spencer's phrase the undifferentiated differentiates itself. The homogeneous puts on heterogeneity. However it may be in special cases, then, we must suppose that as a rule the continuum has been derived from a more general continuum, a continuum of higher generality.
>
> (Peirce 1935(VI): para. 191)

It follows that continuity cannot be derived from the existing universe. For all the facts of this universe involve generalities which can be derived, not from those facts, but only from higher generalities.

> From this point of view we must suppose that the existing universe, with all its arbitrary secondness, is an offshoot from, or an arbitrary determination of, a world of ideas, a Platonic world; not that our superior logic has enabled us to reach up to a world of forms to which the real universe, with its feebler logic, was inadequate.
>
> (ibid.: para. 192)

It follows that the evolutionary process with which we are familiar 'is not a mere evolution of the *existing universe* but rather a process by which the very Platonic forms themselves have become or are becoming developed' (ibid.).

Now it is imperative *not* to suppose that Peirce is here advocating the Platonic theory of transcendent reality. He is not proposing *any* direct theory of transcendent reality; rather he is indicating, indirectly, that reality is transcendent. The Platonic forms are a symbol for, not a theory of, transcendent reality. (There is abundant evidence, we may note in passing, that they had the same function in Plato's own philosophy.) Thus, he says explicitly that we have no logic superior to that of the universe by which we can reach up to the world of forms. He says, again, that we cannot suppose the universe began 'elsewhere than in the utter vagueness of completely undetermined and dimensionless potentiality.' In other words, we can conceive of transcendental reality only in terms of *potentiality* not in terms of *existence*. That is because we can conceive of existence in positive terms only by reference to the physical universe. Transcendent reality is not this universe but it is only in terms of this universe that we can refer to it. Consequently we can refer to it only *relative* to the universe. We cannot conceive of transcendental reality as *being* this universe, so we conceive of it as being *potentially* so. It is that which the universe comes from. The terms are not positive but negative and relative. Peirce's thought is the same as is found in the lines we quoted from the *Tao Te Ching* (Lao Tzu 1985):

> 'Non-existence' I call the beginning of Heaven and Earth
> 'Existence' I call the mother of individual beings.'

Peirce next offers a sketch of how the universe has emerged from a state which he characterises in terms of sense-qualities or Firsts.

> Imagine a magenta colour. Now imagine that all the rest of your consciousness – memory, thought, everything except the feeling of magenta – is utterly wiped out and with that is erased all possibility of comparing the magenta with anything else or of estimating it as more or less bright. That is what you must think the pure sense-quality to be. Such a definite potentiality can emerge from the indefinite potentiality only by its own vital Firstness and spontaneity.
>
> (Peirce 1935(VI): para. 198)

Now it is essential to grasp that Peirce does not take himself to be giving a literal description of how the universe originated. In another place he says: 'Our conceptions of the first stages of the development, before time yet existed, must be as vague and figurative as the expressions of the first chapter of Genesis.' He is attempting, in figurative terms, to convey two ideas. The first is that the fundamental features of the universe are more comparable with processes of mind than with those normally associated with matter and consequently that there is no absolute gulf between matter and mind. This is the doctrine of Objective Idealism, according to which the objective universe may be seen ultimately as mental in character. But, again, the word 'doctrine' must be taken with reservations. When in this paper, Peirce discusses the view that the world exists in the mind of God, he comments as follows.

> I really think there is no objection to this except that it is wrapped up in figures of speech ... For all you know of 'minds' is from the actions of animals with brains or ganglia like yourselves, or at furthest like a cockroach. To apply such a word to *God* is precisely like the old pictures which show him like an aged man leaning over to look out from above a cloud.
>
> (Peirce 1935(VI): para. 199)

The reality which is the source of our being transcends both what we think of as mind and what we think of as matter. But of the two it is 'mind' which the better expresses that reality.

The second idea Peirce is attempting to convey is that the universe involves the particularisation, in some measure arbitrarily, of a higher or more general reality. In this respect, it is important to note that qualities or Firsts do not hold, as Gallie supposes, out of relation to law or continuity. Peirce is explicit on the point:

Yet we must not assume that the qualities arose separate and came into relation afterward. It was just the reverse. The general indefinite potentiality became limited and heterogenous. Those who express the idea to themselves by saying that the Divine Creator determined so and so may be incautiously clothing the idea in a *garb* that is open to criticism, but it is, after all, substantially the only philosophical answer to the problem.

(Peirce 1935(VI): para. 199)

Peirce goes on to illustrate this point by means of a striking example:

Let the clean blackboard be a sort of diagram of the original value potentiality, or at any rate of some early stage of its determination. This is something more than a figure of speech; for after all continuity is generality. This blackboard is a continuum of two dimensions, while that which it stands for is a continuum of some indefinite multitude of dimensions. This blackboard is a continuum of possible points; while that is a continuum of possible dimensions of quality, or is a continuum of possible dimensions of a continuum of possible dimensions of quality, or something of that sort. There are no points on this blackboard. There are no dimensions in that continuum. I draw a chalk line on the board. This discontinuity is one of those brute acts by which alone the original vagueness could have made a step towards definiteness. There is a certain element of continuity in this line. Where did this continuity come from? It is nothing but the original continuity of the blackboard which makes everything upon it continuous.

(Peirce 1935(VI): para. 203)

It may be noted in this passage that Peirce is not interested in details. He is attempting to illustrate not the details of the universe but its *logic*. That logic cannot be understood until we grasp the relation between continuity and discontinuity. What he is attempting to convey is that discontinuity emerges through the particularisation of a continuum which is still present in those particulars, as the continuity of the blackboard is present in that of the chalk line. He next comments that the chalk mark is not, strictly speaking, a line. For example, it is not a line in the geometrical sense, since it has dimensions. Rather it is a surface. The only line present is that which forms the *limit* between the white surface and the black surface.

> Thus the discontinuity can only be produced upon that blackboard by the reaction between two continuous surfaces into which it is separated, the white surface and the black surface. The whiteness is a Firstness – a springing up of something new. But the boundary between the black and white is neither black, nor white, nor neither, nor both. It is for white the active Secondness of the black; for the black the active Secondness of the White.
>
> (Peirce 1935(VI): para. 203)

Peirce is here attempting to convey the nature of Secondness or contingency. To see what he means, consider a contingent or fortuitous occurrence, such as the falling of a tile which injures a passer-by. The occurrence is fortuitous because the causation which brought the passer-by to this spot contains no reference to the causation which produced the falling tile; and vice versa. Nevertheless there is law or continuity in each of those causal chains taken separately. The contingency is, as it were, the running into one another of different continuities. Thus continuity is everywhere present. It is present in white (First) which cannot exist without the continuity of the blackboard and in the relation between white and black (Second) which is formed by a reaction between its surfaces. Moreover, continuities amongst particulars are always manifestations of higher continuity (see Peirce 1935(V) para. 9: 75). 'There is a certain element of continuity in this line. Where did this continuity come from? It is nothing but the original continuity of the blackboard which makes everything upon it continuous.'

Thus everywhere in the universe transcendent reality shows itself. This is the very view which Peirce expresses elsewhere in the following terms.

> Therefore, if you ask me what part Qualities can play in the economy of the universe, I shall reply that the universe is a vast representamen, a great symbol of God's purpose, working out its conclusions in living realities. Now every symbol must have, organically attached to it, its Indices of Reactions and its Icons of

Qualities; and such part as these reactions and these qualities play in an argument that, they of course, play in the universe – that Universe being precisely an argument.

(Peirce 1935(V) para. 119: 75)

As Joseph Brent remarks, Peirce's views are the same as those which Plato expressed in one of the most famous passages in *The Timaeus*. Plato says that the universe is a 'Living Being' whose:

character it was impossible to confer in full completeness on the generated thing. But he (the creator) took thought to make, as it were, a moving likeness of eternity, and at the same time... he made, of eternity... an everlasting likeness moving according to number – that to which we have given the name Time.

(Brent 1993: 345)

A sign is precisely a moving image. Brute matter in itself, the sign, in movement, takes on meaning; and the greatest of signs is the universe itself, the moving image of eternity.

The point may be clarified further if we consider a paper of Peirce's entitled *A Neglected Argument For The Reality of God* (Peirce 1935(VI): 313–39). At first sight the paper is an odd one. Peirce spends much of it, not on religious issues, but in analysing scientific reasoning. Moreover, the argument itself seems not to have been neglected; it seems to be a mixture of two familiar types of argument for the existence of God, the cosmological argument and the argument from design. I do not think that commentators have made clear what its essential point is.

Peirce begins by describing a state he calls Musement. By this he means a state in which certain topics are given a free play of the mind. The play is free because the mind has no ulterior motive. It follows wherever it may be led by the play of thought itself. He then argues that if in this way we reflect on the general features of the world, and especially on its three pervasive categories, we shall find ourselves led to the idea of God.

in the Pure Play of Musement the idea of God's Reality will be sure sooner or later to be found an attractive fancy, which the Muser will develop in various ways. The more he ponders it, the more it will find response in every part of his mind, for its beauty, for its supplying an ideal of life, and for its thoroughly satisfactory explanation of his whole threefold environment.

(Peirce 1935(VI): para. 465)

It may be wondered how this differs from the cosmological argument, according to which God's existence is inferred from the existence of the world. The essential point is that the movement from the world to God, which Peirce describes, is not in the ordinary sense an inference. For example, it is neither deductive nor inductive. Thus Peirce is not suggesting that we arrive at the existence of God by analogy with our past experience, nor that there would be a contradiction in denying the existence of God, having affirmed the existence of the world. Nevertheless the movement of thought, which he describes is not illusory. It is precisely in order to show this that Peirce devotes the middle sections of his paper to an analysis of scientific reasoning. The points he makes are already familiar. He argues that in science both induction and deduction are subsidiary processes, neither of which can explain the discovery of a single scientific theory or law. A theory or law is discovered at a more fundamental level of the mind; moreover it is precisely at this level that the mind moves from the world to God. Thus a genuine discovery in science is made only when a scientist frees his mind of ulterior purpose and allows his attention to be absorbed by the world itself. In attending to the details of an empirical phenomena, he may then find that the law which is the fundamental reality of that phenomenon takes shape in his mind. That law will then show its reality by the sense it enables the scientist to make of further empirical phenomena, and then of phenomena further still, and so on endlessly. The law itself will never be exhausted by the phenomena in which it shows itself. The relation, of course, is just like that between a sign and its meaning. The law is not inferred as an entity separate from its instances. Rather, the scientist, as it were, 'reads' the law *in* those instances, which nevertheless do not exhaust the law. This process is by no means confined to science. It is this process which is at work, for example, in our awareness of Second, which gives us our very sense of existence. This awareness is not inferred; nevertheless it is mediated through sensation, which like any sign draws attention not to itself but to what it signifies. Moreover, the physical reality which sensation reveals can never be reduced to it. There is more to physical reality than can ever be analysed in terms of sensation. The process is even more evidently at work in our knowledge of other persons. We read a person's thoughts or feelings in his features or in his behaviour. The process is neither deductive nor inductive. We see in a person's features that he is in pain. But we do not infer the pain from the details of his features. We are less certain of those details than we are of his being in pain. The details call attention not to themselves but to the reality they embody. Moreover, there is more to that reality than can ever be embodied in those details. There is more to any person than can be read in his features or behaviour. In just that way, Peirce argues, we are led from the world to God. We do not construe the world according to our own purposes but give it our purest attention and then we find in the world the reality which transcends it, which the world itself can never exhaust. The process is neither arbitrary nor illusory. It is the same process by which, through ordinary sensation, we are given our sense of existence itself.

It will be useful in conclusion to consider a further criticism, often brought against Peirce. The criticism is that his metaphysical views are in conflict with his Pragmatism, because they are not amenable to scientific testing. Now if by scientific testing is meant the procedures of some special science, such as physics, this may be true. As we have seen, Peirce did not believe that metaphysical views are in that way scientific. It does not follow that they lack consequences, nor even that they lack consequences for science. We may take an obvious example. The Positivists of the nineteenth century, who discarded metaphysics, proved quite mistaken in their views about the future course of science itself. Peirce, by contrast, was remarkably prescient. Moreover, he was assisted in this by views that were central to his metaphysics. We may take a further example. The relation between body and mind has been a problem throughout the history of inquiry. In Peirce's terms, the reason why the problem seems altogether baffling is that it is framed entirely as a matter of Second. It becomes less baffling when we find a mediating Third. Thus the problem is to find how body and mind act on one another. But no reaction, no Second, is intelligible when taken in itself. It must always be mediated by some law, habit or purpose, some Third. Thus instead of asking how mind and body act on one another, we should ask how mental and physical events are related within some wider system. In this case, the system is evidently the organism as a whole. The brain, for example, serves the function of co-ordinating the responses of the organism to the environment. But then whatever the relation between a mental event and an event in the brain it cannot be *brute*. The one can be related to the other only if both are related to a Third, the functioning of the whole body. So the question is not how mind and body affect one another but how the mental and physical aspects of the body are related to its functioning as a whole. As we shall see, the most fruitful work of the later Pragmatists was in philosophical psychology. Moreover, the inspiration for their work was derived, whether directly or indirectly, from this idea of Peirce's. The point will become evident when we turn in the next chapter to the work of William James.

Chapter 5

James: background and *The Principles of Psychology*

William James is unusual amongst great men in that one often needs to remind oneself of his greatness. That is because he had the substance without its usual manner. Unlike the typical sage or prophet, for example, he always addresses us as equals. That was a quality he shared with Dewey, his fellow Pragmatist. Sidney Hook has written as follows of Dewey.

> The Vermont and the New England of Dewey's boyhood and youth are gone. But he still carries with him traces of its social environment, not as memories but as habits, deep preferences, and an ingrained democratic bias. They show themselves in his simplicity of manner, his basic courtesy, freedom from every variety of snobbism, and matter of course respect for the right of everyone in America as a human being and a citizen.

Much of that description would fit James as well as Dewey. Each had a faith in democracy and embodied its values. In this, they were influenced by the traditions of their country and especially by its protestant heritage. The faith in equality is not immediately justified by the facts. Human beings tend to fasten on to differences amongst themselves and especially on any differences in talent, gift or social status. God, however, according to the old protestants, is less impressed by our differences, judging us on the whole to be of equal worth, saving those who turn to him, not because of their especial merit but out of his mercy. James's democratic spirit appears even in his style of writing, which is easy and, by the standard of the time, extremely informal. His phrases, though often brilliant, seem never to have been created for effect but only because, at the point where they occur, they were the best way of explaining what he meant. Again, one has often to remind oneself of how brilliant a writer he is. His style is so entirely natural that one forgets to give him credit for it.

James's education was an unusual one. His father was a wealthy man who had been trained for the ministry but had turned against orthodox Christianity. Subsequently, he cultivated unorthodox thought and encouraged his children to think for themselves and to follow their own inspiration. The family was often on the move, frequently visiting Europe. From an early age, the children were familiar with cultural issues, and especially issues in philosophy and religion, not through explicit instruction, but as common topics raised at the family table. Their precociousness may be illustrated by an incident involving William's brother Henry, the famous novelist. As a small boy he was sent into the garden to play with his sister; surveying the scene, he remarked, 'That might certainly be called pleasure under difficulties.'

William at first was trained as an artist. He acquired some skill, but did not persist with his training because he believed he lacked real talent. Instead, he enrolled as a medical student, graduating in 1867, when he was twenty-five. His medical studies had been interrupted for fifteen months, when in 1865 he had taken part in a scientific expedition to the Amazon, led by the famous botanist Louis Agassiz. Throughout the period, however, when he was acquiring a thorough scientific training, his main preoccupations had been personal and philosophical, the two being related. In his adolescence, he had become affected with bouts of depression. Problems of this kind were common in his family. In the 1840s, his father had suffered a severe nervous breakdown and his sister Alice suffered from nervous problems throughout her life. In William's case, the causes were in part philosophical. He had become oppressed by the outlook on the world of Scientific Positivism: its strict or universal determinism, much advocated at the time, being for him a special problem. It is possible that he encountered this view as it was presented in a famous lecture by T. H. Huxley. Huxley held a view termed 'epiphenomenalism'. This is the view that mental events, though real enough, belong, as it were, to the surface, having no effect on human life, which may be explained wholly by mechanical principles. Huxley illustrated his views by taking a frog whose brain had been almost wholly removed. In that condition, the frog was incapable of sensation or indeed of initiating action. Placed in the palm of the hand, it would stay there for ever. Curiously enough, however, on a slight turning of the hand, the frog's legs would adjust to maintain balance. Turning the hand over, so that the palm faced the ground, one would find that the frog had retained its hold and was now perched on the back of the hand. This delicate balancing act was performed, Huxley emphasised, entirely without the benefit of mind. Moreover, if one threw the frog in a pond it would swim away, indistinguishable from any other frog.

In March 1870, James underwent a terrible experience, which he later described, though not under his own name, in his *Varieties of Religious Experience.*

> Whilst in a state of philosophical pessimism and general depression of spirits about my prospects, I went one evening in a dressing room in the twilight to procure some article that was there; when suddenly there fell on me without warning, just as if it came out of the darkness, a horrible fear of my own existence. Simultaneously there arise in my mind the image of an epileptic patient whom I had seen in the asylum, a black-haired youth with greenish skin, entirely idiotic, who used to sit all day on one of the benches, or rather shelves against the wall, with his knees drawn up against his chin, and the coarse grey undershirt, which was his only garment, drawn over them enclosing his entire figure. . . . This image and my fear entered into a species of combination with each other. That shape am I, I felt, potentially. Nothing that I possess can defend me against that fate, if the hour for it should strike for me as it struck for him. There was such a horror of him, and such a perception of my own merely momentary discrepancy from him that it was as if something hitherto solid within my breast gave way entirely, and I became a mass of quivering fear. After this the universe was changed for me altogether. I awoke morning after morning with a horrible dread in the pit of my stomach and with a sense of the insecurity of life that I never knew before, and that I have never felt since.

> (James 1959:166–7)

Jacques Barzun (1983: 18) remarks that in the figure of the idiot on his bench, James had, like a painter 'objectified Huxley's view of man as automaton, giving visual equivalents for the horror, vacancy and desolation that the conception implied.'

James's struggle against his nervous depression and terror was indistinguishably intellectual and personal. He determined that if he could overcome them by the exertion of his own will, he would thereby have disproved the idea that fed them, namely, the idea of man as an automaton. That idea would be disproved by the very *act* of overcoming the terror and depression. His success in doing so left him with an idea which was of great importance in his later philosophy. Often in his later work, he argued that the scientific attitude, or what is often taken as such, was in certain areas not only false but pernicious. By the scientific attitude, he meant, roughly, the view that one should withhold belief, on any issue, until one had acquired conclusive evidence of the truth. Against this, he argued that on many issues, and especially on the most important ones, the truth can be established only by those who have the faith to take it as such.

In 1872, James was appointed as an instructor in Harvard, his subjects being anatomy and physiology. In succeeding years, he expanded his experimental interests to include psychology, and later concentrated on the main issues of philosophy. All his work, however, is imbued with philosophical reflection and his specifically philosophical work is informed by his scientific interests. Moreover, no academic thinker has been less academic, in the pejorative sense of abstract, remote from life. All his work is an extension, at the reflective level, of his passionate engagement with life itself.

THE PRINCIPLES OF PSYCHOLOGY

James's first great work, indeed his chief masterpiece, is *The Principles of Psychology*, published in 1890. It is a large work, as befits its subject, which is the human mind. It is an inexhaustible source of instruction and entertainment. Jacques Barzun says, correctly, that it should be read at least once by anyone professing to be educated. Here we are forced to be severely selective. We shall pursue those themes already touched on, showing how James, in his work on mind, is elaborating ideas introduced by Peirce. For example, we shall note how James, in emphasising that mind is active on nature, is developing Peirce's view of inquiry. We shall note, too, how James like Peirce is seeking to undermine the categories of Victorian science. Common to both is the view that nature in its inexhaustible variety is imperfectly represented by those categories. Fresh categories are needed and pre-eminently in the study of mind.

Thus, taken in one way, the work is an attack on the view of man as an automaton. Its originality is that it combines the attack with an approach which is strictly experimental, naturalistic, scientific. Thus James, in describing the workings of the mind, does full justice to its physiological conditions but he refuses to reduce its workings to those conditions. For example, he begins his work with a detailed study of the brain and of the nervous system more generally. But he treats it as a fallacy to *identify* the mind with the brain. Now it is puzzling how often the two are in fact identified. The brain is a physical object ('a blood soaked sponge' as James calls it) which is located in the skull. The skull can be opened and the brain lifted out. Taken in itself, it betrays no trace of the mental. It may be said, however, that the brain is a condition of mental activity and that anyone who appreciates this will be inclined to identify the two. But people do not usually identify a thing with the conditions for its working. For example, suppose it could be shown that no one plays the piano well unless he has fingers of a certain shape, say, slender and tapering. Then, having a certain shape of finger would be a condition for playing the piano well. Still no one would be tempted to suppose that playing the piano well *is* a certain shape of finger. Yet identifying the mind with the brain is a confusion just as gross. To explain how the confusion arises, one must turn yet again it seems, to the influence of the scientific outlook. At least it is hard to see why people should identify the mind with the brain unless they were already convinced that such categories as fit the brain are the only ones to be allowed in explaining the mind.

James is concerned also with a reductionist fallacy which is somewhat less gross, namely, that of admitting the reality of the mental and proceeding to explain it *on the model* of the physical. An example will be found in the Empiricist philosophy. As we have seen, Locke explained ideas as the residue of perception. One perceives, say, a white object. This leaves in the mind an image of whiteness. An objection immediately suggests itself. The image is particular, being an image of a particular object, say, a cup. But whiteness as an idea is surely general. Whiteness is a quality that applies not simply to a cup but to innumerable other objects. How does this generality obtain? Locke argues that our general idea of whiteness is an abstraction from our particular ideas. In other words, after perceiving a number of white objects, after receiving many particular images of white, I am left with an idea of what is common to them and that is my general idea of whiteness. Thinking is explained as the combining of such ideas, according to the principle of association. One idea calls up another through various associations, such as those of visual resemblance, occurrence at the same time and place, and so on. For example, a knot in your handkerchief calls to mind something you want to remember, because, earlier, when you wanted to remember it, you tied the knot in your handkerchief. Thinking is a grouping of ideas according to such associations. To take another example, you think that Jack loves Jill because the ideas of Jack and Jill and love come together in your mind, and they come together because of some incident or report in which they were associated.

Now such an account is framed on the model of the physical, because it assumes throughout that the workings of the mind are entirely mechanical. It assumes, in short, that the idea is governed solely by chance and mechanical causation. But the account, as James makes clear, is riddled with difficulties. Take, for example, Locke's account of generality. He assumes that we obtain a general idea of whiteness simply through our acquaintance with white objects. In fact, however, some contrast is needed. Strange as it may seem, our idea of whiteness requires acquaintance with what is not white. In a world entirely white, we should not know what whiteness is. One will grasp the point if one recalls how quickly one loses one's sense of a sound, however loud, which simply persists. On the other hand, the moment it stops, one is aware of its having occurred. In short, we notice by contrast. Whiteness mechanically accumulated would deaden the mind. We discriminate what is white as different from what is not white. In other words, the mind is not mechanical; it is discriminatory, active. The connection here with Peirce's views will be evident.

Take again the idea that the general is an abstraction from the particular. Given this, that and the other particular colour, we mechanically form an image of what they have in common. But can a general idea so mechanically arrive? Do we not, in some respects, make our general ideas. For example, consider blue. There is navy blue, royal blue, light blue. Now would the contemplation of these shades suggest an image of what is common to all three? As a matter of interest, what would such an image be like? Surely it must have some shade. How, for example, can it simultaneously be both light and dark? We *take* those shades together, *take* them as blue, as the same colour. *Need* we do so? Might we not, if only for certain purposes, be more struck by the *differences* between them?

Finally, take the view that one thinks 'Jack loves Jill' by having in mind the ideas 'Jack', 'Jill' and 'love'. Now 'Jack loves Jill' is not the same as 'Jill loves Jack', unrequited love, alas, being not uncommon. But in both cases we will have in mind the ideas of 'Jack' and 'Jill' and 'love'. How does one determine who loves whom? The difference between the two propositions is one of *meaning*. The difficulty is to see how a difference in meaning can be captured in a mechanical succession of images. Association by resemblance, for example, is not in itself meaningful. One tulip may exactly resemble another but no meaning is involved. It is true that a resemblance may be *used* meaningfully. For example, a picture can represent a person. Representation is a meaningful relation; but it is not equivalent to resemblance. For one thing, as we have seen, the resemblance works both ways. A person resembles his picture as much as the picture resembles him. Why do we say the picture represents the person rather than the other way around? Well, one reason is that we may carry a picture to identify a person but not a person to identify a picture. In other words, the difference comes out in the *use*. It is not simply because the picture resembles the person that it represents him; rather it is because one can make use of its resemblance in order to identify him, celebrate him, remember him, and so on. Similarly, the difference between 'Jack loves Jill' and 'Jill loves Jack' comes out not in the images associated with those words but in the different uses they have in the language, the different circumstances in which they would be uttered, the different consequences which would follow from uttering them, the different ways that people would take them. Here, in dealing with meaning, we inevitably evoke concepts of purpose, use and interest. These are integral to the workings of the mind but they cannot be understood in purely mechanical terms.

The same point can be made by emphasising an aspect of James's thought that was later developed by the so-called Gestalt psychologists. Perception is not a mechanical reaction but a making sense of things. Thus we do not take in a scene by picking out individual details and then building up the whole scene. Rather we take in the scene as a whole and only later dwell on its details. We perceive in intelligible wholes, the details taking their sense from the perceived whole, the whole order. What makes a puzzle picture puzzling, for example, is that we are frustrated in this natural tendency of our minds. The difficulty is not in the details, for they are all before us. Rather, we can make no sense of them as a whole. Perhaps the picture appears to us as just a collection of dots. We keep scanning the dots, viewing them from different angles, trying to bring them into relation with one another so that they assume intelligible forms. Thus one group takes the form of a head, another of a shoulder, and we keep going until the whole picture becomes intelligible. This, again, shows that the mind is purposive; we do not just register the world; we scan it, seeking for intelligible forms. Which forms are intelligible will depend on what James calls the apperceptive mass. He had in mind what Peirce meant when he talked of our being laden with a mass of cognitions already formed. The apperceptive mass is the assumptions, beliefs, tendencies one has acquired in the course of one's life. It is this which determines what one notices, what one sees. Barzun nicely illustrates the point by what he calls the rubber band effect. Convince a person that he is wrong in one of his fundamental beliefs and you will find, fifteen minutes later, that he has snapped back into holding it. He cannot help himself; his belief has formed a channel in his mind, from which his thoughts may momentarily be diverted but along which they will soon flow again.

One reason why these points have been overlooked is that one is inclined to slip into what James calls 'the psychologist's fallacy'. That is the fallacy of supposing that experience occurs in the form one might use to report it. For example, someone describing a room, say, over the telephone, will list it item by item; there is a chair in one corner, a table in the middle, the curtains are such-and-such a colour, and so on. But that is not how he experienced the room. Rather he took in the room as a whole and only later dwelt on its details. The form in which he describes the room is the opposite of how he experienced it. Again, the form of exposition, say, in a philosophy essay is not the form in which the author's thoughts occurred to him. For example, the end might have occurred to him before he worked out the beginning. The form of his exposition is the form in which his thoughts are *eventually presented*. Many errors in Rationalism and in Empiricism come from overlooking that point, an evident example being the Empiricist view that thought moves inevitably from the simple to the complex. Precision of detail is what we work towards, not what we start from. Hence Pascal's apology for writing a long letter; he said he did not have the time to make it shorter.

James attempted to characterise thought, as experienced, by speaking, in a famous phrase, of 'the stream of consciousness'. He was attempting, amongst other things, to dispel the idea that thought as experienced takes the form of logical exposition. One can see what he means by reading a page of James Joyce's *Ulysses*, which was written in the so-called stream of consciousness technique. Joyce attempted to portray what his characters were thinking by taking us, as it were, into their minds, so that we can follow the stream of their thought. One is struck, in reading him, by how the mind hops about. An incident starts a thought which by association, rather than through strict logical sequence, suggests another which, linked perhaps by a memory, suggests yet another, and so on.

Sometimes also, along the chain, an earlier thought returns, curiously enriched. The earlier thought is enriched because, on its return, it carries an added significance. The enrichment is curious because it seems to have arisen from a process more arbitrary than logical. But that reveals an important feature of the human mind. One might express it by saying that the associationist philosophers were not entirely mistaken. Chance associations are an important feature of thinking. Where they were mistaken was in not seeing that in the human mind chance itself can work to a purpose. Thus thought, as experienced, hops about according to no sequence known to formal logic, being often governed by chance association; it happens, however, through those associations, that it sometimes finds connections which it would not have discovered in following strict logical sequence. That is one of the ways in which the human mind differs from a computer. A computer works by chance only when it is not working properly.

James's notion has another important feature, which it is not entirely easy to grasp. There is a sense in which the stream of thought is impersonal. One might almost say: it is not that we think the stream; the stream thinks in us. Purpose, in short, is a feature of the stream, or of its elements, not something that stands over and above the stream directing it. More strictly: the stream of one's thought contains purposive and chance sequences, the chance sequences often being integrated into the purposive ones, but there is no overall purpose directing one's thoughts as a whole. At least, it is certainly not the individual himself who stands over and above the stream of his thought, directing it. For any purpose he has in itself part of the stream, directing some elements within it, being occasioned by others. Thus, often enough, we have no control over what passes through our minds and, where we have, that is because some thought has become dominant. For example, the thought of having work to complete helps to control your otherwise wandering thoughts; but you have not decided to have the thought that work needs to be completed; or, if you have, that is because of some previous thought you have not decided to have. The individual's decision and explicit choice cannot direct the stream as a whole because they are part of it and depend on it for their existence.

There is an important truth contained in the above remarks. We are inclined to suppose that human beings are responsible for whatever purposive sequences exist, outside the human sphere all being chance and mechanical causation. Now that is a view not so much false as incoherent. It is true, of course, that human beings are responsible for purposive sequences; but that is because we are purposive creatures. For that, however, we have nature to thank not ourselves. We are certainly not responsible for it, since we have no choice in the matter. We are inescapably purposive, by instinct. Thus, unless a child, in its earliest years, exhibited some purposive behaviour, however primitive, it could not be initiated into those forms of purpose behaviour which are typically human. For example, it will not speak a language. Language is, as it were, an outgrowth of behaviour already purposive. Language, giving us explicit choice, is inconceivable without purposive behaviour not chosen. For that we are plainly not responsible. It is a development of nature – which is to say that nature is purposive. In short, it is incoherent to suppose that purpose is exhibited *simply* in the human sphere, for human life is an evolution of purposive sequences lying more deeply in nature. In the stream of thought we have the point perfectly illustrated. The stream is not *directed* by human purpose; is not its product. So far as it is explicit or chosen, human purpose is the *product* of the stream; so far as it is not explicit or chosen, it is the stream itself, for which no human being is responsible.

Perhaps we have now sufficiently indicated what may be termed the Pragmatist view of mind, foreshadowed in many remarks by Peirce, but given its richest treatment in James's great work. We may note that it stands distinct from both the Rationalist and the Empiricist view. It is distinct from the Empiricist because it makes the mind active and discriminatory; it is distinct from the Rationalist because it treats mind as a *feature* of nature, not something standing over and against it.

There remains to be considered one important section in James's work on psychology, namely, his famous treatment of the emotions. I shall be concerned to bring out the strength of his treatment, criticism being confined to a later stage. James said that we do not weep because we are sad; rather we are sad because we weep. That is sometimes called the James–Lange theory of the emotions, because the Danish psychologist Carl Lange made a similar point, at about the same time. At first, the theory seems entirely paradoxical. Surely we weep because we are sad; sadness is not a consequence of our weeping. But James is not saying we weep first and then, later, become sad. He is not referring to a causal sequence; rather he is seeking to express what *constitutes* an emotion such as sadness. If you weep out of sadness at receiving bad news, wherein does the sadness consist? Is it something in addition to your receiving the news and weeping? James's point is that it need not be. In certain circumstances, your sadness may consist in your weeping at the news.

The point may be clarified by distinguishing between emotion and sensation. Emotions take objects. You are sad *about* something. This means that emotions are interwoven with beliefs. Here there is no sharp division between reason and feeling. Thus you can alter a person's emotions by giving him reason to think that he is mistaken in his belief. For example, if a person is sad because he believes the news is bad, and you give him reason to believe he was mistaken about the news, he will no longer feel sad. Here, as we have said, reason and feeling are interfused, a point that James often emphasised. By contrast, sensations do not take objects. For example, you are not in pain *about* anything, at least in the most usual sense of the term. In the usual sense, you are just in pain. Moreover, your pain cannot be removed by changing the way you think, sensations are not interfused with reason and belief, as emotions are. There is another feature by which the two can be distinguished. There is as it were, a private relation between a sensation and the person who feels it. Some sensations, such as pain, have public manifestations by which they can be detected, at least on some occasions. But the person who feels the sensation does not detect it by noticing its public manifestations. One knows a person is in pain by seeing him writhe and groan; but it is not by detecting his own writhings and groanings that the person himself knows he is in pain. Indeed the person does not *detect* that he is in pain; for there is no sense in supposing that he does not detect it. 'He is in pain but hasn't noticed it' is not a clearly intelligible sentence. The same point applies to feelings of heat, nausea, colour, and so on. Images, also, in this are like sensations. I can find out what image you have in mind (though, usually, that is only because you have told me) but you do not have to find out what your image is; you just have it. Emotions, in that respect, are quite different. Thus you might be *unaware* that you are jealous, malicious, vain, falling in love, or getting angry. Moreover, to find out, say, that you are jealous, you have to consider much the same things that others have to consider in detecting your jealousy. You have to reflect, not on some sensation, but on how you have been acting, thinking and speaking. Emotion, in short, cannot be assimilated to sensation; it is altogether a more complicated phenomenon.

Now emotion and sensation need to be distinguished because there is a common tendency to assimilate the one to the other. Moreover, we may note in passing that this belongs to a more general tendency. There is a common urge to assimilate to sensation not simply emotion but every other feature of mental life. For some reason, it is natural, at least on a first reflection, to treat any feature of the mind as some kind of sensation or image. The Empiricists, for example, evidently treated the meaning of a word as an image in the mind – that is, as something which occurs privately in the mind when a word is uttered. Moreover, it is a point of interest, to which we shall return, that James himself sometimes falls into the same fallacy. For example, in the *Principles* he says at one point that there are feelings which correspond not simply to common nouns but also to prepositions and conjunctions (James

1904(I): 245–6). 'We ought to say a feeling of *and*, a feeling of *if, but, by,* and so on, as much as a feeling of *blue* or a feeling of *cold*.' The tendency to assimilate all features of the mind to some form of sensation or image is here illustrated at its extreme. To someone not in the grip of that tendency, it will appear evident that prepositions and conjunctions derive their meaning from what they contribute to the constitution of sentences. Their meaning, in short, lies in the use they have in the language, not in something private to the mind. So long as we have grasped their employment, we have grasped their meaning, and then it is irrelevant what feelings we associate with them. Note here how the tendency under discussion carries James back into Empiricism – in other words, into direct conflict with his own Pragmatism.

As I have said, the point is one to which we shall return. Meanwhile we must continue to examine James's treatment of the emotions, where he proceeds along sounder lines. We have established that an emotion, though it may contain sensation among its elements, is not itself a sensation. For example, many people when they are angry become heated and go red in the face. Here there is sensation. But anger is not constituted by that sensation, since one may become heated and go red without being angry at all – such as when one has been standing too near to a fire or taken too much to drink. The sensation, in short, does not count in itself as anger but only when taken in a wider context, where it is one amongst a number of elements, constituting a person's attitude to something outside himself. James's example of weeping will serve as a further illustration. Weeping in itself does not constitute sadness, since one may weep out of joy. How does one know whether it is in joy or in sadness that someone weeps. What enables one to tell, is not something *internal* to the person concerned; rather, we shall look at the situation in which the person finds himself. Thus, we shall not take him to be sad if he has just had good news, nor to be joyous if the news is bad. If it is bad news at which he weeps, that will count as his being sad. We do not have to search for something which lies hidden 'behind' the weeping, since nothing that lies hidden can be of greater significance than what has been revealed. That, indeed, is what is essentially sound in James's treatment. Let us grant that the person in his sadness is feeling sensations of which we are unaware. But we are still aware that he is weeping at bad news and, in taking him to be sad, that is just as significant as any sensation he feels. Emotion, in short, is a feature of the whole person, not simply of something 'inside' him.

Now we have already implied that the *Principles*, though masterly, is not faultless. We must now dwell on some faults. In doing so, it will be important to pay special attention to the phrase 'in the mind'. Taken one way, it is synonymous with the mental in general. But in common usage it has a narrower sense, where it signifies what is private to the individual. For example, to go over some issue 'in one's mind' normally signifies, as it were, silent thought; or again, if one distinguishes between reading out loud and reading silently, it is the latter which is 'in the mind'. Now, as I have implied, in reflecting on the mental, there is a tendency to take what is 'in the mind' as fundamental or even to suppose that the mental in general is identical with what occurs 'in the mind'. Many have supposed that if a person is thinking or reading out loud, he is not really thinking or reading unless there is some private process, something in the mind, that corresponds to the spoken words. In short, what occurs in public is only expression; the real thinking or reading is always private. Now that is a serious confusion. Moreover, it is one into which James occasionally falls. Indeed we have already illustrated the point. Thus we have noted his supposing that a preposition or conjunction will have some feeling associated with it. Here the proposition or conjunction, as public expression, as a mark on the page, derives its meaning from what occurs in private, 'in the mind'.

The confusion being serious, it needs to be considered in some detail. There is, of course, no doubt that one can read or think in one's mind, in the required sense. The confusion lies in taking this to be the essence of the mental. For example, a child learns to read out loud; silent reading has to be mastered later. Indeed silent reading seems to be an accomplishment that human beings were somewhat late in acquiring. For centuries, all reading was out loud. Moreover, even where a person does read silently, he is only doing in private what he might have done and has in fact done, in public. There is, in short, no reason to suppose that the private phenomenon is the more significant. The same point applies to thinking. A nervous participant, in a philosophical discussion, may carefully compose in his mind what he wishes to say, before entering the discussion to say it. He thinks in his mind before speaking out loud. It does not follow, however, that whenever someone speaks out loud he is, in addition, thinking in his mind. The confident participant thinks *in* speech. One does not have to suppose a second more nervous self accompanying his speech with private thoughts. Indeed it is evident that private thoughts, in those circumstances, are more of a handicap than an advantage. Hence the phenomenon of the nervous participant who, having carefully composed what he wishes to say, finds that the discussion has moved on and he no longer has the opportunity to speak.[1] Once again that is not to deny the usefulness, much less the reality, of private thought. Often enough, for example, one has to pause in writing in order to call to mind how to spell a word. But the opposite is also common enough. Sometimes one cannot recall how to spell a word, simply in one's mind; one has to write it down. In short there is no reason to suppose that the mental is essentially private. A similar point applies, incidentally, to emotion. One may be sad without revealing it, but that is not the initial accomplishment. It is only as the years go by that one learns, more or less, to control one's emotions. So, as in the case of reading or thinking, it is not the phenomenon in its private form that takes precedence, but in fact in its public form.

Now this confusion in James's thought is serious in its consequences because it works against the main line of his argument. The *Principles*, in its treatment of the emotions, for example, serves to show that the mental is a feature of the *whole person*. In this, its views are to be distinguished not simply from reductionism but also from some forms of dualism, which treat the person as made of radically different parts, a merely physical body to which a mental part is added. Now James's work, at least in many of its details, serves to show that the relation between the physical and mental features of a person is not a relation between parts; it is more like the relations of parts to a whole. One might say that the difference between a human being and a physical object is not that the human being is a physical object with a part added but that he is a different kind of object. Taken as a whole he is different and the mental is a sign of the difference. Thus no mental feature belongs to a part of the person. It is true one may speak of, say, a pain in one's hand. But unlike a bone or a vein it is not a part of one's hand. An image, one cannot locate in any sense. The pain or the image is not occurring in some part of the human being, not even in some 'mental part'. Rather it is the whole person who feels the pain or images.

Now the confusion we are considering has the effect of obscuring that very point. So far as the mental is taken as essentially private, it is not being taken in relation to the person as a whole. In his public aspect, he is ignored. Moreover, the effect of this is to obscure the person's life not simply in its public aspect but also in its private. A simple example will illustrate the point. Suppose I have in mind an image, say, of a dog. What is the significance of that image? What am I doing in having it? Am I *thinking* of my pet? *Remembering* one I kept in my youth? *Worrying* what the neighbour's dog is up to? These are different mental acts, any one of which might involve the image of a dog. The image itself will not inform you of what I am thinking or whether I am thinking at all. For example, an image may simply be the result of a chance association, having no further significance. So far as the image has a significance, it will be in its surroundings, in what is occurring at the time, or has occurred just before, in what I shall go on to say or do, and so on. Here it will be important to remember a point made earlier. The significance of my image is not determined simply by resemblance. For example, suppose I have an image of the dog I kept in my youth. What makes the image represent the dog is not the resemblance between them. For all I know, the image might resemble any number of other dogs. As we have mentioned, an image becomes representative only in the way it is taken. So, only in a wider context is the image in my mind an image of the dog I kept in my youth.

Once again, it will be useful to emphasise that the reality of the private is not being denied. Sensations and images are undoubtedly psychological material. The point is simply that the significance of the material will depend on how it is related to a person's life more generally. Here we may note a danger in James's notion of 'the stream of consciousness'. The danger is in taking the stream of thought not as a person thinking, as the succession of *his* thoughts, but as a separate process within him, which carries its meaning within itself. The stream of thought, in fact, is merely the successive thoughts of some person, which derives its meaning from his life more generally, public as well as private. Remove his life more generally and the succession of his thought will become meaningless. The point may be illustrated by returning for a moment to Joyce's *Ulysses*. Most of its readers find it a difficult book. The reason is that one has to infer from an image or broken phrase in some character's mind what scene he is passing through and then in the light of that scene grasp the full significance of the image or broken phrase. The process is exhausting. It is exhausting precisely because the so-called stream of thought does not carry its meaning in itself.

RADICAL EMPIRICISM

James never did attain an entirely coherent view of the mental. Indeed his later work, or so it seems to me, shows a falling away from the high standards of the *Principles*. To illustrate this point, it will be worth considering his influential paper 'Does Consciousness Exist?' (James 1912). He there argues that the world consists of a single stuff, which he terms experience, the mental and the physical being no more than different ways of taking it. In other words, he abandons the view that the mental has its own features distinct from the physical; the mental and the physical are the same stuff considered, as it were, from different angles. An example he gives is that of observing a room. The room is mental when taken in relation to me, an observer; but it is physical when taken in relation to its wider history, physical so far as there is more to it than appears to any observer in particular. One and the same room is therefore both mental and physical; it belongs to each category, as a point at the intersection of two different lines is common to both.

Now James's view in this paper, as he acknowledges, is hardly distinguishable from Berkeley's (James 1912: 10–11). It consists essentially in identifying experience with the object which is experienced. Thus Berkeley denied there are objects existing independently of our sensory ideas. The sensory ideas *are* the objects. This view rests on a fallacy which was exposed by Thomas Reid. If by 'ideas' Berkeley means sensory experience, this is not *what* we perceive but that *whereby* we perceive other things. For example, my visual experience is not what I see but that whereby I do so. James's view rests on the same fallacy. Thus if my visual experience of the room is identified with the room I see, this entails that what I see is my visual experience.

An example will further clarify the point. Suppose my optician asks me to tell him what I see on his chart. I describe the first few lines and then tell him the rest is blurred. Now it seems evident that this is not an objective description of the chart. I am not claiming for example that the chart is blurred in the sense that the surface of a pond is blurred when the wind blows across it. It would, in any case, be difficult to understand why I should in that sense describe the chart to my optician, when he knows very well what it contains and when I know very well that he does so. I am not, it is true, describing some object other than the chart which I see instead of it. But that is because I am not in that sense describing any object; rather I am describing *how* I experience the chart. If it is a confusion to identify this with some object other than the chart, it is equally a confusion to identify it with the chart itself. Indeed both confusions rest on the same fallacy, namely that of supposing that my visual experience is some object that I see.

The views expressed in this paper belong to the years when James was developing the philosophy he called Radical Empiricism. We have already considered this philosophy, in discussing Peirce, but it will be worth considering it in further detail.

The essence of Radical Empiricism, as we have seen, is that nothing can transcend human experience. James frames this view by means of three postulates (1912: ix–xii). The first is that of empirical method; issues are to be debated in terms drawn from experience; the second is that of Nominalism; not just objects but also their relations are matters of direct particular experience. The third is that 'the parts of experience hold together from next to next by relations that are themselves parts of experience'. This last postulate is in the nature of a general conclusion which expresses a metaphysic, its essence being that it excludes 'the hypothesis of trans-empirical reality'.

Let us concentrate, in this general conclusion, on what it says about relations. For this is a topic to which James returns repeatedly in his later work. He is concerned to establish that not simply objects but also the *relations* between them fall wholly *within* experience. In defence of this view, his style frequently turns virtuosic.

> Propositions, copulas, and conjunctions, 'is', 'isn't', 'then', 'before', 'in', 'on', 'besides', 'between', 'next', 'like', 'unlike', 'as', 'but', flower out of the stream of pure experience, the stream of concretes or the sensational stream, as naturally as nouns and adjectives do, and they melt into it again as fluidly when we apply them to a new portion of the stream.
>
> (James 1912: 95)

The description, it may be noted, is somewhat metaphorical. Let us by means of an example attempt to sharpen the issue. A train's whistle changes in pitch as the train approaches. One experiences both the earlier and the later pitch but does one experience the change from one to the other? In short, does one experience the temporal *relation* between the two pitches? The question is by no means trivial. Indeed, in effect the credibility of Empiricism depends on it. For unless 'experience' is to be turned into a superfluous synonym for knowledge itself, we need to determine whether all knowledge really can be reduced to what might usefully be termed 'experience'. Now anyone who reflects will find that when he hears the second pitch he certainly knows that it was preceded by a different one but that there seems to be no particular experience which corresponds to that knowledge. Indeed on further reflection he will find it difficult to see how there could be. For either he experiences the pitches simultaneously in which case there can have been no change from the one to the other, or he experiences them successively. But if he experiences them successively, he cannot know there has been a change from one pitch to the other unless he knows there has been a change from one experience to the other. It is difficult to see how this knowledge can consist in the experiences themselves. Against this, James argues, in effect, that there is an *experience* of continuity between the two pitches. He is referring to the so-called 'specious present'. There is a stretch of time in which whilst hearing the present pitch one is still hearing the past one. We may grant the point. But since in this experience the pitches are heard simultaneously, how does one know that one of them belongs to the past? It is evident that this question cannot be answered simply by reference to the pitches *as experiences*. However one considers the matter, it is evident that our knowledge of temporal relation cannot be reduced to pure experience. The experience, in some manner, must be adulterated by a knowledge which transcends it.

This is a general truth. As the Logical Positivists discovered, when they made the attempt, no statement about a physical object, however simple, can be reduced to a set of statements about pure experience, however complicated. All knowledge transcends experience, taken purely as such. The point is especially evident in the case of the causal relation. In the vernacular, one may certainly speak of a causal relation as experienced. For example, one may speak of seeing the first ball's moving the second. Moreover, one may provide a phenomenological description of what one experiences on such occasions. To suppose, however, that this solves the philosophical difficulties about causation is to mistake their nature. The difficulties are epistemological not phenomenological. Thus in saying that the first ball causes the movement of the other, one implies that in the appropriate circumstances it will always do so. The difficulty is to see how one's knowledge that it will always do so can be derived simply from one's present experience of what it does.

It is hard to dissent from John Skorupski's view that in his later work James ventured into areas where he lacked a grip on the philosophical issues (Skorupski 1993: 109–17). He repeatedly resorts to the description – often brilliant – of psychological processes that are irrelevant to the problem. In short, the faults we noted in the *Principles* have become pervasive. The description of experiences which accompany the use of a concept are taken as an analysis of the concept itself; the subjective is treated as significant independently of the objective context which alone gives it significance. Nevertheless these views are of great historical interest, because they are ones which are characteristic of later Pragmatism.

Chapter 6

James: 'The Will to Believe'

It may be remembered that James had become convinced in early manhood, through his struggle with nervous depression, that one is entitled to believe independently of reason. Some truths, or so he came to believe, can be discovered only by those who have the faith to take them as such. 'The Will to Believe' (James 1918: 99–125) is his mature treatment of that theme. The title is not a happy one. James himself wished he had entitled it 'The Right to Believe'. 'Will' suggests choice, which in its turn has suggested to some that in James's view one may choose to believe whatever one wishes. James in fact assisted that view not only in his title but by occasional turns of phrase in the body of his essay. We must be clear, from the start, that James is not suggesting belief may simply be chosen. What he argues is that the conditions for knowing the truth are wider than the simply rational and that some of these conditions may on occasions take precedence over it. His aim is to attack the view expressed by W. K. Clifford in the following sentence: 'It is wrong always, everywhere, and for anyone, to believe anything upon insufficient evidence.' On Clifford's view, one should withhold assent, as a matter of duty, from any belief until one has conclusive evidence or reason for taking it as true. Now James notices that this view is itself not simply intellectual; it is expressive of an attitude. Clifford is advocating that we cultivate the habit of doubt. We must hold back, set ourselves against belief, wait to be persuaded. This attitude is as much affective as intellectual. What James wonders is whether it is an attitude which is necessarily conducive to discovering the truth. The habit of doubt, like any other, perpetuates itself, indeed reinforces itself, as time passes. Is that the attitude most conducive to recognising the truth? Thus habituated, may one not eventually be in a condition whereby one is unable to recognise the truth even when one sees it?

Those are the questions that James's paper may suggest to our minds. He wishes to consider what tendency, bent or bias is most conducive to discovering the truth. Note that simply in raising the question he does us a service. For he forces us to recognise that no inquiry is conducted in terms of pure reason. Take, for example, the term bias. An intellectual instinctively takes the term as pejorative. But the term simply means bent or tendency. In bowls, for example, every wood has a bias. That is not a flaw; it is indispensable to the game. James argues that some bias is also needed if one is to discover the truth.

One other point needs to be noted at the outset. James is working in a particular context. His essay was originally delivered as a lecture to an audience at Harvard. In short, he is addressing the educated, who were influenced by the intellectual trends of the nineteenth century. He is well aware that his remarks, in other contexts, might encourage credulity. But he does not believe that credulity is the chief peril for the audience he is addressing.

As we have suggested, James has two aims. He wishes to show, first, that inquiry has its affective as well as its intellectual conditions; and, second, that in some circumstances the affective may take precedence over the intellectual. The second view, as we shall see, is related to Peirce's views that doubt is not real unless it is *felt* as such.

James's first aim is easily achieved. He distinguishes between what he calls a live and a dead option. An option is dead for a person when it is not something he would even consider. For example, in Britain, at least until very recently, anyone who had been converted to a belief in God would almost certainly have become a Christian. It would never have occurred to him to adopt, say, Sufism, though Sufis also believe in God. On the other hand, it might well have been an issue for him whether he should become a Catholic or a Protestant. For him the latter option would have been live, the former dead. It is worth emphasising that the difference between a live and a dead option cannot be drawn simply in intellectual terms. To do so, the individual would have to examine all those options he considers dead in order to confirm that they are not intellectually respectable. But the whole point about a dead option is that one does not so consider it. That is what makes it dead. It may be thought regrettable that any option should be so treated. Whether or not it is regrettable is precisely the topic that James considers in the second part of his essay. For the moment, he emphasises that it is in any case inevitable. Any inquirer who treated every option as live would be paralysed in his inquiry. One is prompted to inquiry by the sense that one's beliefs are unsatisfactory and by the desire to search among alternatives so that one might find more satisfactory ones. But there must be some limit to what one counts as an alternative. A belief cannot so count just because it is coherent and can be defended by some show of reason, for then one's life will have passed before the alternatives have been exhausted. An inquirer, of any merit, must have or develop an instinct for which alternatives are worth considering. He must develop a *bias*, so that he fastens, without having to consider the matter, on some issue or belief whilst ignoring others. One develops, as it were, a nose for what is plausible. But the use of the phrase indicates that the ability cannot be conveyed in explicit terms to one who lacks it. Thus, although it may be cultivated, it cannot be chosen. Rather than being chosen, it develops. James's point is that it is indispensable; without it, genuine inquiry is impossible:

> Evidently, our non-intellectual nature does influence our convictions. There are passional tendencies and volitions which run before and others which come after belief, and it is only the latter that are too late for the fair; and they are not too late when the previous passional work has been already in their own direction.
>
> (James 1918: 107)

It will be worth attending to the way James phrases that conclusion. He distinguishes between passional tendencies which come after and those which come before belief. A passional tendency comes after belief, and therefore too late, when what one wishes to believe is not what one does believe. If what one wishes is a belief one lacks, it is idle to suppose one can simply choose to believe it. In other words, James makes clear that he is not supposing beliefs can simply be chosen. Nevertheless the last sentence is disquieting. Here James seems to allow, misguidedly I believe, that one's wanting to believe something is *some* reason for believing it. His idea seems to be that where one is *already* inclined to believe something, one may remove whatever doubts remain by considering that one wants to believe it. As we shall see later, James seems to be confusing the question of what is so with that of what one is to do. If one is strongly inclined to a belief then obviously one will believe it, unless one is still not entirely convinced. But if so, one can hardly convince oneself by thinking that one would like to be. If a father has some doubts about his son's honesty, he cannot remove them by wishing that he wholly trusted him. On the other hand, he can *decide* to trust him, in the sense of *treating* him as wholly reliable, *acting* as though he wholly trusted him. But those are points to which we shall return.

James now turns to his second aim. He states as follows the thesis he wishes to defend:

Our passional nature not only lawfully may, but must decide an option between propositions, whenever it is a genuine option that cannot by its nature be decided on intellectual grounds; for to say, under such circumstances, 'Do not decide, but leave the question' is itself a passional decision – just like deciding yes or no – and is attended with the same risk of losing the truth.

(James 1918: 108)

I shall now consider how James defends that thesis, leaving my own comments, for the most part, until later. He makes a preliminary distinction between two ways of looking at our duty in the matter of opinion. According to one, we must know the truth; according to the other we must avoid error. These are two attitudes, says James, not a single attitude differently expressed. For example, suppose A is the truth on some matter and B a falsehood. In believing A we escape the falsehood B. But in escaping B, we do not thereby believe the truth, A. We may believe some other falsehood. Indeed we may escape B by withholding any belief.

It makes a difference, therefore, how our minds are set, whether they are set on finding the truth or avoiding error. Clifford, in the passage quoted, exhorts us to the latter course; James himself is in favour of the former.

He concedes, however, that there are areas where Clifford's attitude may usefully predominate. He takes the sciences as his example. He says that Clifford's attitude may there be recommended because the issues involved are not intrinsically important (James 1918: 115): 'What difference, indeed, does it make to most of us whether we have or have not a theory of the Röntgen rays, whether we believe or not in mind-stuff, or have a conviction about the causality of conscious states?' In those cases, where the issues are not urgent, we may take the side of doubt, treating each theory as guilty until it has proved its innocence, being content, if need be, to withhold belief indefinitely.

One may wonder, at this point, whether James is not conceding too much to his opponents. The cultivation of doubt may have become common in science but it seems not to have characterised science during its greatest periods of creativity. An example will illustrate the point. During the lifetime of Copernicus there was evidence which conflicted with the truth of his theory; indeed, some of it appeared decisive. For example, using the instruments of his time, one could easily falsify his theory by showing that the distance between the stars and the earth was not as great as his theory required. Copernicus was aware of this and had no way of explaining it; nevertheless he remained convinced that his theory was true. After his death, Galileo showed that the instruments of his time had been inadequate to make a correct estimate of the distance involved. Using better instruments, Galileo showed that Copernicus had been correct. It might be said that Copernicus was therefore justified in sticking to his theory. But that is ambiguous. He was justified by James's criterion, since he found the truth. By Clifford's criterion, however, he was not justified, since he did not exactly proportion his belief to the evidence available to him; he affirmed his theory where he might have doubted it.

Still, James himself wishes to concentrate on issues other than the scientific. In particular, he wishes to consider what he calls *genuine* options. An option is genuine, as defined by James, when it has three characteristics, being *living*, *forced* and *momentous*. A living option we have already defined; it is one that you can seriously consider might be true. An option is forced when, in postponing your decision about it, you are in effect rejecting it. You have to decide for or against it. An option is momentous when the opportunity is unique and there is something at stake.

Now James's argument is that an option of the above kind may lawfully be settled by the sway of our passional nature. An example from an earlier paper, 'The Sentiment of Rationality', will illustrate what he has in mind.

> Suppose, for example, that I am climbing in the alps and have had the ill-luck to work myself into a position from which the only escape is by a terrible leap. Being without similar experience, I have no evidence of my ability to perform it successfully; but hope and confidence in myself make me sure I shall not miss my aim, and nerve my feet to execute what without those subjective emotions would perhaps have been impossible. But suppose that, on the contrary, the emotions of fear and mistrust predominate, or suppose that having just read the *Ethics of Belief*, I feel it would be sinful to act upon an assumption unverified by previous experience – why then, I shall hesitate so long that at last, exhausted and trembling, and launching myself in a moment of despair, I miss my foothold and roll into the abyss. In this case (and it is one of an immense class) the part of wisdom clearly is to believe what one desires; for the belief is one of the indispensable preliminary conditions of the realisation of its object. *There are then cases where faith creates its own verification.*
>
> (James 1918: 153)

As James implies, it would be evident folly, in those circumstances, to withhold belief in myself and to leap into space in an experimental fashion. But that means it would be evident folly to reason in the way Clifford recommends. Obviously, I must put doubt from my mind and summon up confidence in my own power. Indeed there is no other way to discover whether I have it in me to leap the gorge. If I lose confidence in myself I shall fall in the abyss and it will never be discovered whether I had it in me to make the leap. A condition for finding whether I have it in me is my believing I have it in me. Faith, in short, is a condition for finding the truth.

James now extends that point to cover morality and religion. His discussion of religion will be of special interest. He begins by presupposing that his readers consider the religious hypothesis a living issue. For those who think the hypothesis not worth considering he has nothing to say. He is addressing those who can give it some credence. Given that it is a living issue, it presents itself as a genuine option, for not only is it living, it is forced and momentous. It is momentous because it offers us a vital good. It is forced because we cannot evade it.

> We cannot escape the issue by remaining sceptical and waiting for more light, because although we do avoid error in that way *if religion be untrue*, we lose the good, *if it be true*, just as certainly as if we positively chose to disbelieve. It is as if a man should hesitate indefinitely to ask a woman to marry him because he was not perfectly sure that she would prove an angel after he has brought her home. . . . Scepticism, then, is not avoidance of option; it is option of a particular kind of risk. *Better risk loss of truth than chance of error* – that is your vetoer's exact position. He is actively playing his stake as much as the believer is; he is backing the field against the religious hypothesis, just as the believer is backing the religious hypothesis against the field.
>
> (James 1918: 120)

Moreover, the religious hypothesis brings into play an additional factor:

> The more perfect and more eternal aspect of the universe is represented in our religions as having personal form. The universe is no longer a mere *It* to us, but a *Thou*, if we are religious; and any relation that may be possible from person to person might be possible here. For instance, although in one sense we are passive portions of the universe, in another we show a curious autonomy, as if we were small active centres on our own account. We feel, too as if

the appeal of religion to us were made of our own active good-will, as if evidence might forever be withheld from us unless we met the hypothesis half way. To take a trivial illustration: just as a man who in a company of gentlemen made no advances, asked a warrant of every concession, and believed no one's word without proof, would cut himself off by such churlishness from all the social rewards that a more trusting spirit would earn – so here one who would shut himself up in a snarling logicality and try to make the gods extort his recognition willy-nilly, or not get it at all, might cut himself off forever from his only opportunity of making the gods' acquaintance.

(James 1918: 121)

James's point might be put another way. There is a peculiarity about the religious hypothesis which distinguishes it from any in science. The aim of science is knowledge or understanding; the aim of religion is salvation and it is not on knowledge or understanding that salvation depends. It is not we who understand God; it is God who understands us and offers the salvation we seek. The condition is that we take it. The condition, in short, is not that we understand but that we have the faith to act. It follows, on the religious hypothesis, that the man who withholds assent, cultivating his doubts so that he may be certain not to fall into error, has developed the very attitude which will prevent his receiving the salvation offered, of finding the truth he seeks. Moreover, it may be remarked that such a state of affairs hardly conflicts with one's idea of a wise providence. That salvation should be most easily available to the simple and open-hearted seems not unreasonable or unfair. Why should salvation be available only to intellectuals?

That, at least in outline, is the argument that James develops. Let us consider it in some detail. We may begin with a point already mentioned. Throughout his argument, James runs together the question of what is so with the question of what is to be done. For example, consider the man who is trapped in the mountains, contemplating a leap. We may grant that he is entitled to suppress whatever doubts he may feel about his own ability. But to what end? It is evident, on reflection, that he suppresses his doubts not in order to find the truth but in order to save his life. His procedure is practical not theoretical, the theoretical question of what ability he has being entirely subordinate to the question of how to get out of a dangerous spot. So far, then, we have no evidence that a man whose interest is entirely theoretical would be justified in suppressing doubt. I say *so far*. Not for a moment am I suggesting that the questions, thus distinguished, can always be sharply separated. In fact they are evidently connected even in the example we are considering. Thus suppose I were capable, in the circumstances envisaged, of retaining a theoretical interest in my own ability. Still, I should need to have faith in my ability in order to put it properly to the test. Unless I believe I can save my life, I shall never discover even on theoretical ground that I have the ability to do so. Nevertheless the questions I have distinguished, though connected on some occasions, are wholly separable on others and it is a confusion on James's part simply to run them together. As we shall see the effect of removing that confusion is not to weaken James's argument but to strengthen it.

To illustrate the point let us return to the religious issue. It is necessary to distinguish between types of case. In James's time there were people who had real faith but were beginning to suffer from scruples simply because they could not supply their faith with an intellectual foundation. In other words, what made such people uneasy was not their faith in itself but arguments about intellectual duty, put forward by Clifford and others, which suggested that they ought not to have it. They were beginning to wonder whether they ought to be as certain as in fact they were. Now James's point here would be the same as Peirce's. In any activity, inquiry included, one cannot be expected to give a reason for everything and one is required to answer not every conceivable doubt but only those one feels. In short, one can show on purely theoretical ground that the people in question have no obligation to doubt.

But the type of case on which James concentrates is significantly different from the one above. He concentrates on the type of person who is torn between faith and doubt. There are considerations which incline a man, say, towards Christianity. But there are also doubts which prevent his doing so. He is torn in this way back and forth and becomes convinced, let us suppose, that he will never settle the matter on an intellectual level. Now here we can hardly tell the man that he has no real cause for doubt, since precisely what we are supposing is that he has. Moreover, it would evidently be confused, not to say reprehensible, to say that he can answer his doubts by recalling that he has an interest in believing. We should, in effect, be encouraging him to deceive himself. James's point, properly understood, is not that his wanting to believe is a reason for his doing so, but that it is a reason, in *his* circumstances, for changing the question. In other words, there is a practical as well as a theoretical issue involved. Thus he has become convinced on the theoretical level that he will never settle the issue. Well, the question is, what is he going to do about it? The issue now is a practical one. If he goes on in the same way, he is in effect rejecting Christianity, the life of worship and prayer. Thus he must decide for or against, and the issue, being practical, is evidently to be settled by his determining what he really wants. By this we do not mean what he likes or what is in his interest. Rather, he has to determine whether what is fundamental in him is faith or disbelief. If it is faith then, however imperfect his belief, he is entitled to commit himself to the life of worship and prayer. Let no one suppose, incidentally, that there is something confused or disreputable about worshipping or praying with an imperfect faith. One might as well suppose that it is irrational to cry for help unless one is convinced there is someone to hear. Obviously the best way to find out if there is someone to hear is to cry out. In any case it would be equally confused or disreputable for him to commit himself to a life of disbelief, since his disbelief is at least equally imperfect. But, as James points out, whether in effect or explicitly he has to commit himself one way or the other.

Note, however, the essential point, namely, that what entitles him to commitment are considerations which do not answer but which take precedence over his theoretical doubts. The confusion in James's account is that he makes it appear as if the man's theoretical difficulties were themselves answered by those considerations which entitle him to commitment. Yet, as I have said, the effect of removing that confusion is to strengthen, rather than to weaken James's argument. Thus it should be clear, in both of the above cases, that it is James, not Clifford, who is correct. He is correct in the first case, because even on theoretical ground one is not obliged to answer every conceivable doubt. He is correct in the second, because there are considerations which take precedence over the theoretical, so that one is sometimes entitled to ignore doubts which, simply on the theoretical level, one would be obliged to answer.

SCEPTICISM

The above points, it will be important to note, apply not simply in the religious sphere but in any sphere of life. The point will bear elaboration. It will be useful to consider so-called philosophical scepticism, which is not confined to the sphere of religion but which seeks to cast doubt on every certainty. In doing so, we shall find further support, I believe, for James's position, for we shall see that his points are relevant wherever scepticism appears. Besides, it will be salutary to recognise that the doubts which are commonly raised in philosophy about the foundations of religion may as easily be raised about the foundations of any other activity. Take, as an instance, the foundations of physical science. A scientific law is commonly formed as an induction from, comparatively speaking, a handful of cases. The amount of arsenic, let us say, which has never been examined by scientists is far in excess of the amount they have examined. Nevertheless they confidently affirm that all arsenic is poisonous, not only the arsenic they have examined but all that they never have and never will. It is evident that their sample cannot be justified as reliable simply in numerical terms. Their procedure is reasonable, it would seem, only on the assumption of a uniformity in nature, on the assumption that substances which are alike in certain respects will be alike also in others. 'Assumption', perhaps, is not the right word, nor even 'presupposition', since both may connote an element of conscious choice, as if scientists deliberately made the assumption, or adopted the presupposition that nature is uniform. In fact, they never think about it. Still, it is assumed or presupposed in some sense, for it is entailed by what they do affirm. Thus assume that nature is not uniform and it follows necessarily that every scientific conclusion is dubious.

Now in philosophy one attempts to reason, so far as one can, independently of commitment. One attempts, as it were, to stand outside any body of belief and to ask oneself what reason one might have to accept those beliefs, were one not already committed to them. Reflecting in that way, one might ask oneself what reason one has to suppose that nature is uniform. Many philosophers have attempted to supply such a reason. What they say does not convince me, which may not be significant; what is more significant is that they do not convince one another. There is, in short, no agreed solution to this problem. Some philosophers, it is true, have argued that the problem does not really exist. The Logical Positivists, for example, used to argue that inductive reasoning is what we mean by reasoning about matters of fact. It would therefore be a confusion to seek some further reason for accepting it. But that argument is entirely dubious. A contrast between scientific and mathematical reasoning will reveal why. In mathematics there is no difference between a proposition's being true and its being validly inferred. Truth and validity come to the same thing. Wittgenstein put the point by saying that in mathematics one can work out on the blackboard what is true; one does not have to check what one has written against the world outside. In science, however, it is the world outside that concerns us. We seek, for instance, to predict the course of some natural process, that process being not our own invention but something that exists quite independently of us. However correctly our prediction is framed, according to our own procedures, it will still be false if nature goes differently. In short, truth is not the same as validity. Truth depends on what happens, not on how we follow our own procedures. But then, what guarantee do we have that in following our procedures we shall arrive at the truth? Philosophical reflection persists in raising the problem. It can hardly be removed, in the manner of the Logical Positivists, by defining what is reliable or reasonable in terms of our procedures, since it is precisely those procedures that philosophical reflection is now holding in doubt. In effect, the Logical Positivists are forsaking the theoretical level and resorting to commitment. They are simply affirming what they are resolved to take as reasonable or reliable. Now, I do not say, let it be noted, that their procedure cannot be justified. What is clear, however, is that it cannot be justified on the theoretical level as an answer to the problem raised there.

It is tedious to multiply examples but let us consider two more, chosen more or less at random, in order to show how easily, at the theoretical level, one may question the foundations of any activity. Take the study of history. An event occurs; someone records it; he passes on his report to someone else and eventually it reaches the historian. That, one may be inclined to suppose, is how history gets written. There is, as it were, a chain stretching from an event in the past to the historian who reports the event. In fact, however, the historian is acquainted only with one end of the chain; how does he know that it stretches back to an event in the past? He has no independent access to the event itself in order to check the report against it. Moreover, history is recorded by people who have an interest in doing so. It is not easy to believe that they are invariably, or even usually, moved by a disinterested love of the truth. Often enough, it is reasonable to suppose, they are moved by the desire to justify themselves or in some other way to increase their fame. How much is their testimony worth? When Robert Walpole was in retirement, his son, to keep him amused, would often read to him. One day he asked his father whether he would like him to read some history. Walpole declined. 'There'll be no truth in it', he said. Walpole had an unparalleled experience of the political events of his time, being for more than twenty years at their very centre. His experience was that events do not get reported in the way they occur; indeed, the most important of them occur in such a way as to ensure that they do not get reported.

Anyone who attempts to reason about the study of history, independently of any commitment to it, will easily find sufficient cause for scepticism. Historians, it is true, attain certainty but that is because they do not reason independently of commitment. They will question certain testimonies but only on the basis of others which they would never think to question. One may note that the certainty which is attained both in science and history depends on their being, as it were, imperfectly theoretical. They are theoretical; but only within limits, reasoning without commitment in certain areas but leaving others unquestioned. Moreover, it is their leaving certain areas unquestioned which enables them to attain certainty in the areas where they do question. It is only in philosophy, where commitment is at a minimum, that scepticism flourishes without limit. That is a point insufficiently noted by those in philosophy who reason about religion. Their conclusions are often sceptical; but it never occurs to them that their scepticism might be occasioned, at least in part, by the stance they have adopted, so that they would have come to similar conclusions had they adopted the same stance towards any other activity.

For a final example, we shall take everyday or non-technical knowledge. On being asked the location of your car, you are entitled to answer with certainty if you clearly remember where you parked it, say, twenty minutes earlier. Judged by ordinary standards, that would be correctly termed knowledge. But it is conceivable that during the last twenty minutes your car has been towed away by the police. Judged by ordinary standards, you could not be correctly said to *know* this has not occurred since during the time in question you have not seen your car. But now we have an antinomy. You know that your car is parked, say behind the supermarket. On the other hand, you do not *know* whether the police have towed it away. But if they have done so, it is not behind the supermarket. Consequently you do not know where it is. The example is trivial but it has a significance in being typical of our knowledge in general. In short, an antinomy can be made to appear whenever someone claims knowledge. For example, you are entitled to claim with certainty that you will be at a meeting this evening, if you have made definite arrangements and fully intend to be there. But you will not be at the meeting if, in the meantime, you crash your car, walk into a bus or suffer some other serious accident. You surely cannot claim to *know* that these accidents will not occur to you. But then we have the same antinomy. You know p, but you do not know q; yet if q then ~ p; so you cannot claim to know p. The antinomy can be made to appear wherever we claim to know, since our knowledge is always relative to normal conditions that pass beyond our knowledge. For example, in each of the cases mentioned above, knowledge is relative to normal expectations – normally, the police do not tow away cars, accidents are out of the common run of things. But on a perspective wider than normal, it will appear as if we have no knowledge at all. For the conditions to which our knowledge is relative are themselves uncertain. One is certain relative to normal circumstances but one cannot be certain that present circumstances are normal. You are not certain that the police have not towed away your car or that you will not suffer an accident. Stepping outside normal standards and reflecting on them, adopting the theoretical perspective, we find that our certainty has disappeared. We have become sceptics.

Within philosophy, there have been innumerable attempts to show that scepticism is fallacious or incoherent. What they have in common is that they address scepticism on a theoretical level, that is, on its own ground. James's strategy in effect is to change the ground, to show that there are considerations which take precedence over the theoretical. Thus, let us grant the perspective adopted by the sceptic. On a perspective wider than normal, we can see that our knowledge is always relative to what passes beyond knowledge. The point might be expressed by saying that we have no absolute certainty. But what consequences are supposed to follow from that point? For example are we supposed in practice to face the future with no expectations whatever, treating everything as uncertain? But in that case we should be unprepared to cope even with normal circumstances, even where events take their normal course, so that had we reasoned in the normal way we should have known what to do. In practical terms, the attitude is evident folly. If we reason in the normal way we may lose, but, on the alternative, we cannot win. Moreover, we have to adopt some attitude, since even if we evade a decision, we have in effect decided to let things drift, to treat everything as uncertain. The option, as James would put it, is forced.

It may be remarked, however, that the attitude we normally adopt can hardly be reasonable if it involves us in contradiction, in what we have called an antinomy. But the appearance of contradiction or antinomy arises only on the assumption that we are aiming in the first place at absolute certainty. A little reflection will reveal that our certainty is well understood to be relative. For example, when I am asked where I have parked my car, or what I shall be doing this evening, it is presupposed that I am not to count exceptional circumstances. The untoward is always possible, but for that very reason discounted. I am to state what will occur only so far as I can be expected to foresee it. If the unforeseen occurs, we have a different ball game, and no one will blame me for being wrong. In short, the words 'know' and 'certainty' are practical instruments; in using them, we are not committed to omniscience.

To put the essential point another way: scepticism is the inevitable consequence of confining oneself *simply* to the theoretical sphere. Moreover, Pragmatism explains precisely why that should be so. As Peirce argued, our certainty rests ultimately on certainty in practice. Our reasons are convincing because they rest on certainties for which no reasons are required. Scepticism is therefore inevitable for one who confines himself to the theoretical sphere and demands a reason for everything. What makes it inevitable is not the rigour of his reasoning; his conclusion is guaranteed by the attitude he has adopted before he starts to reason. For, in requiring a reason for everything, he refuses to accept the very condition for achieving certainty. He refuses to trust anything until it is proved; but the condition of such a proof is that he put his trust in something.

Further reflection will now reveal that there is no incompatibility between the perspective adopted by the sceptic and that of ordinary practice, *just so long as neither is taken as absolute.* It is not the perspective that the sceptic adopts but his refusal to accept any other that occasions his scepticism. There is no incompatibility in admitting that perspective *along with* that of ordinary practice. Indeed it can be salutary to do so. It is sometimes useful to remind oneself that our normal expectations are not guaranteed, that our certainty is not absolute.

Let us elaborate the above point by looking again at the theoretical stance. In adopting that stance, we step outside our beliefs; we reflect upon them. The usefulness of doing so may be illustrated by metaphor. It is as if, for the first time, we move outside the wood where we have always lived and view it from above. In that perspective we shall notice much that we have never noticed before. For example, we shall acquire a clear view of how one part of the wood is related to another and how the whole is related to what surrounds it. It is evident, however, that the knowledge thus acquired, though it may supplement or even correct, cannot wholly replace the knowledge that has been acquired from within. The view from above, taken in itself, is partial; indeed it may even be delusive. The following example may illustrate the point. On returning to my home, when I lived on a hill overlooking the town of Swansea, I used sometimes to pause and look back on the distance I had covered. Human beings in the middle distance were mere dots; at the centre of the town, from where I had walked, only vehicles could be seen and they were the size of toys. Sometimes I had the curious feeling that it was impossible for a human being to cover so vast a distance. I say 'curious', because the distance is only some two miles and, on the very occasion of having the feeling, I had just covered the distance myself. The feeling was induced by a trick of perspective. On the wider perspective, presumably because the figures are so diminished in size, the distance is exaggerated and a comparatively easy accomplishment is turned into an impossibility.

Analogous points apply to the theoretical perspective. When one ceases to be immersed in human life, and reflects upon it, viewing it in relation to its surroundings; when one considers the variability and conflict in human opinion, the sources of human reason in causes apparently blind, the limits of human experience both in space and time, the vastness of the universe – considering all this, one no longer feels impressed by what passes for human certainty. Closer to the ground, however, much goes on; in practice, certainty is attained; the apparently impossible, when viewed from afar, is occasionally accomplished. It is possible, in other words, that the wider perspective is only one amongst the others, useful but not absolute or final. The point is reinforced by reflection, since the wider perspective is itself the product of human practice, of that very certainty which, when viewed from the wider perspective, appears so unimpressive. Consequently, if the view it presents were the last truth, we should have no reason to accept it. In short, viewing life from another point, one becomes somewhat sceptical about scepticism; it, too, has its limits.

Chapter 7

James: *The Varieties of Religious Experience*

We must now consider James's second great work, *The Varieties of Religious Experience*. The aim of the book is to give an account of religion from the standpoint of psychology, where psychology, as is usual with James, includes philosophical reflection. In an introductory chapter, James says that he will consider religion in its subjective or individual rather than in its social or institutional aspect. That distinction has attracted some criticism. It has been pointed out, for example, that the individual and the social are not sharply divided. Any individual is a social creature, who is influenced in his private activity by what he has acquired from the public sphere. The point is sound but I doubt that it invalidates James's approach. He has a preference for one of two approaches which may be found in the study of any social phenomenon. The two approaches may be called that of the sociologist and that of the novelist. The approach of the one is abstract and general; that of the other, personal. For example, suppose one is studying contemporary driving conditions in Britain. The sociologist will describe conditions in general, laying out the rules for motorists, statistics of accidents, and so on. Here, the conditions being common to any number of motorists, it is unnecessary to mention any motorist in particular. No individual motorist, for example, need be mentioned in describing the Highway Code. On the other hand, one could proceed by giving examples, taking a number of individuals and recreating the conditions they encounter, say, during a given day. Similarly, one may study a religion by considering the details of its ritual, ceremony and theology; or, again, one may do so by considering the way it enters into the lives of a number of individuals. Both of these methods have their advantages and their disadvantages. The sociologist's approach, for example, has the disadvantage of inducing boredom. Examples need to be introduced at some point, if only to retain the attention of one's readers. Moreover, in remaining at the level of the abstract and general, one will miss those individual variations which, on occasions, have a decisive effect on the general development. The disadvantage in confining oneself to particular examples is that one may lose common features or leave uncovered important aspects of the field. Moreover, without the references to general features, the individual case becomes unintelligible. For example, your re-creation of a driver's experience during a given day, will not be fully intelligible to your readers unless they have some knowledge of the Highway Code. In practice, the two methods will usually be mixed in some measure; nevertheless, there will often remain a real difference in emphasis. In James, the emphasis is on the particular example. He is attracted to that method, partly because, like many Protestants, he has no taste for the details of ritual and ceremony, but also because he has a native preference for the concrete and vivid.

James's introductory remarks cover his first two chapters. It will be valuable to consider some of his points, because he often gives them classical expression. At the beginning of his second chapter, for example, he insists that we shall not be assisted in our understanding of religion by giving it a definition. That is an important point, often missed, because it is not sufficiently recognised that the knowledge provided by a definition is purely verbal and is therefore useless to someone who is puzzled by the idea or concept for which the word stands. For example, one may usefully define a bachelor as an unmarried man only to someone who already has the concepts of being a man and being unmarried. The definition simply gives him an additional term to stand for those concepts. But suppose a person who comes from a society in which marriage is either unknown or takes a form radically different from our own? The definition is now useless to him. To understand 'bachelor' , he needs to understand the institution of marriage, which cannot be conveyed in a phrase. Similarly, a definition of 'religion' would only give us a verbal equivalent. That is no substitute for understanding the phenomena covered by the term. Nor need we be worried if there is no very sharp boundary between the phenomena that count as religion and those that do not. There is no sharp boundary, at least in Britain, between day and night. Nevertheless, the two may usefully be distinguished. There is a clear enough difference between midnight and midday. Similarly, says James, we may ignore borderline cases and proceed in our study of religion by taking what is central. That, again, is a reason for proceeding not in general terms but by means of examples.

From the outset, James is concerned that we distinguish questions of fact from questions of value. The two, of course, are connected. For example, suppose you hold that the Bible is a revelation from God. That is an estimate of its spiritual value. Now suppose you become convinced that the Bible contains errors of fact. That is a factual or scientific judgement. It may be that the latter judgement leads you to give up the former. You change your estimate of the Bible's spiritual value as a result of the judgement of fact. That shows that the two types of question, the evaluative and the factual, are connected. But, though connected, the two are different, and there is no immediate inference from the one to the other. For example, in holding that the Bible contains errors of fact, you are not bound in logic to change your opinion of its spiritual value. You might, instead, change your idea of what constitutes a revelation from God. You may hold, quite reasonably, that any revelation must be adapted to the understanding of those who receive it, and, in consequence, you may continue to believe that the Bible is a revelation from God even though it contains errors of fact.

One consequence of confusing fact with value is the so-called genetic fallacy. That is the fallacy of supposing that in explaining how a phenomenon has arisen, in giving its genesis, one has thereby explained it away. For example, in James's time it was common to explain certain religious phenomena as arising from frustrated sexuality. As evidence for this, critics of religion pointed to the use of sexual imagery in describing mystical experience. St John of the Cross, for example, has a famous poem in which the union of the soul with God is described in the language of an erotic encounter. James points out that to explain religion as a perverted form of sexuality is no more plausible than to explain it as an aberration of the digestive function. 'Language drawn from eating and drinking is probably as common in religious discourse as is language drawn from the sexual life. We "hunger and thirst after righteousness"; we "find the Lord a sweet savor"; we "taste and see that it is good".' It is not surprising that religious imagery and symbolism should draw upon sexuality, since sexuality is one of the common facts of life on which all imagery and symbolism draw. But, in any case, suppose it could be shown that certain religious phenomena are based in sexuality, that they are connected, say, with the development of sexuality in adolescence. That is a judgement of causation, of fact. One has not thereby shown the phenomena to be valueless, unless one has independent grounds for supposing that anything is valueless which arises in that way. Thus in connecting certain religious phenomena with the development of sexuality in adolescence, one has shown them to be valueless only if anything is valueless which is connected with such a development. But, as James points out, the entire higher mental life may plausibly be connected with the development of sexuality in adolescence, that being the time when the mind typically begins to raise questions about the meaning of life. To put the point another way: showing how something arises will not in itself settle any question of value, since those who differ in their values, will differ also about whether what has arisen in that way is valuable.

In clarifying the difference between fact and value, James reinforces the point we made earlier, namely, that the theoretical standpoint is only one amongst others. Thus, in reflecting theoretically on religion, one may establish certain facts and trace causal connections, and, in that way, one may be assisted in evaluating the phenomenon. But though theoretical reflection may assist one's evaluation, it cannot in itself determine it. One must already possess some sense of value; and, once again, those who differ in their values may differ in their estimate of the phenomenon, even though they agree about the facts that theoretical inquiry discloses. Theoretical inquiry, in short, cannot settle all questions. In this respect, it will be useful to consider the limits of the theoretical, as James draws them in his third chapter. An inquiry such as physical science presupposes: (1) definitely statable abstract principles; (2) definite facts of sensation; (3) definite hypotheses based on such facts; and (4) definite inferences logically drawn. One may add that its aim is to establish conclusions that will be accepted by all reasonable persons, so that it is forced to appeal only to what such persons hold in common, that being a restriction which a little reflection will reveal as severe. Now James pays tribute to the achievements of inquiry, thus characterised, but he rejects the rationalist claim that all knowledge is confined within such limits.

Nevertheless if we look on man's whole mental life as it exists, on the life of men that lies in them apart from their learning and science, and they inwardly and privately follow, we have to confess that the part of it of which rationalism can give an account is relatively superficial. It is the part that has the *prestige* undoubtedly, for it has the loquacity, it can challenge you for proofs, and chop logic, and put you down with words. But it will fail to convince or convert you all the same, if your dumb intuitions are opposed to its conclusions. If you have intuitions at all, they come from a deeper level of your nature than the loquacious level which rationalism inhabits.

(James 1961: 81–8)

These are points we must have in mind when we come to consider James's own conclusions. We shall find them negative, so far as they are definite and, so far as they are positive, highly tentative. But we must remember that James is confining himself to the theoretical standpoint. He is attempting, for example, to isolate what, in religion, may be accepted even by those who stand outside it. It will help us to appreciate the point if we recall an earlier conclusion, namely, that the theoretical approach will draw conclusions, hardly more positive, whatever activity it considers. The caution or scepticism, in short, is integral to the standpoint.

One final point, of a preliminary nature, has to be considered. James repeatedly states that the only criterion for estimating the value of religion, which is likely to be persuasive to someone uncommitted to the religious life, is that of utility. 'By their fruits shall ye know them.' But here, once again, we encounter the difficulties, earlier raised, about James's theory of truth. As we have seen, James came perilously close, at least in his later work, to identifying truth with utility. That may be one cause of the impression, gained by some readers, that James, in his account of religion, was not concerned with its objective truth but only with those religious states, however subjective, which have useful consequences. For example, in a number of pages, he appears to suggest that religious belief is valuable just so far as it saves the believer from depression, makes him useful to society, and so on. Against this, it has been pointed out that a religious belief might have those consequences even if it were false. If a man believes he is in touch with the source of all things and will be taken into paradise, one can explain why he has ceased to be depressed simply by indicating what he believes; it is not necessary, in addition, to suppose that his belief is true. The point is entirely sound. Nevertheless two further points need to be taken into account. First, James is indicating a criterion that will be persuasive to someone who stands *outside* religion. He is not suggesting, indeed he explicitly denies, that the believer himself has no other ground for his conviction. Second, utility is one criterion of truth. Granting, in other words, that James is indiscriminate in his use of utility as a criterion, it does not follow that a more discriminating use was not available to him. It will be important to consider the point in some detail. We need to be clear about where the utility of a belief will serve as a mark of its truth. Consider the following example. St John of the Cross spent much of his life absorbed in prayer. From a non-religious point of view, he was therefore absorbed for much of his life in a state of delusion. On the other hand, in the remainder of his life, he was remarkable not simply for his virtue but also for shrewdness and for outstanding gifts as a prose writer and poet. Now that is not usual. One would expect a delusion which occupies so much of a life, which is prolonged, indeed cultivated, to have some unfortunate effect on the life more generally. Yet that seems not to have occurred. St John's gifts seem not to have declined but to have flourished the longer he was occupied with his state of delusion. Evidently we have *some* reason to suppose that he was not deluded at all. I don't say the reason is conclusive; nevertheless we have some reason. Why in this case is utility a sign of truth? Because our supposing St John's state not to be deluded makes it easier to explain why it flourished. In other words, utility is not invariably a sign of truth; yet sometimes it is, because sometimes our supposing a belief true provides the best explanation for why it is useful.

James begins his survey of religious phenomena in his third chapter, entitled 'The Reality of the Unseen'. He says that 'were one asked to characterise the life of religion in the broadest and most general terms possible, one might say that it consists of the belief that there is an unseen order, and that our supreme good lies in harmoniously adjusting ourselves thereto' (1961: 69). His method in this and subsequent chapters is to present us with a variety of cases, having a family resemblance, in which the religious cases are not sharply divided from the non-religious. Thus, in the present chapter, he begins by giving examples, not in themselves religious, in which people have become convinced of the presence of objects not perceived by the senses. He then shows that these cases shade into the religious, where people have had vivid experiences, for example in contemplating the beauty of nature, that have convinced them of the reality of God. A clergyman, whom he quotes, after recalling such an experience, says that

> since that time no discussion that I have heard of the proofs of God's existence has been able to shake my faith. Having once felt the presence of God's spirit, I have never lost it again for long. My most assuring evidence is deeply rooted in that hour of vision, in the memory of that supreme experience, and in the conviction, gained from reading and reflection, that something of the same has come to all who have found God.
>
> (James 1961: 81–2)

One important conclusion, of a negative kind, emerges from this chapter, namely that religious experiences exist which for those who have them are entirely convincing, more convincing, indeed, than any conclusion is likely to be which is based on argument. That in itself, of course, is not likely to convince those who lack such experience. Nevertheless the point, though negative, is philosophically important, because it leads to a criticism of Rationalism. On the Rationalist view, those who gain conviction from such experiences must in addition have the support of argument, not simply to convince others but in order to be entitled to their *own* convictions. James's point is that they are entitled to their convictions simply on the basis of their experiences. Their having those experiences will not convince the Rationalist, but the arguments of the Rationalist will not convince them. On a priori ground, either may be right. But that in itself conflicts with the Rationalist view that conviction in this area *must* be supported by argument. On a priori ground, there is no reason to suppose that truth in this area is more likely to be acquired by argument than by experience. James's own view is that experience in this area is the more fundamental:

> The truth is that in the metaphysical and religious sphere, articulate reasons are cogent for us only when our inarticulate feelings of reality have already been impressed in favour of the same conclusion. Then, indeed, our intuitions and our reason work together, and great world-ruling systems, like that of the Buddhist or of the Catholic philosophy, may grow up. Our impulsive belief is here always what sets up the original body of truth, and our articulately verbalised philosophy is but its showy translation into formulas. The unreasoned and immediate assurance is the deep thing in us, the reasoned argument is but a surface exhibition. Instinct leads, intelligence does but follow. If a person feels the presence of a living God after the fashion shown by my quotations, your critical argument, be they never so superior, will vainly set themselves to change his faith.
>
> (James 1961: 88–9)

James now proceeds to distinguish between different types of religious temperament, the once-born and the twice-born. The once-born, also called the healthy minded, are those who find it natural to adopt a religious attitude. For them, faith is easier than doubt, the good of the world more obvious than the evil. For the twice-born, it is the evil of the world which is the more obviously impressive. For them, faith emerges out of the struggle with doubt and takes something of its tone from that struggle. James devotes a number of chapters to each. In describing the healthy minded he draws freely on pamphlets supplied by the mind-cure and Christian Scientist movements, which were popular in America at the time he wrote. The academics of James's time would have considered much of this as belonging to the underworld of religion. These considerations had no effect on James. He believed in giving everyone a chance and took a delight in examining phenomena, such as spiritualism, which his academic colleagues considered disreputable. At the end of his book, he distinguishes between two types of religion which he terms crass and refined. He indicates that his preference is for the crass variety.

One reason for his distinguishing between different types of religious temperament is that it enables him to illustrate one of his main themes, namely, that variety is a permanent feature of religion. Religion needs to be various because human nature is various. Thus, in comparing the once-born with the twice-born, James's sympathies are evidently with the latter; it is the experience of the twice-born that is the more profound, that takes in the greatest range of significant fact. Nevertheless, he insists that the mind-cure movement has something to offer. It is valid for those who are suited to it. The once-born are better off being true to themselves than trying to be something else.

James begins his examination of the twice-born, or sick soul as follows:

> To begin with, how can things so insecure as the successful experiences of this world afford a stable anchorage? A chain is no stronger than its weakest link, and life is after all a chain. In the healthiest and most prosperous existence, how many links of illness, danger and disaster are always interposed? Unsuspectedly from the bottom of every fountain of pleasure, as the old poet said, something bitter raises up: a touch of nausea, a falling dead of the delight, a whiff of melancholy, things that sound a knell, for fugitive as they may be, they bring a feeling of coming from a deeper region and often have an appalling convincingness. The buzz of life ceases at their touch as a piano string stops sounding when the damper falls upon it.
>
> (James 1961: 145)

The mind-cure movement recommends that we free ourselves from morbid thoughts, concentrate on the good in the world, think positively. Faith thus sustained, though real, will strike the reflective as shallow, because the evil which it ignores is a permanent, not incidental, feature of the world. The faith of the twice-born is more profound because it has been put to the test. In his seventh chapter, James gives many cases of people who have been afflicted by the evil of the world, some of them, such as those of Tolstoy and Bunyan, having classic status. Also included in this section is the passage, quoted in Chapter 5, in which James describes the terrible experience that came upon him in early manhood. In the next chapter, he describes a phenomenon which is important in understanding the twice-born, namely, that of the divided will. 'What I would, that I do not,' said the apostle Paul, 'but what I hate, that I do.' The sense of division is well brought out in a quotation from Augustine:

> The new will which I begun to have was not yet strong enough to overcome that other will, strengthened by long indulgences. So these two wills, one old, one new, one carnal, the other spiritual, contended with each other and disturbed my soul. I understood by my own experience what I had read, 'flesh lusteth against spirit, and spirit against flesh'. It was myself indeed in both wills, yet more myself in that which I approved in myself than in that which I disapproved in myself. Yet it was through myself that habit had assumed so fierce a mastery in me, because I had willingly come whither I willed not. Still bound to earth, I refused, O God, to fight on thy side, as much afraid to be freed from all bonds, as I ought to have feared being trammeled by them.
>
> (James 1961: 177)

This sense of division, of not liking on reflection what one does, how one lives, yet not refraining, or refraining only imperfectly, from what one dislikes is of great importance in understanding one of the most striking of religious phenomena, namely, that of conversion. In many cases, afflicted souls have suddenly come into the light, have found faith. Moreover, this has been accompanied by the most remarkable transformation of character. Vices that held them in subjection have simply disappeared, virtues that seemed impossible to attain have become settled features of their characters. James gives many examples. There can be no doubt the phenomenon is real. The question is whether we can obtain any understanding of it in theoretical terms.

CONVERSION

James devotes two chapters to the phenomenon of conversion. We have already seen that he is anxious to make connections between religious and non-religious phenomena. In dealing with conversion he continues with the method, placing cases of non-religious conversion alongside cases of religious. James gives an example of a young man who had wasted a large patrimony in profligate living:

> Reduced to absolute want he one day went out of the house with an intention to put an end to his life, but wandering awhile almost unconsciously, he came to the brow of an eminence which overlooked what were lately his estates. Here he sat down and remained fixed in thought a number of hours, at the end of which he sprang from the ground with a vehement exulting emotion. He had formed his resolution, which was that all those estates should be his again.
>
> (James 1961: 183)

The man's life was genuinely transformed. Formerly profligate, he became close-fisted, acquired a fortune, regained his estates and died an inveterate miser. From Tolstoy, James takes a striking case of conversion to disbelief. A young man, who had been on a hunting expedition, knelt at the end of the day to say his prayers.

> His brother, who was hunting with him, lay upon the hay and looked at him. When S had finished his prayers and was turning to sleep, the brother said, 'Do you still keep up that thing?' Nothing more was said. But since that day, now more than thirty years ago, S has never prayed again; he never takes communion and does not go to church. . . . The words spoken by his brother were like the light push of a finger against a leaning wall already about to tumble by its own weight. These words but showed him that place wherein he supposed religion dwelt in him had long been empty and that the sentences he uttered, the crosses and bows which he had made during his prayers were actions with no inner sense. Having once seized their absurdity, he could no longer keep them up.
>
> (James 1961: 183)

Tolstoy's example suggests that a transformation sudden in its effect, at the conscious level, may nevertheless have been long in preparation. The brother's words transform the young man's conduct because they make him realise that, in effect, he has, for a long time, ceased to believe. James's view is that the pattern of religious conversion is similar. The transformation of a person's character in religious conversion, though sudden in its effect, has often been long in preparation. Hence the importance of that division or conflict which so often precedes conversion. The conversion is in fact the resolution of the conflict. The desire for deliverance, long present, though hitherto blocked, overcomes resistance. In this connection, James points to the importance in conversion of a further feature. Often a person's conversion is immediately preceded by his *giving up* the struggle for deliverance. He has desperately wanted deliverance from sin. He strives for deliverance but does not get it. Eventually, he gives up. At that point, he is delivered. The process has its parallels in ordinary experience. For example, striving to recollect a name often seems to prevent one's recalling it. Thus often enough, when one gives up trying the name comes into one's mind of its own accord. Or consider the joke about the centipede who was asked which leg he moved first and never moved again. One's purposes, so far from being assisted, are often frustrated by conscious striving. Similarities in the case of religious conversion suggest to James that the phenomenon exhibits a resolution in full consciousness of purposes or desires which have been working at the subconscious level.

Now the notion of the subconscious must detain us for a while. It figures prominently in James's book and especially in the chapters we are considering. The theory of the subconscious had greatly interested psychologists since the 1880s, as the result of studies in hysteria carried out, amongst others, by Janet, Binet and Freud. The cases these psychologists study are very remarkable. Indeed it seems to me a pity that they are now remembered simply as having given rise to the theory of the subconscious. The theory of the subconscious, in my view, is less remarkable than they are. For the notion of the subconscious, so far as it is valid, is a device for emphasising features of human life which, in many cases, are already familiar. An example appears in the above paragraph. Often enough, when asked a person's name, one simply answers. The name is not consciously recalled. It just comes to mind. Indeed, as we have seen, conscious recall, the deliberate effort to remember, so far from assisting, will often frustrate the process of recall. This will seem surprising only on the supposition that purposive behaviour is primarily conscious or explicit.

But, as we have had occasion to notice, that supposition is erroneous. Conscious or explicit behaviour is simply the outgrowth of purposive behaviour in general. In general, purposive behaviour is not explicit or conscious. Indeed, even where explicit or conscious, it always depends on behaviour that is tacit or non-explicit. For example, suppose you make a conscious effort to remember an appointment, say, by tying a knot in your handkerchief. In doing so, you presuppose that you will not need consciously to recall the appointment when you see the knot. Otherwise, the device is useless and you might just as well try to carry the appointment in your head.

There is, however, a further reason why the theory of the

subconscious appears more striking than it really is, namely, that people associate with it images that are entirely inappropriate. To illustrate the point, consider the case of a person under hypnosis who is told to perform a particular act, say in an hour's time. An hour later he performs the act, though he cannot recall being told to do so. Now there is evidently a difference between that case and one in which a person is asked to perform an act and later performs it, having explicitly recalled what to do. The trouble is that the difference is misconstrued. Thus it is often assumed that the hypnotised person does exactly what is done in the other case, except that he does it unconsciously. In other words, it is assumed that he is recalling what he was told to do, though he does not know he is recalling it. That is merely a variation on the prejudice mentioned above, namely, that all purposive action is conscious or explicit. Confronted by purposive action where no conscious or explicit purpose appears, those who think in that way assume it is present, but is occurring subconsciously. That, in fact, is a contradiction – what is occurring subconsciously is conscious or explicit purpose – but the contradiction is not noticed as such; rather, the phenomenon is taken to be strange and remarkable. In fact, what the behaviour of the hypnotised person shows is that behaviour does not have to be at the explicit or conscious level. Thus the hypnotised subject does not *need* to recall what he was told, in order to do it. That is the real difference between the cases. In the case of the hypnotised subject the causes of his purposive behaviour are sufficient to ensure that those purposes will be carried out. Moreover, in that respect, though not of course in others, his behaviour does not differ so very markedly from behaviour found in ordinary experience. Many a person, for example, has found himself looking though a drawer in his kitchen without immediately being able to recall why he does so. In his living room, he decided to fetch a screwdriver kept in the kitchen. On the way, a problem from earlier in the day returned to his mind and completely engrossed him. Nevertheless, his original purpose carried on regardless; he still opens the drawer and starts looking for his screwdriver. In many cases, the original purpose can be entirely carried through. A person may open the drawer, search it, locate the screwdriver and return to the living room, his mind engrossed throughout with a problem entirely distinct from what he is doing. It will be recalled that these points are implicit in what Peirce said about the continuity of purpose.

The above reflection will reveal that James's view of conversion is not as striking as it may at first appear. To say that it exhibits, at the conscious level, a resolution of purposes or desires that have been at work in the subconscious is merely to assimilate the phenomenon to many others in common experience. Tolstoy's example illustrates the point. Belief may ebb away, before one has made it explicit that one no longer believes. So might love, before one has formulated that one no longer loves, and so on. What, however, is an interesting question is whether one may accept James's view and simultaneously take a religious view of conversion. James's view would suggest that conversion is simply the product of forces hitherto at work in the mind of the converted person. The religious view, often at least, is that conversion is a miraculous process involving the direct intervention of the divine, and therefore not explicable in psychological or, at least, natural terms. It will be useful to take the issue in two stages. First, we shall consider whether James has disproved the religious view, thus characterised. One can show very easily that he has not, at least with regard to many cases of religious conversion. But then we shall consider whether James's view, even if it were true, would necessarily deprive conversion of its religious significance. James would say that it does not, and in this I think he is entirely correct.

The reason why James's view does not disprove the religious one, which is given above, is that he is selective in the cases he cites in support of it. For every case that fits his view there is another which does not. The point can be proved by reference to his own pages. Here is a passage quoted by James from the confessions of Colonel Gardiner, former drunkard and womaniser.

> I was converted in my own bedroom in my father's house at precisely three o'clock in the afternoon of a hot July [13 July 1886]. I was in no way troubled about my soul. In fact, God was not in my thoughts that day. A young lady friend sent me a copy of Professor Drummond's *Natural Law in the Spiritual World*, asking me my opinion of it as a literary work only. Being proud of my critical talents and wishing to enhance myself in my new friend's esteem, I took the book to my bedroom for quiet, intending to give it a thorough study, and then write her what I thought of it. It was here that God met me face to face and I shall never forget the meeting. 'He that hath the Son hath life eternal, he that hath not the Son hath not life.' I had read this scores of times before, but this made all the difference. I was now in God's presence and my attention was absolutely 'soldered' on this verse, and I was not allowed to proceed with the book till I had fairly considered what these words really involved. Only then was I allowed to proceed, feeling all the while that there was another being

in my bedroom, though not seen by me. The stillness was very marvellous, and I felt supremely happy.

(James 1961: 223)

That was the moment of conversion. It was not preceded by any struggle nor by anything that could be described even as latent belief. Neither was it accompanied by any sense of deliverance; quite the contrary, the immediate effect of his experience was to convince Gardiner that he was lost.

> I felt God's love so powerfully upon me that only a mighty sorrow crept over me that I had lost all through my own folly; and what was I to do? What could I do? I did not repent ever; God never asked me to repent. All I felt was 'I am undone', and God cannot help it, although he loves me. No fault on the part of the Almighty. All the time I was supremely happy: I felt like a little child before his father. I had done wrong but my Father did not scold me, but loved me almost wondrously. Still my doom was sealed.
>
> (ibid.)

The case of Alphonse Ratisbonne is also relevant. Ratisbonne was a Jew and a sceptic, indifferent to all religion. On a visit to Rome he fell in with a traveller from his own country who gave him a religious medal and asked him to read a short prayer to the Virgin. He complied out of politeness. On the following day at noon, with time on his hands, he wandered into a church.

> The church of San Andreas was poor, small and empty; I believe that I found myself there almost alone. No work of art attracted my attention, and I passed my eyes mechanically over the interior without being arrested by any particular thought. I can only remember an entirely black dog which went trotting and turning before me as I mused. In an instant the dog had disappeared, the whole church had vanished, I no longer saw anything... or more truly I saw, O my God, one thing alone.
>
> (ibid.)

Ratisbonne does not describe what he experienced, but it appears to have been a vision of the Virgin. At any rate, the effect of the experience was to transform him for the rest of his life into a devout Catholic.

> You may ask me how I came to this new insight, for truly I had never opened a book of religion nor even read a single page of the Bible, and the dogma of original sin is either denied or forgotten by the

Hebrews of today, so that I had thought so little about it that I doubt whether I ever knew its name. But how came I, then, to this perception of it? I can answer nothing save this, that on entering the church I was in darkness altogether, and on coming out of it I saw the fullness of the light.

(James 1961: 226)

The above case is in conflict with James's account on every significant detail. The experience of conversion breaks into a life unprepared for it by any struggle or desire for deliverance. Someone who holds James's view may, of course, argue that the appearances are deceptive. The desire for deliverance, in such a case, lies too deeply in the subconscious for it to appear on a single survey. But that is to approach the case with the truth of the view presupposed. There is nothing in the case, as it appears, to *substantiate* the truth of that view.

Let us suppose, however, that the experience of conversion were confined to those cases that do fit James's view. Would it follow that those cases are deprived of religious significance? It would not in fact follow. Suppose that conversion results simply from prior psychological conditions, such as conviction of sin, repentance and the desire for deliverance. Why should those not be the conditions that God has ordained, if not by direct intervention then by the workings of his general providence, as the conditions under which people will truly find him? It might be said that we have no reason to assume the truth of the converted person's belief if we can account for it simply in psychological terms. But the answer to that has already been given by James: the truth or falsity of a belief can never be accounted for simply by reference to its psychological origins. Whatever the origins of a belief, we shall suppose it true if it has consequences which are best explained on that assumption. An example may illustrate the point. Cameron Peddie, who had a ministry in the slums of Glasgow, was recuperating in hospital when he found himself in the next bed to a man who was dying. He recalled that the gift of healing is taken in the New Testament as one of the normal consequences of faith. He felt that his own faith was deficient in that he did not have that gift and could do nothing for the man who was next to him. He resolved that he would pray for the gift, devoting an hour every day to the task. He persisted for some two years. Then one day, as he was preparing a meal, he experienced a change in his body and felt that he had been granted the gift. The feeling at first he did not trust. He attempted a healing, by laying on of hands, but failed through lack of confidence. He succeeded on a second attempt and never failed thereafter. He did not always succeed in effecting a complete cure but he never failed to bring relief of suffering. His gift had nothing to do with psychological suggestion. It was irrelevant whether his patients had confidence in his power and he could relieve the pain not simply of human beings but also of animals. There can be no reasonable doubt that he had this gift. Witnesses are innumerable and they include members of the medical profession with whom he was always happy to work. Now let us suppose that the conditions for acquiring this gift are simply psychological. In other words, we shall eliminate divine intervention and suppose that anyone at all who had Peddie's belief, desire and persistence would also have acquired his gift. Still we have not thereby eliminated a further question, namely, whether Peddie's belief is true. The gift appeared as the result of sustained prayer in which Peddie showed his faith in God and his desire to serve him. If God is non-existent, faith vain and prayer a delusion, it becomes not easier but altogether harder to explain why Peddie's gift appeared. To see the point, contrast Peddie's case with one mentioned earlier. We said earlier that the satisfaction often produced by religious belief does not in any way count towards its truth. If a person believes he is going to Paradise, we do not have to suppose his belief true in order to explain why it brings him satisfaction. We have only to suppose that he thinks it true. The difference in Peddie's case is that his beliefs brought satisfaction not simply to himself but also to others who did not share them. For example, he cured them of their suffering. It is somewhat more difficult to argue that the same thing would have happened even if his beliefs were deluded, just so long as he believed them. Note, I do not say impossible; but some argument is required.

Here we return to points that James made in his preliminary remarks. The value of a belief does not depend on its origins. It is true, as we have remarked, that the source of a belief may sometimes be suspect. Self interest, for example, is not in general a reliable source of the truth. Nevertheless, on a given occasion, what it is in a person's own interest to believe may be true. Consequently, if one wishes to determine the truth of a belief, it is always wiser to address the belief directly rather than to concern oneself with its origins. The same point applies to religious belief. Whatever its source, we shall have reason to think it true if it proves itself in experience. Consequently, it is to the value of religious belief, rather than to its origin, that James next turns, giving special attention to that transformation of the character which issues in saintliness.

SAINTLINESS

In his two chapters on saintliness and in the next on mysticism, James deals with the full flowering of the religious spirit. Saintliness manifests itself in devotion, charity, strength of soul, purity, obedience, poverty, humility. Not all these phenomena, in James's view, are valuable. In this world, for example, evil is as often encouraged as thwarted by charity. Moreover, fanaticism is often exhibited by the saintly character in the pursuit of austerity and purity. James quotes the case of St Louis of Gonzago who whilst still a boy took a vow of chastity. It was said of him that:

> if by chance his mother sent one of her maids of honour to him with a message, he never allowed her to come in, but listened to her through the barely opened door, and dismissed her immediately. He did not like to be alone with his own mother, whether at table or in conversation, and when the rest of the company withdrew, he sought also a pretext for retiring. . . . Several great ladies, relatives of his, he avoided learning to know even by sight; and he made a sort of treaty with his father, engaging promptly and readily to accede to all his wishes, if only he might be excused from all visits to ladies.
>
> (James 1961: 342–3)

James is severe on the ascetic qualities. He suggests that in an inverted form they place too much importance on the life of the body. 'Anyone who is genuinely emancipated from the flesh,' he said (ibid.: 351), 'will look on pleasures and pains, abundance and privation as alike, irrelevant and indifferent. He can engage in actions and experience enjoyments without fear of corruption or enslavement. As the Bhagavad Gita says, only those need renounce their worldly action who are still unworldly attached thereto.' The argument, it may be noticed, is somewhat curious. We may grant that anyone may safely engage in a worldly life who is genuinely emancipated from worldly attachment. What James does not explain is how one becomes genuinely emancipated from worldly attachment whilst leading a worldly life. Here we touch on a fault running though these chapters. James's strategy is to distinguish between the saintly qualities in terms of social utility, praising those which would find a ready place within a Protestant society at the end of the nineteenth century. The effect is to turn religion into a branch of the social services. The fault, as usual, lies in the indiscriminate use of utility as a criterion of truth. It is one thing to point to the social consequences of religion in order to show those who stand outside it that it contains something valuable. It is quite another to suggest that the value of religion lies wholly in the social consequences. Religion offers itself not as a supplement to ordinary life but as a transformation of character. It could not be true unless in some respects it appeared to the ordinary person not simply as strange but even as repugnant.

Nevertheless, James decides, on balance, that even the ascetic is a force for good. He manifests strength of will, creates energy and power. It is a mistake, says James, to suppose that man will ever live at ease in nature. He lives and grows only by maintaining and increasing human energy. His very existence depends on continual self-renewal and recreation, by an exertion of the ascetic qualities. Moreover, if the saint is at variance with his time that, often enough, is because he is in advance of it. He strives to fit himself for a more perfect society; and in thinking of it as already existing he contributes towards its realisation.

With regard to the weird or occult phenomena, often associated with sanctity, James, in a later passage, notes that scientists have the tendency first to dismiss such phenomena and then to admit them under different terms:

> Miraculous healings have also been part of the supernatural stock in trade and have always been dismissed by the scientists as figments of the imagination. But the scientist's tardy education in the facts of hypnotism has recently given him an apperceiving mass for phenomena of this order, and he consequently now allows that healings may exist, provided you expressly call them 'suggestions'. Even the stigmata of the cross of Saint Francis's hands and feet may on those terms not be a fable. Similarly the time-honoured phenomenon of diabolical possession is on the point of being admitted by the scientist as a fact, now that he has the name 'hystero-demonophy' by which to apperceive. No one can foresee just how far this legitimation of occultist phenomena under newly found scientist titles may proceed – even 'prophecy' even 'levitation' may creep into the pale.
>
> (James 1961: 478)

PHILOSOPHY OF RELIGION

James's next chapter is entitled 'Philosophy'. It deals not with philosophy in general but with the attempt to give religion a philosophical base. In effect, it deals with rationalism on its religious side. As a critic of rationalism, James is entirely consistent. If he concentrates on the form of rationalism termed scientific, that is simply because it is the form most prevalent amongst the educated people of his time. But he is equally critical of rationalism when it takes a religious form. In its religious form, rationalism attempts to prove the existence of God, relying simply on reason; more strictly, starting from premises that would be accepted by all reasonable people, it attempts by valid reasoning to arrive at the conclusion that God exists. Thus the most famous of such arguments, the cosmological, takes as its premise the most obvious of facts, namely that the universe exists. If the conclusion that God exists can be validly inferred from such a premise it will be coercive; all sane people will be forced to accept it. Another famous argument is the argument from design, which draws an analogy between general features of the world and those objects we know to be designed; it then concludes that those features likewise require a designer.

There is difficulty, however, with all such arguments. They all proceed on the basis of arguments that apply to familiar objects, extending them to apply to the world as a whole. Unfortunately, the world as a whole transcends our understanding. Consequently there is an evident difficulty in knowing what in this area counts as a cogent argument. For example, the cosmological argument, in one of its forms, treats the whole world as an object, or as a collection of objects, asks, by analogy with reasoning about an ordinary object, how we are to account for its existence and concludes that its existence must have a cause, namely, God. But if we are to proceed by analogy with ordinary reasoning, we are entitled to ask for the cause of God's existence. If it is said that ordinary reasoning does not apply to God, one might reply by asking why it should apply to the world as a whole.

The argument, however, has a subtler form which evades that difficulty. In the subtler form, the argument states that everything in our experience is contingent – that is, depends for its existence on something else. But, it continues, if everything in the world depends on something else, we have no way of explaining the existence of the world as a whole, except by supposing the existence of something non-contingent. For a world of contingent things cannot explain itself. Its existence would therefore be inexplicable unless there were a non-contingent being, God, which brought it into existence. This argument, it is often claimed, commits the fallacy of composition. One commits the fallacy of composition in supposing that an explanation for A, B and

C must consist of a single explanation for all three elements. But if one has a complete explanation for A, one for B, and another for C, one does not need a further explanation for them all; one has already explained them. The above argument, or so it is claimed, commits that fallacy because it supposes that there must be a single explanation for the whole of the world. In fact one has completely explained the existence of any contingent thing by reference to some other contingent thing and no single explanation for the whole is needed. But that is to misunderstand the argument. The argument is precisely that one has not completely explained the existence of a contingent thing simply by reference to some other; without some explanation for the order of contingent things, no explanation of the existence of any contingent thing is in fact complete. In other words, it is not that having a complete explanation for A and B and C, we need a further explanation for the whole. The argument, rather, is that where A, B and C are contingent elements then, without an explanation for the whole, something will inevitably be left unexplained. In other words, one will *not* have a complete explanation for A, B and C. For example, suppose a series of A, B and C in which A depends on B and B on C . Now suppose, just for the sake of the argument, that C has no explanation. The interesting question is whether we have nevertheless explained the existence of A and B. In one sense, yes. We have linked A to B and B to C. But in another sense, no. For A and B depend for their existence on C and the existence of C, we are supposing, is inexplicable. If there is no explanation of where C came from, then, in the end, there is no explanation of where A and B came from, for they came from C. No doubt their existence can be explained, in the sense that one can link them within the series; unfortunately, one has no explanation for the existence of the series. Moreover, it is easy to see that the same problem arises even if one does have an element to explain the existence of C, so long as the element is equally contingent. Thus suppose that D is the explanation for C. We have now extended the series to A, B, C and D. But if D is itself contingent we have still not explained how the series came into existence; nor shall we ever do so, however we extend it, so long as its constituents are contingent.

The cosmological argument in this form says that the world is like a series in which every element depends on another. Each element may be explained in the sense of being linked to what precedes it. Nevertheless something is left unexplained, namely, why there should be such a series, why there should be a world at all. Moreover, we cannot explain it by adding more links to the chain; it can be explained only on the supposition that the chain is not exhaustive of reality. There is something that transcends it.

The argument is not easy to fault in formal terms. But is it coercive? Not if a coercive argument in this area is one that settles disagreement about religion by directly inducing belief. Consider the following statement: the world can be explained only by supposing the existence of something we know not what, except that it is not like anything we do know. That is not a statement calculated to induce religious belief. But, on reflection, does it differ so very strikingly from the conclusion of the cosmological argument? The conclusion is that the existence of the world can be explained only by assuming the existence of a non-contingent being. But what is the positive content of non-contingent? We know what such a being is not like: not like anything contingent. But that is only to say, not like anything we are acquainted with. Are we not exchanging one mystery for another? That is hardly ground for solid faith. Similar difficulties confront the argument from design. We may grant the argument a certain force. No doubt there are analogies between human purpose and many processes in nature; indeed, it would be hard otherwise to account for human purpose. Nevertheless, Hume's verdict seems just. The most the argument can establish is that between the human mind and the source of all things there is probably some remote analogy. Here again we have little inducement to religious belief. Moreover, we must remember that this is the most that can be expected from a proof strictly theoretical.

Now James's conclusions about religion have in large part already emerged. Nevertheless it will be useful to consider his last chapter, in which he presents them in summary form. The first conclusion which is supported by a theoretical survey of religious phenomena is that if there is value in religion, it does not lie in any single form. In short, variety in religion is likely itself to be valuable. The second concerns the limits of the theoretical. James expresses the point vividly as follows:

> the science of religions may not be an equivalent for living religion; and if we turn to the inner difficulties for such a science, we see that a point comes when she must drop the purely theoretic attitude, and either let her knots remain uncut, or have them cut by active faith.
>
> (James 1961: 467)

But what, then, about the main issue, namely, the objective truth of religion? Granting that the theoretical attitude, of its very nature, cannot settle the matter, what indications can it provide? James's conclusion is that a theoretical survey of religious phenomena gives some reason for accepting the reality of the divine. The reason lies, of course, in the fruits of religion, these being a sign of its truth. But in his concluding chapter James adds a fresh consideration. On his view, the study of subconscious phenomena reveals that the human mind has access to a reality which is not simply wider than ordinary experience but which includes elements of the divine. James emphasises, however, that this conclusion provides no support for any religion in particular. The various religions affirm in common the reality of the divine, but differ about how the divine is to be interpreted. James calls these differing interpretations 'over-beliefs'. One's over-beliefs are determined by living experience, not by theory. It is with an account of his own over-beliefs that James ends his book.

One may distinguish, he suggests, between crass and refined forms of supernaturalism. The crass variety mixes the natural with the super-natural, admitting miracles and providential leanings and interpolating influences from the supernatural amongst the forces that causally determine the real world's details. The common people, amongst whom the crass variety flourishes, tend also towards polytheism. For them reality forms no single system, the details of which are controlled by an absolute authority. Rather, there are a variety of forces, natural and supernatural, a battle is in progress and the outcome is still uncertain. For the refined, by contrast, the miraculous and the providential are not dramatic interventions into the natural world. The world forms a single system, of which the natural and the supernatural are different aspects. The supernatural, or better spiritual, supplements rather than interferes with the natural world; the spiritual and the scientific, when properly understood, being entirely compatible. To the refined, the crass variety is superstition; to the crass, the refined variety is naturalism in religious clothing. James sides unequivocally with the crass.

The Varieties of Religious Experience may be seen as a sustained application of Pragmatism to a particular case. Peirce had insisted that we view the world from the midst of it, having no total conception. Our knowledge, however theoretical, always depends on certainty attained in practice. Certainty on the religious issues is similarly obtained. It is not based on any theoretical conception of the world and its relation to God, for we possess no such conception. It is based on practice or on experience, where that is taken not in the empirical way, as bare sensation, but pragmatically, as our general engagement with life. Reasoning will enter into experience, thus conceived, but it cannot replace it.

Reasoning, on the religious issues, as on others, has its limits, resting finally on what we simply acknowledge to be so. Theoretical reasoning has a place, so far as it clarifies, isolates inconsistency, makes connections, elaborates upon what is found in experience. But the decisive issue will be settled on a different level. It is, so far as it proves itself in practice, that religion will be taken to be true.

In the last three chapters, we have considered James's work in the field where he was a master – philosophical psychology. In this field, Peirce's Pragmatism received fruitful development. But we must recall that in his more general philosophy, James seriously misunderstood Peirce's ideas. The point will be important as we proceed to examine how Pragmatism has fared during the twentieth century.

Chapter 8

Dewey: background and philosophical psychology

The most influential Pragmatist in the twentieth century has been John Dewey. There is, however, a change in the spirit of Pragmatism as it appears in Dewey's work. This change has been indicated by Flower and Murphey in their excellent history of American philosophy:

> In the modern world, pragmatism is viewed as a variant of empiricism, and even as a hard-headed empiricism; its connections with religion are forgotten. But it needs to be stressed how important these connections were historically, and how modern pragmatism is indebted to the religious concerns of men like Peirce and James. Both of these men were fundamentally religious and Peirce was an idealist; both vigorously rejected any form of reductionist empiricism and laid great stress on the freedom and spontaneity of the mind. Both abhorred materialism – then so popular as an alleged implication of science – and fought to maintain a view of man as a creature of values and interests, of imagination and insight far transcending anything possible in the crude mechanistic psychology of Spencer and his followers. Most important, both men saw science as a test by which the mind creates order and beauty out of the chaos of experience.
>
> (Flower and Murphey 1977: xvii)

In the twentieth century, Pragmatism has figured, sometimes in alliance with Logical Positivism, as a species of Scientific Positivism or Naturalism, the very doctrine against which Pragmatism, in the hands of Peirce and James, was very frequently directed. It was John Dewey who was largely responsible for this change. This does not mean that he reverted to a reductionist Empiricism. His aim, rather, was to transform Empiricism, using the insights of Peirce and James. But what he produced, in effect, was a defence of the Scientific Positivism which they had attacked. In short, we are confronted by two Pragmatisms. To consider in detail how this situation arose, we must turn to the work of Dewey himself.

Commentators are agreed that the philosophy of Dewey was formed under the influences, first, of Hegel and then of Darwin and James. Dewey himself mentions a further influence which helps explain what is common to the other three. In an autobiographical sketch (Dewey 1930(II): 13–27), he recalls the pleasure he received when, in studying a textbook on philosophy, he discovered how the various organs of the body are related so as to sustain the body as a whole. This feeling for the organic, for unity amidst differences, appeared when he was young and remained with him throughout his life. Nothing in his later work is more striking than his aversion to discontinuity; indeed it would be difficult to find a dualism, hitherto thought important in philosophy, which he does not attempt either to modify or to undermine. Mind and matter, means and end, reality and appearance, fact and value, theory and practice, art and life, all these are modified in his hands and shown to differ only as aspects of a greater whole. The appeal of Hegel to a mind of this stamp is not difficult to explain. For Hegel offers such a mind the supreme pleasure of seeing the whole of reality develop into a single system. In the same autobiographical sketch, Dewey wrote as follows of Hegel's philosophy:

> It supplied a demand for unification that was doubtless an intense emotional craving and yet a hunger that only an intellectualised subject matter could satisfy… Hegel's synthesis, of subject and object, matter and spirit, the divine and the human, was, however, no mere intellectual formula; it operated as an immense release, a liberation. Hegel's treatment of human culture, of institutions and the arts, involved the same dissolution of hard-and-fast dividing walls, and had a real attraction for me.

What attracted Dewey to the Hegelian system, however, was not its details, which he soon came to abandon, but its central ideas. The most important of these, as we have said, is that of the organic, of unity amidst differences. The radical dualisms which plague philosophy and throw it into confusion, such as that between reality and appearance or between mind and matter, are the result of taking in the abstract what are different aspects of a single reality. These dualisms appear radical or irreconcilable because they are abstractions from the living reality which unites them. The idea was to remain with Dewey in all his later philosophy.

The influence on Dewey of Darwin's theory may be put shortly: he saw in it Hegelianism naturalised. Dewey's generation was the first to feel the impact of Darwin's theory. *Origin of Species* was published in 1859, the year when Dewey was born. We must remember that the theory, for the people of that generation, was much more than a theory in biology. On scriptural authority, it had been held that the species were fixed, having their origin not in the play of natural causes but in the work of God's creation. Their origin, in short, lay in a world over and above the natural. For many, Darwin's theory destroyed the possibility of belief in such a world. The species were not fixed and separate but related to one another through their having evolved from earlier forms, this having occurred precisely through the play of natural causes. The supernatural was removed and there remained only the natural world, a single system in continual change but holding within itself the explanation for all its changes. Here, as in Hegel, the world is revealed as a developing process; but the details in Darwin's theory, unlike those in Hegel's system, are based on the observation of concrete fact and have behind them the authority of the scientific method. It is this vision of the world which is expressed in the philosophy of Dewey's mature years. It is expressed at first with unconstrained vigour. As the years pass, however, there appears a certain unease, a sense of difficulties inherent in the system. It is this which explains the notorious complications of Dewey's later prose. These are caused not by failing powers but by a sense of difficulties which Dewey is too honest a thinker to suppress. In his old age, under the pressure of these difficulties, his philosophy takes a form hardly to be anticipated by those familiar with it only in its earlier stages.

What influenced Dewey in the work of William James was precisely its interpretation of Pragmatism as a form of Radical Empiricism. We must emphasise again, however, that in the spirit of their work the two were very different. Thus, in his later work, James advocated not Naturalism but the right to believe in the supernatural. Moreover, he was a vigorous opponent of the Hegelians, having a native preference for variety over unity. Whereas Dewey, like the Hegelians, looked instinctively for unity in apparent difference, James looked instinctively for difference in apparent unity. It was James's work on the mind which first influenced Dewey. As we have seen, James, in his great work, was anxious to show that the mind is active on the world. In this, he was an opponent of traditional Empiricism, which treated knowledge or belief, for example, as a mechanical effect of outside forces. James, by contrast, analysed knowledge or belief as features of the whole person's activity in pursuit of his needs or purposes. In Dewey's eyes, this was to treat the mind according to a functional or biological model. Mental features were explained through the role they played in preserving the organism as a whole. Moreover, Dewey had James's own authority for supposing that his criticism of Empiricism applied not to the doctrine as such but to the doctrine in an inadequate form. The weakness in traditional Empiricism was that it treated the mind according to the *wrong* empirical model. James had found the right one. It lay in biology rather than in physics. Thus Dewey took James's work to constitute a reconstruction rather than a criticism of Empiricism or Scientific Naturalism. We may note here, in the shift from physics to biology, an important change in Scientific Naturalism itself, one which Dewey was amongst the first to appreciate. In its older forms, Scientific Naturalism or Positivism had taken its model from Newtonian mechanics. In the Newtonian system, changes in phenomena are explained by differences in the configuration of atoms, these being discrete units which underlie the phenomena and are themselves changeless. In the late part of the nineteenth century, the model shifts from physics to biology and the important notions are process and function. On this model, the stable features are *relations* between changing elements rather than permanent features underlying those changes. The importance of this move may be seen if we return for a moment to the religious view of the world. On that view, the natural world is merely a fragment of reality which in its essence is supernatural and therefore inaccessible to the human mind. This distinction between the nature of reality and the way it appears to the human mind, or between phenomena and the reality which underlies them, was preserved in the work of the older Empiricists, not simply because many of them still held a religious view of the world but because they retained the view that human knowledge is in principle limited and fragmentary. In Locke, for example, matter in its substance is entirely unknown, a something we know not what, so that our knowledge, even of the physical world, is inevitably approximate. The contrast with some of the more audacious thinkers of the late nineteenth century is very striking. In Nietzsche, for example, this distinction between reality and appearance is entirely abolished. The reality of the world is constituted by the changing phenomena which appear to our senses. Science reveals no reality underlying these phenomena but simply traces relations between the phenomena themselves. As we shall see, Dewey's own philosophy moves precisely in this direction.

PHILOSOPHICAL PSYCHOLOGY

In considering Dewey's work, it will be useful to begin with the ways in which he developed James's ideas in psychology. Here we have one of Dewey's most solid achievements, for he succeeds not simply in developing what was sound in James's work but also in removing some of its defects. As we have seen, James in explaining the development of the mind gives insufficient weight to the social element. Dewey, by contrast, together with his colleague, G. H. Mead, emphasised that the most distinctive features of the human mind develop only within a social context.

As an example of Dewey's work in psychology, we may take his celebrated article on the reflex arc (1896: 357–70). He takes James's example of a child's reaching for a candle flame. Within a mechanistic psychology, the sequence would fall into the following divisions: light (stimulus), grasping (response), burning (stimulus), withdrawal (response). Dewey condemns this as an abstraction from a living sequence. We must take into account that the child is already active, so that the sight of the flame cuts into and disturbs prior experience. As such, it appears as a problem: bright light (what is this?); grasping hand (let me find out). In short, the stimulus is not mere cause, nor the response mere effect. The relation is rather purposive or functional. The grasping hand is the means of resolving the problem posed by the bright light. Moreover, the further sequence is to be similarly construed. The child is burned and withdraws. This again is not simply a mechanical sequence. Rather the child has come to see the bright light as something to be avoided. The withdrawal is a response to what he has found in exploring the problem of the bright light. Each element in the sequence gets its point from what precedes it and the sequence itself from the way it enters in the experience of the child. The proof of this may be found in what occurs when the child next encounters a bright light. If the elements were mechanical, the sequence would simply repeat itself. But that is just what does not happen. The bright light now evokes the response not of grasping but of hesitation or withdrawal. This shows that the stimulus derives its significance, derives its status *as* a stimulus, from the way it enters into the child's life. On the first occasion, it is a stimulus to grasping; on the second, a stimulus to withdrawal. On other occasions, when the child is preoccupied or has come to take such a light for granted, it may be no stimulus at all. Thus stimulus and response are not absolute categories. Their status is relative to the way they enter into the life of the child.

A similar relativism is involved in distinguishing between means and end. It will be useful to consider in some detail Dewey's analysis of this notion, because it constitutes one of his finest achievements. As he shows, the notion of means and end is the source of confusion in many areas of philosophy because philosophers take it in a grossly simplified form. For example, I want to go to London. Here we have a fixed end not itself subject to reasoning; rather my reasoning is evaluated relative to that end. For example, if I adopt such-and-such a means and I get to London, I have reasoned correctly. The means has no value in itself; rather it derives its value from the end to which it leads. Here we have a model of the relation between means and end which appears in the work of innumerable philosophers. Nevertheless it is grossly misleading. In the first place, the end – my going to London – is fixed for my reasoning *only in that moment*. Take that moment out of my life and the end will seem permanently fixed, in itself impervious to reasoning. Put it back into the flow of my life and take into account my other desires or purposes and it will not seem fixed at all. For then I shall have occasion not simply to evaluate the means in relation to the end but also to re-evaluate the end in relation to the means available. To take a simple case, I may find that the only means of my getting to London will involve more expense than I can afford. As a result, I change my mind and do not go to London. Here, what I evaluate is not the means in relation to its end but the end in relation to its means. In other words, I do not properly appreciate the end I pursue until I appreciate the means involved in getting it. Until I appreciate the means involved in going to London, I do not properly appreciate what is involved in going there. Indeed, as a little reflection will reveal, our ends or purposes in pursuing various activities are more often made clear after rather than before we pursue them. It is only later that we can appreciate what is involved in our purposes and can make clear to ourselves what we really want. It is therefore false to suppose that the value of a means lies wholly in its serving its end, that it has no value in itself. Dewey argues that when we think in this way, we very frequently have in mind the example of manual labour. Such labour is valueless in itself and derives its value only from what it produces. But what this shows, according to Dewey, is not the true relation between means and end but rather the degradation of manual labour. Consider, by contrast, a work of genuine craftsmanship. This has about it a certain beauty. But the beauty appears only when means and end are taken together, seen as forming a whole, each element being as necessary as the other. The relation between means and end need not be seen as rigidly hierarchical; the two may be seen as working together in partnership. Moreover, it is easy to show that certain ends can be achieved only where the means for achieving them are afforded an independent value. For example, pleasure may be obtained from music, but only by someone who has an independent interest in music and is not concerned simply with his own pleasure. Or again, great art can teach one about life but only if one is not concerned simply with life but also has a genuine interest in art.

It is remarkable how fertile Dewey's analysis can prove in removing philosophical confusion. Take as an instance, H. A. Pritchard's celebrated argument to show that morality is an end in itself. The argument is that one cannot give a person a reason for being moral, since only a person who was not already moral would require such a reason. But he would still not be moral even if he were given a reason for acting morally. Rather he would simply be using morality as a means for something else. It is then concluded that moral reasons are entirely internal, that morality is an end in itself. Now this argument evidently presupposes that if morality were a means to something else, it could not have an independent value. Taken as a means it would be valueless in itself. Consequently if we do not wish to place the value of morality *wholly* without, we must place it *wholly* within itself. But, as Dewey has shown, this assumption is fallacious. Take again the famous dispute in aesthetics between those who claim that the value of art lies wholly in what it teaches us about morals or about life in general (the didactic view) and those who claim that art has no purpose outside itself (the art for art's sake view). Here we have what in effect is precisely the fallacy we have just considered. We are offered no choice but to place the value of art either wholly without or wholly within itself. But on reflection it should be evident that art may be valuable because it can teach us about life in *its own distinctive way*. In short, even if art were a means to teaching us about life, it need not be valueless in itself. Perhaps it is precisely because it has a value of its own that it can teach us something distinctive about life.

Dewey's treatment of the means–end relation falls into the category of what used to be called conceptual analysis. He takes a notion much used in philosophy and contrasts its use in philosophy with its use in life. At once the philosophical use appears as a distortion of the real one. For example, the elements of the relation have now lost their absolute quality. What appears at one moment as an end reappears at another as a means. Thus having London in view as an end, I work out the means to get there. Having done so, London reappears not as the end I had in view but as a means for squandering my resources. It is evident that in philosophising with the notion we lose sight of its complexity. As we shall see in a moment, it is a striking illustration of this point that Dewey himself, on occasions, slips back into simplifying the relation between means and end.

Dewey's treatment of the notion, however, is intended not simply to remove confusion but also to advance his more general philosophical purposes. Among the dualisms he is especially concerned to modify or undermine is that between theory and practice. An absolute distinction between these two had already been undermined by the work of Peirce and James, who had shown that theoretical activity presupposes practical certainty. Indeed it is of the essence of Pragmatism that the distinction between the two cannot be absolute. That is one reason why Dewey was attracted to Pragmatism in the first place. For, as we shall see, he took it as one of the main benefits of Scientific Naturalism that it enables us to see theory as continuous with practice. On his view, we no longer have to suppose that there is a gulf between the problems of science, on the one hand, and, on the other, the practical problems of life. The best means of dealing with the problems of life is to be found in the methods of science. To rephrase the point, science is not an end in itself *as distinct from* a means to something else. It is both an end and a means. It is an *end* so far as one is concerned with its problems but also a *means* so far as the solutions to those problems will have consequences for life more generally. Dewey's analysis of means and end as relative makes it easy for him to attribute a similar relativity to the distinction between theory and practice. The point is especially important for Dewey in the philosophy of education, a field in which he exerted an enormous influence. Here it is ruinous to suppose that schooling should be concerned with a subject matter of its own *as distinct from* preparing students for life. The student should be prepared for life *in* his schooling, which comes alive only when it deals with problems which are relevant to life more generally.

To develop these points, it will be useful to consider Dewey's account of inquiry. The elements of this account are already in our hands. Thus the child is already engaged in a primitive form of inquiry in reaching for the candle flame. We must recall that the experience of the flame cuts into or disturbs his prior experience. Dewey is here developing the account given by Peirce. Inquiry begins with a felt difficulty. The movement of the child's arm is a kind of exploration. When the inquiry is explicit or reflective, the exploration will take the form of an attempt to locate and define the difficulty felt. In the case of the child, exploration quickly established the situation as one to be avoided. In more developed inquiry, the location of the difficulty will be followed by an explicit hypothesis as to its solution. This will be followed in turn by its testing, which occurs in two stages. First there is developed the implications of the hypothesis. These implications are then subjected to observation or experiment and the hypothesis itself either accepted or rejected. Like Peirce, Dewey emphasises that developed inquiry is communal. It proceeds on the basis of funded experience and through mutual criticism.

Now we have here distinguished five stages in the process of inquiry. The stages, of course, are to be taken as typical, not as invariable. Dewey summarises them as follows:

> (i) a felt difficulty; (ii) its location and definition; (iii) suggestion of possible solution; (iv) development by reasoning of the bearings of the suggestions; (v) further observation and experiment leading to its acceptance or rejection; that is, the conclusion of belief or disbelief.
> (Dewey 1910: 72)

There are a number of points here to be noticed. Dewey has emphasised that inquiry arises out of a felt difficulty or disturbance of customary experience. As we shall see later he confines the term knowledge to what is found in the course of inquiry. This means that ordinary experience is not a matter of *knowing*; rather, ordinary experience is *had*. The point will have considerable significance in his later work. For the moment, we shall note simply that knowledge for Dewey is only one element in experience. Indeed, it is one of his complaints against traditional philosophers that they place too much importance on knowledge. Human life is not consumed in knowing.

The second point is related to the last. Inquiry has a logic which may be termed instrumental. It has its significance in what it contributes to the life of the organism as a whole. The point follows, of course, from Dewey's functional or biological view of the mind. Being an element in experience, knowledge derives its significance from what it contributes to the enlargement of that experience. As we shall see in a moment, this is amongst the most controversial of Dewey's views.

The third point is that Dewey intends his account to cover inquiry in all its various forms. Thus it covers inquiry both in its practical and in its theoretical aspects. Moreover, it applies as much to value as to fact. Here again Dewey's point is somewhat controversial. Very many philosophers have argued that scientific inquiry is competent only in the realm of fact, not in that of value. For example, it is competent to ascertain what *is* desired but not what *ought* to be. For Dewey, by contrast, it is competent to determine both. His argument is that any desire is implicitly evaluative. If I desire something, I value it. It is true that in the light of further experience, I may no longer desire what I desired earlier. I conclude in the light of my experience that I did not *really* want it. But that is only to acknowledge that I *ought* not to have wanted it. Thus the distinction between what *is* desired and what *ought* to be desired, or is truly desirable, merely reflects the difference between a desire that has not yet faced the test of experience and one that has done so successfully.

Dewey's point can be seen more clearly if we consider his *Human Nature and Conduct*, which is his most substantial work in psychology (Dewey 1930). Here he traces the origin of desire to instinctive or native impulse. He emphasises, however, that such impulses are of secondary importance in explaining the development of any human being. That is because a human being is a social creature. How he develops will depend on what form his impulses take and this will inevitably be influenced by the society in which he lives.

> Exaggerate as much as we like the native differences of Patagonians and Greeks, Sioux Indians and Hindus, Bushmen and Chinese, their original differences will bear no comparison to the amount of difference found in custom and culture. Since a diversity cannot be attributed to an original identity, the development of native impulse must be stated in terms of acquired habits, not the growth of custom in terms of instincts.
>
> (Dewey 1930: 91)

Instinct, then, depends on custom for its form or significance. Dewey argues, however, that a given set of customs may fail to give satisfactory form to available impulse, and this impulse may then serve as a force to reorganise custom. At first, it may not be clear how impulse, which depends on custom, can serve as a force to reorganise it. Dewey's argument is that custom, however apparently rigid, is never wholly so. That is because in order to persist it has to be continually relearned, and this very process will bring about its modification. He gives as an example the way a language is modified over several generations by a series of changes which in any given generation may seem imperceptible. Moreover, no custom can determine all its future applications. Conditions change, throwing up the unusual or novel. There arise periods of extraordinary stress releasing impulses hitherto denied full expression. Problems of value will therefore inevitably occur. For example, there may be a conflict between what others expect me to desire and what I desire myself, or between what I desire and the means available for my satisfying it. How then am I to proceed? I have a felt difficulty which disturbs me in my customary behaviour. I can proceed only by framing a hypothesis of what in these new circumstances will satisfy me, by tracing its implications and by testing those implications in experience. In short, my procedure falls into the familiar pattern of scientific enquiry. At this point, Dewey takes up the theme of social reform:

> We have depended upon the clash of war, the stress of revolution, the emergence of heroic individuals, the impact of migrations generated by war and famine, the incoming of barbarians, to change established institutions. Instead of constantly utilising unused impulse to effect continuous reconstruction, we have waited till an accumulation of stresses breaks through the crust of custom.
>
> (Dewey 1930: 101)

On Dewey's view, it is possible, through the use of the scientific intelligence, to anticipate the need for social reconstruction so that our institutions may change, not by chance, but under intelligent supervision. What he means is not that social affairs should be run by a group of scientists, a view entirely foreign to his democratic instincts. He means rather that the critical or scientific spirit should be suffused throughout society. Democracy, in fact, is superior to other forms of society because it requires that spirit and seeks to make it general. In such a society, the citizen will stand to his institutions rather as the scientist stands to his theories. He will appreciate that they need continual renewal and will submit them to the test of criticism. In this way – or so Dewey argues – social affairs will be brought under scientific control.

We have now given a survey of Dewey's philosophical psychology. Some of its virtues have been emphasised; it will be useful to consider also some of its difficulties. We may begin with a criticism of Dewey's so-called instrumental view of inquiry. The criticism is that the view is essentially philistine, knowledge being valuable in itself and not simply for the sake of its consequences. This was a criticism often urged by Morris Cohen, a vigorous opponent of Dewey in the 1920s and 1930s. Peirce himself made a similar criticism late in his life, when he discovered the use that Dewey had made of some of his views. As we shall see, there is some truth in this criticism, but as it stands, it seems to me misplaced. In the first place, knowledge is not valuable in itself, for it is often trivial. Scientists study the stars or the atomic structure of matter; they do not spend their time counting the grains of sand on the sea-shore. If science is valuable that is not simply because it provides us with knowledge but because there is some value in the knowledge it provides. Dewey seems, to me, correct in emphasising that science would be deprived of value if it were taken entirely in isolation from the rest of life. In the second place, there is nothing in Dewey's view of inquiry which prevents his attributing to inquiry a measure of autonomy. The point is especially evident if one takes into account what he says about means and end. As we have seen, he emphasised the flexibility of the elements involved. What appears in one context as a means may appear in another as an end. Thus amongst the Egyptians, geometry was developed as a means employed in building operations. We do not have to suppose that geometry, though employed as a means, was entirely devoid of intrinsic interest to those who developed it. Indeed, as Dewey said, where a means has its own value or interest, it is the more readily employed in order to bring about its end. Geometry will be more readily employed in building operations where it has an interest of its own. The Greeks developed this interest, independently of building operations, so that geometry became a study in its own right. There is nothing mysterious in this process, given that there is a flexibility in the relation between means and end and given also that a means can have an independent value. Dewey emphasised both those points.

The real difficulties in Dewey's work arise not so much from error as from inconsistency. The point was well expressed by Scheffler when he said that there is in Dewey a conflict between the psychologist and the moralist. Scheffler had in mind a conflict between Dewey's view of inquiry and his view of social reform. Inquiry arises, on Dewey's view, when people are disturbed in their settled experience or behaviour and achieves its aim when they return to settled experience or behaviour, having resolved what disturbed them. This suggests that people will resolve their difficulties when they feel them and will relax when their difficulties are no longer felt. His view of social reform, however, requires in people a habit of incessant critical activity. Indeed it is essential to his view that people should be set to anticipate their difficulties; in short, that they should be set to cope with them *before* they are felt. For this, in his account of inquiry, he has provided no motive. What he requires as a moralist is in conflict with what he has found as a psychologist.

There is a related difficulty in Dewey's attempt to show that the problems of value are amenable to scientific inquiry. On his view, desire is implicitly evaluative. But when I desire something, I am set to get it. I am not set, in a disinterested spirit, to frame a hypothesis about what for me will prove truly desirable. I cannot stand inside and outside myself simultaneously. Perhaps I shall be stung into reflection, if things go badly, but then, as Scheffler pointed out, I reflect about the difficulty felt; I am not set to anticipate future difficulties. The point is even more evident if we consider the problems of social and political life. Who can suppose that these problems are tackled in anything like the spirit of science? Interests are in conflict; each seeks to exert power over the other. Neither party is in a condition to inquire, in an impartial spirit, which arrangement between them will prove truly desirable. Indeed it is not clear that there need be an arrangement which is truly desirable in the sense of being satisfactory to both of them. Perhaps the interests are irreconcilable. In that case, it would be difficult to see what would *count* as a scientific solution to their problems. This is not to deny that a society which is suffused with the scientific spirit might find it easy to resolve the problems which afflict our own. But then, in such a society, the problems which afflict our own are not likely to arise in the first place. Moreover, any society with problems such as our own will find it as difficult to introduce the scientific spirit, at least in a general way, as to resolve its own problems.

These difficulties are not incidental to Dewey's social philosophy; they are pervasive. As we shall see, his analysis of particular points, which are often of great subtlety, are repeatedly in conflict with his more general moral and philosophical purposes. Those purposes are set by his view of science, which figures for him as a mode of deliverance. He is convinced that mankind has found in science a means of coping not simply with the problems of philosophy but with those of life in general. This forms his apperceptive mass. The apperceptive mass, as James indicated, is highly resistant to change. In Dewey, it is impervious. In his analysis of particular points he often wanders from his overall view, but he snaps back when the view itself is in question. Of the view itself, he sometimes writes in religious terms:

> Faith in the power of intelligence to imagine a future which is the projection of the desirable in the present, and to invent the instrumentalities of its realisation, is our salvation. And it is a faith which must be nurtured and made articulate: surely a sufficiently large task for our philosophy.
>
> (Dewey 1960: 69)

Philosophy is to be instrumental in articulating a faith in intelligence which, in its turn, will be instrumental in solving the problems of life. This faith would be easy to sustain were the instrumentalities themselves easy to formulate. And Dewey sometimes writes as if this were so. On the one hand, we have our problems; on the other, we have the method of science. We have only to apply the latter to the former. The relation would seem as simple as that between a can and a can-opener. At his best, of course, Dewey knows that the relation is not at all simple. Indeed, it is not as simple as all that even in the case of a can-opener, which sometimes leaves us with the can unopened and a damaged finger. No means, however simple, is inert to our purposes. It has its own characteristics and contains some element of unpredictability. The point is especially evident in the case of science, which has a life of its own, is largely unpredictable, and has its own values and disvalues. We may acknowledge that it is likely to affect our purposes in life more generally. What seems certain, however, is that it will do so in ways not easy to anticipate and with consequences *both for good and ill.*

We may express the central point by saying that Dewey's faith requires that people have a control over their lives which in his detailed work he shows to be impossible. Thus, it is he himself who emphasises how often our purposes become clear to ourselves only in the course of our activities, so that in the nature of the case we cannot formulate beforehand what difficulties we shall encounter in advancing those purposes. Indeed where the activity involved is inquiry then by its very nature, so far as it is genuine, it cannot anticipate its own results. And if it cannot anticipate its results, how can it anticipate their consequences? As a moralist, Dewey wants science to have beneficial effects of the simplest and most direct kind. The tendency of his more detailed work is to show that this is impossible. But he is unable to abandon either tendency.

THE PHILOSOPHY OF EDUCATION

The resulting confusion is especially evident in his philosophy of education. In this area, as we have said, he exerted an enormous influence. For example, the movement in American education some-times called child-centred, or new or progressive, referred to him as an authoritative source for its ideas. The progressivist view of education is normally contrasted with the so-called liberal view. On this latter view, education is based on a curriculum or set of central subjects, these being valuable for their power in stimulating critical thought and raising problems central to inquiry. The progressivists, by contrast, took education to be a more direct instrument of social improvement, the subjects studied being of secondary importance compared with the development in the child of values not specifically educational. We may note that those who hold the liberal view need not deny that schooling may also be a means for affecting certain social purposes. For example, if students acquire from their schooling a habit of critical thinking, they will take this into their later lives and it will have its effect on whatever social purposes engage them. The point, however, is that the effect is indirect; it does not arise from a direct study of social improvement itself. Moreover, educational values, on the liberal view, need not be conducive to every social purpose nor even to those which predominate in a society. To take an obvious example, during Dewey's lifetime there was a rapid development of capitalism within American society and an increasing commercialisation of the society itself. Now commercial activity, whatever its benefits, is not necessarily conducive to critical inquiry, at least in an unrestrained and disinterested form. Commerce is primarily concerned, and perhaps rightly, with immediate profit. We must note, also, that if people in American society had been asked to choose between the value of critical inquiry and the benefits of commerce, they would not necessarily have chosen the values of critical inquiry. Thus, on the liberal view, the values of schooling may be in conflict, not simply with other social values, but also with some of those which predominate in the whole society. In short, we seem confronted by two clearly distinguishable views of education. According to the first, schooling has its own subject matter and values and may be in conflict with other social activities; according to the second, it is an instrument for developing values not themselves specifically educational but shared by society as a whole. The progressivists assumed that Dewey, like themselves, held the second view. In this, as we shall see, they were not altogether correct.

Dewey's philosophy of education rests on assumptions which by now are familiar. Antiquated thought has given rise to various dualisms, such as those between child and society, interest and discipline, vocation and education, knowledge and action. These dualisms, as Richard Hofstadter has remarked (Hofstadter 1963: 387), are seen by Dewey 'not as a clue to the nature of human problems but as an unfortunate legacy that could be done away with.' They must be resolved or harmonised through the introduction of ideas that are genuinely scientific. Dewey's view, roughly, is that schooling should be a means by which society is suffused with the critical or scientific spirit. Schools therefore should not simply reproduce the features of the larger society.

To avoid this, the emphasis in schooling should be on the regenerative potentialities of the child rather than on the authority of the teacher or of the curriculum. The impulses of the child, not as yet moulded by custom or habit, are to be mobilised in the exploration of new social forms so that schooling will no longer be a means for repeating the errors of the past or reproducing the flaws in existing society. Moreover, such a reconstruction of schooling will have its effects on society at large, so that the reconstruction of the schools will be a means to the reconstruction of society. One may feel that Dewey here is working against the line of causation. Schooling occurs within society and is subject to its numerous influences; how can the part reconstruct the whole? For Dewey, however, this is not a problem, for he believes that society is already progressing, by which he means becoming more democratic and more subject to the influence of science. Schools, therefore, will serve to accelerate a process already at work. They will serve to develop and make concrete values already present, at least in an ideal form, within society as a whole.

It was not simply the progressivists, but also the public at large, who took Dewey to be advancing the second of our views on education. They had considerable evidence for this assumption, not simply in the drift of his views but even in his explicit statement. For example, in *My Pedagogic Creed* (Dewey 1929: 9–17) he says that education 'is the fundamental method of social progress and reform'. Of the teacher, he says that he is 'engaged not simply in the training of individuals but in the formation of the proper social life.' Consequently, he should consider himself 'a social servant set apart for the maintenance of proper social order and the securing of the right social growth.' In the same work, he says also: 'We violate the child's nature and render difficult the best ethical results by introducing the child too abruptly to a number of special studies, of reading, writing, geography, etc, out of relation to his social life. The true centre of correlation on the school subjects is not science, nor literature, nor history, nor geography, but the child's own social activities.' These quotations surely suggest that schooling is subservient to wider social purposes; indeed that independent of those purposes it has no definite subject matter.

Nevertheless what Dewey was advancing was not the second view. At any rate, there is considerable evidence for this assumption. For example, in the work from which I have just quoted, he says that setting up any end outside education tends 'to deprive the educational process of much of its meaning and tends to make us rely upon false and external stimuli in dealing with the child.' In *Democracy and Education*

(Dewey 1916: 5, 59), he is equally emphatic: 'The aim of education is to enable individuals to continue their education', or again, '...the educational process has no end beyond itself; it is its own end.' Here he is attempting to acknowledge that the educational process, where it is genuinely critical, cannot take its ends from outside but must have its own values, must be productive of its own problems and solutions, and therefore cannot guarantee what it will provide for the public.

This might suggest that what Dewey is advancing is the liberal view. But that too is mistaken, as the reader may verify by re-reading the earlier quotations. The truth is that he believes he can have it both ways. The educational process is at once an end in itself and an instrument for social improvement. The dualism between these functions has been overcome. The difficulty is to see how he has done it. Sometimes he seems to think that the dualism is overcome just in so far as we recognise that learning and critical thought can be valuable in social life more generally and that a person may continue with profit to learn and to think long after his schooldays. But that view was common to all the parties. Everyone believed, or at least hoped, that there was *some* relation between schooling and social improvement. The issue was over how direct that relation should be. Now Dewey sometimes wrote as though it were entirely direct. In the passages quoted earlier, and in many others, he conveys the impression that schooling is an immediate instrument of social reconstruction. Here, it is the moralist who is in charge and he gives free rein to his faith in the power of science to regenerate the educational process and, along with it, society as a whole. He tends to change ground, however, when challenged to be more specific and to state what precise solutions the educational process would provide for this, that, or the other concrete social problem. He then argues that it is not the business of education to provide such solutions, since it is engaged in fostering critical thought, whose results cannot be anticipated. The truth is that he has not overcome the opposing positions. He has merely created the illusion of doing so by a rapid oscillation between both. He is the moralist, in one moment; the psychologist, in the next; but he is still unable to reconcile the two.

The story of Dewey's influence on American education is a melancholy one. Richard Hofstadter (1963: 384), for example, has noted the influence of his ideas in undermining the status of the curriculum within American schools. It was through invoking Dewey's principles of immediacy, utility and social learning that some teachers were enabled to replace traditional problems in literature or geography or mathematics with such problems as 'How can I be popular?' or

'What can I do with my old-fashioned parents?' or 'Should I follow my crowd or obey my parents wishes?' The followers of Dewey have vigorously repudiated the charge that he was responsible for these developments. They have argued that in many cases the developments would have been offensive to him. In this, they are entirely correct. What they neglect to mention, however, is that, through his own confusions, he was himself largely responsible for the misunderstanding of his views. Indeed his defenders sometimes perpetuate those confusions in the course of defending him. Richard Bernstein, for example, writes as follows:

> We see, then, that adapting ourselves to the existing social environment where this entails simply accepting the current values that are ingredient in it would be the very antithesis of Dewey's proposal. On the contrary, we must attempt continually to reform and rebuild social institutions so that our ideal values become concretely realised.
>
> (Bernstein 1960: xiii)

The first sentence suggests that schooling may serve to criticise the values current in a society. The second that it serves to embody values which, in an ideal form, already exist in that society. But then its criticism of the values already current can hardly be fundamental. It is limited to suggesting better ways to embody what people already value.

Chapter 9

Dewey: philosophy and Empiricism

So far, we have confined ourselves, very largely, to Dewey's work in philosophical psychology. We must now consider his views on the more central issues in philosophy. His main work in this area is *Experience and Nature*. But we shall begin with two works written a few years earlier: *Reconstruction in Philosophy* and 'The Need for a Recovery of Philosophy'. The views of the larger work are here anticipated and expressed in a livelier style.

The two works have a common theme which is indicated by their titles. Dewey's argument in both is that philosophy needs a radical renewal. In its traditional form, it is misconceived not simply in the solutions it offers but even in what it considers to be its problems. It should therefore be replaced by a philosophy which is inspired by science:

> This essay may, then, be looked upon as an attempt to forward the emancipation of philosophy from too intimate and exclusive attachment to traditional problems. It is not in intent a criticism of various solutions that have been offered but raises a question *as to the genuineness, under the present conditions of science and social life, of the problems*.
> (Bernstein 1960: 21)

Dewey is here expressing a view that had become familiar during the course of the nineteenth century, and we shall appreciate him the better if we consider for a moment how that view developed. Early in that century, Comte had argued that human beings in their view of the world pass through three stages, which he called, the religious, the metaphysical and the scientific. In the first, speculation about the world is dominated rather by feeling and imagination than by intellect and observation. In the second stage, the products of the earlier are subjected to criticism and we find the beginnings of genuine inquiry. But inquiry at this stage is deficient in systematic observation. It confines itself to reasoning on the basis of notions which are a priori. It is only in the third, or scientific, stage that inquiry finds the correct method, which consists in ignoring a priori notions and confining itself to phenomena, to the world as it appears to the senses. Here, through the observation of phenomena, the framing of hypotheses, tested again by the phenomena, inquiry issues at last in positive knowledge. For Comte, however, there are stages beyond the scientific. Indeed, the stages are repeated in reverse order, returning in a purified form to their source. Thus science, when taken in itself, is limited. It progresses, for example, by splitting into specialisms, which follow their own way. The result is that much scientific knowledge is devoid of human significance. There is the need for a purified philosophy, which will be attentive to the methods and results of the various sciences but which will serve to co-ordinate them and to direct the attention of those sciences to the knowledge which will be beneficial to mankind. Comte, indeed, envisaged a still further stage in which this work would issue in a purified theology, stripped of its supernatural elements and devoted to the service of humanity.

These views were elaborated, in a significant way, first by Feuerbach and then by Marx. Feuerbach argued that religion is a form not of error but of confusion, having its origin in the desire for consolation rather than for truth. The supernatural world is merely the natural in a mystified form. It serves as a consolation for what we do not find in the natural world. Yet the consolation is false. For it is in the natural world, the only real one, that we *want* to find our consolation. Why then do we not find it there? Because we are too easily seduced by consolations that are false. Here we have the significant idea that a body of views may properly be criticised by elucidating its source rather than by engaging with the views themselves. Thus to engage in the criticism of religious views is already to make an error in tactics. For one is thereby drawn into the mystification they involve. The correct tactic is to elucidate, to show how the phenomenon arises, the needs to which it caters. Necessarily this is conducted from the outside, for those who believe in religion do not understand why they do so and when they do understand they will no longer believe. Marx applied similar views to philosophy in its traditional or metaphysical form. The problems of philosophy are to be eliminated rather than solved. For they are essentially a mystification of the real world, having their significance not in themselves but in the function they perform. For Marx this function is essentially social. Metaphysicians locate the problems of life in an unreal world thereby diverting attention from those problems, which can be solved only by a transformation of the real world. In this, they further the interests of the ruling classes. As we shall see, Dewey's view is in many respects strikingly similar.

The above views are typical of nineteenth century Positivism. Positivism, as we have said, constitutes a world-outlook or Weltanschauung and, as such, involves a number of interrelated elements. Thus one may note a metaphysic, which is naturalistic: the natural world is the only real one. We may note, also, an epistemology, which is Empiricist: the source of knowledge lies in the experience of the senses. But the most potent element is the moral. It is essential to this view that religion and metaphysics are the product not of error but of false consciousness. Here the moral element is supported by the empiricist. The real world is not difficult to find; it is evident to any person in the exercise of his senses. If earlier thinkers have not seen this, it is because they have not *wanted* to see it. They have *preferred* illusion to reality. They have been predisposed to treat as mere appearance what is true reality and as reality what is mere illusion. Moreover, the effect of their activities has been to protect privilege and foster ignorance. In short, they have worked against the true interests of humanity.

Now those are views which Dewey follows very closely in the works under consideration. To see how closely, we have only to consider the opening chapter of his *Reconstruction in Philosophy* (1920). Here, he is concerned to trace how philosophy has developed out of more primitive forms of thought. In its primitive form, human thought is dominated rather by feeling and imagination than by intellect and observation. 'Savage man recalled yesterday's struggle with an animal not in order to study in a scientific way the qualities of the animal or for the sake of calculating how better to fight to-morrow, but to escape from the tedium of to-day by regaining the thrill of yesterday' (ibid.: 2). The original material of human thought, thus construed, has to pass through at least two stages before it becomes philosophy proper. The first is where it acquires a social as distinct from an individual significance. 'The piecemeal adventure of the single individual is built out till it becomes representative and typical of the emotional life of the tribe' (ibid.: 8). Here, we find the development of myth and ritual; poetry becomes fixated and systematised; the story becomes a social norm. The myth or legend as it passes from one generation to another loses its personal and purely individual features and retains only those which serve to express and to guide the life of the community. It thus helps to form a body of rite and doctrine. But alongside the development of rite and doctrine, there develops also a certain measure of positive knowledge. For the 'requirements of continued existence make indispensable some attention to the actual facts of the world' (ibid.: 10). Fire burns; water drowns; some things nourish, others poison; there is a regularity in the change from night to day. Some things force themselves upon the human mind and there inevitably develops some body of empirical fact. Here we arrive at the second stage. We have two systems: rite, on the one hand; empirical knowledge, on the other. According to Dewey, it was through the interaction between those two systems that philosophy arose.

It arose most evidently in Ancient Greece. Dewey takes as especially significant the development there of the Sophistic movement. For it was the Sophists who emphasised the elements of *incompatibility* between the two systems. The effect, of course, was subversive. The traditional system, being the product of feeling and imagination, was vulnerable to any criticism which was based on positive knowledge. The point was evident to those in Greek society who represented the conservative interest. But the most acute amongst them, such as Plato, were not content to defend the old beliefs in the old ways. 'The growth of positive knowledge and of the critical, inquiring spirit undermined those in their old form' (ibid.: 16). What then was to be done? 'Develop a method of rational investigation and proof which should place the essential elements of traditional belief upon an unshakeable basis; develop a method of thought and knowledge which while purifying tradition should preserve its moral and social values unimpaired . . . ' (ibid.: 17). In developing this method, the essential element is the distinction between two realms, the realm of appearance and that of reality. On the basis of this distinction, traditional values may be assigned to a realm distinct from sense-experience, which figures as mere appearance. In that way, they are made safe from any criticism based on positive knowledge. Moreover, it is here, according to Dewey, that one finds the origin of metaphysical philosophy. 'Metaphysics is a substitute for custom as the source and guarantor of higher moral and social values – that is the leading theme of the classic philosophy of Europe, as evolved by Plato and Aristotle' (ibid.: 17).

It may be noted that philosophy, on this account, arises in a state of false consciousness. It has about it the air of disinterested inquiry but is really directed towards pre-determined ends. Dewey is explicit on the point. 'The result has been that the great systems have not been free from party spirit exercised in behalf of pre-conceived beliefs. Since they have at the same time professed complete intellectual independence and rationality, the result has been too often to impart to philosophy an element of insincerity, all the more insidious because wholly unconscious on the part of those who sustain philosophy' (ibid.: 20). The effect of this may be seen, according to Dewey, in the over-elaboration of philosophical systems:

> In dealing with matters of fact, simpler and rougher ways of demonstration may be resorted to. It is enough, so to say, to produce the fact in question and point to it – the fundamental form of all demonstration. But when it comes to convincing men of the truth of doctrines which are no longer to be accepted upon the say-so of custom and authority, but which also are not capable of empirical verification, there is no recourse save to magnify the signs of rigorous thought and rigid demonstration. Thus arises that appearance of abstract definition and ultra-scientific argumentation which repels so many from philosophy but which has been one of its chief attractions to its devotees.
>
> (Dewey 1920: 20)

It will be noted how thoroughly Dewey has absorbed the view that metaphysics should be criticised by exposing its origins rather than by engaging directly with its problems. Indeed he is quite frank on the point:

> Common frankness requires that it be stated that this account of the origin of philosophies claiming to deal with absolute Beings in a systematic way has been given with malice prepense. It seems to me that this genetic method of approach is a more effective way of undermining this type of philosophic theorising than any attempt at logical refutation could be.
>
> (ibid.: 24)

It is a method which he recommends to students in the history of philosophy. They should consider the various philosophies as arising not out of intellectual but out of social and emotional material:

> Considered in this way, the history of philosophy will take on a new significance. What is lost from the standpoint of would-be science is regained from the standpoint of humanity. Instead of the disputes of rivals about the nature of reality, we have the scene of human clash and social purpose and aspirations. (ibid.: 25)

Commentators on Dewey too often treat his Scientific Positivism as though it were of incidental importance, or as though it belonged to his immaturity. The stress, or so they imply, should be on the doctrines of his last years. But this is entirely mistaken. The work from which we are quoting was not written in his immaturity; he wrote it when he was sixty. Moreover, as I hope to show, the doctrines of his last years arose as an attempt, in the face of considerable difficulties, to retain the essentials of his Scientific Positivism.

So far, we have considered Dewey's account of how metaphysics developed out of primitive or religious thought. According to Comte's scheme, the metaphysical stage should give way to the positive or scientific one. In a measure, this has occurred, with the development in the sixteenth and seventeenth centuries of modern science. On Dewey's view, however, it has occurred only in an imperfect form. We possess a body of knowledge far superior to any found amongst the Greeks. But philosophy has not made a comparable progress. Even in its most progressive form, such as in the Empiricism of the eighteenth century, it has retained too many of the assumptions of Greek thought. The most ruinous of these, according to Dewey, is the so-called spectator view of knowledge. For the Greeks, knowledge was achieved rather through contemplation than through active engagement with its material. Dewey believes that this is the result of the class divisions in Greek society. Active engagement with the world was associated with the trades and crafts, which were treated as servile. The Greek idea of knowledge has infected modern Empiricism. It treats experience as occurring to a mind entirely passive. In this respect, an Empiricist such as Locke is hardly distinguishable from a Rationalist such as Descartes. Both identify knowledge with ideas occurring in the mind of a subject standing over and against the world. Between the subject and the world, there is interposed a veil of ideas. This gives rise to a host of problems, such as the problem of how the subject can know an external world, or of how the mind is related to the body. These are the problems which plague modern philosophy. Yet they are entirely unreal. They may be traced to confusions in the thought of such philosophers as Locke and Descartes and those confusions, in their turn, to an inadequate idea of experience. Now a more adequate view of experience is precisely what Dewey believes has been supplied by the Pragmatism of Peirce and James. In the psychology of James, for example, we find the perfect antidote to the spectator view of knowledge. This psychology, of course, will not *solve* the problems of philosophy. Rather it will show that there is nothing to solve: we shall see that the problems need never have arisen in the first place. Philosophy, thus liberated, will then become truly positive or scientific. In this, Dewey is at one with Comte. A purified philosophy will be attentive to the results of the various sciences, will interpret their significance, and will ensure that they are used in solving the real problems of mankind.

We must now consider precisely how the traditional idea of experience will be changed by the new psychology. The matter is dealt with in considerable detail in the opening chapter of *Experience and Nature* (1925). But the essential points are already contained, and expressed more briefly, in *The Need for a Recovery of Philosophy* (1917). Dewey there states five ways in which the traditional view of experience needs to be corrected:

1 The traditional view treats experience as primarily a matter of knowledge. In fact, knowledge is merely one element within experience, which covers the whole intercourse between a living being and his physical and social environment.

2 On the traditional view, experience is essentially subjective. But experience since it covers every relation between a living being and its environment involves an *interaction* between subject and object.

3 On the traditional view, experience is exhausted in registering what has occurred. In fact, it is experimental and anticipatory. Its primary concern is with the future not the past.

4 On the traditional view, there is a problem about how experiences are related since the relations between them seem not to be experienced. For example, I experienced *that* sound before *this* one. But my knowledge that one came before the other seems to be independent of both. This, however, is no problem. Experience being 'an undergoing of an environment and a striving for its control in new directions is pregnant with connections.' Relation, in short, is an integral element in experience.

5 On the traditional view, experience is often contrasted with inference. But experience, being anticipatory, is full of inference.

Now the full significance of these points will emerge as we proceed. But one may already catch something of Dewey's intention. One must recall that, for him, there is no conflict between Empiricism and Pragmatism; rather, Pragmatism *is* Empiricism in its truest form. Thus his aim, in the above points, is to describe and to extend the notion of experience so that it no longer gives rise to the sceptical problems which plagued the older forms of Empiricism, thus placing Empiricism itself on a secure footing. In the second point, for example, he seeks to eliminate the distinction between experience and the world whereby the latter as objective is contrasted with the former as subjective. To achieve this, he construes experience as covering the interaction between subject and object, the two figuring as elements *within* experience. In this way, he seeks to eliminate the distinction between reality as it is in itself and as it appears in experience. Reality and appearance are merely different aspects of experience itself.

There is, however, an obvious objection to this procedure which was vigorously expressed by Morris Cohen (1931: 453). If we glance through the above points, we find that Dewey has so extended the notion of experience that it is difficult to find anything which it does *not* cover. *Everything* seems to be experience. But then, having no contrast, it seems to mean nothing in particular. The criticism, at first sight, is not entirely fair to Dewey. His use of 'experience' is at least roughly comparable with one which is often found in ordinary speech. Suppose I describe someone as an experienced motorist. I mean that he has mastered the activity, through much practice, this involving the use of all his faculties of inference, memory, physical dexterity, grasp of relations, and so on. Moreover, it is evident that this is a use of 'experience' which is strikingly different from that of traditional Empiricism. Nevertheless Cohen's criticism is essentially correct. That is because Dewey does not stick to that use of 'experience'. Rather, he switches between a number of uses, so that in the end, as Cohen suggests, we lose our grip on what he means by the term.

To see the point, let us grant that 'experience' has a use in which it signifies something like a person's general engagement with the world. This use, as we have said, is evidently different from that of traditional Empiricism. What Dewey suggests, however, is that it is essentially an improved version of the same use and that it will serve not in criticism of Empiricism itself but in its defence. For example, Dewey tells us that experience is 'pregnant with connections' and 'full of inference'. He states this in criticism of the older Empiricists and the impression conveyed is that he is pointing to features which they have overlooked but which have been present, all along, in what they mean by experience. In fact, however, he has switched to a different usage. To say that experience is pregnant with connections and full of inference is merely to say that in their general engagement with the world people make inferences and are aware of connections. On any normal understanding of Empiricism, one is supposed to show that these powers are derivative from sense-experience. Dewey makes no attempt to show this. He merely adds these powers to sense-experience and applies the term experience to the resulting sum. The effect is to cause confusion, to obscure rather than to resolve serious problems. For example, suppose I infer that tomorrow it will rain. On the most common usage, the conclusion I infer is not something that falls within my experience. Tomorrow it may do so. But then tomorrow it will no longer be a matter of inference. In short, so far as it is a matter of inference, it does *not* fall within my experience. The point is equally evident with regard to the past. For example, a geologist may make an inference about the conditions that applied on earth before the existence of sentient life. In doing so, he may draw upon his own experience. But the conclusion itself, at least in the most usual sense, would seem to pass beyond that experience. Indeed, in this case, it seems in addition to pass beyond the experience not simply of the human species but of every form of sentient life. Moreover, were inference confined to what falls within experience, it would be difficult to see its point. With regard to matters of fact, the very point of inference seems to be in its supplying us with information about phenomena we cannot experience for ourselves. It is evident that there are problems here for any philosophy that seeks to explain inference in terms of experience. Now Dewey's answer to these problems is merely to add inference to experience and to claim that the problems disappear once one sees that experience is full of inference. The solution is purely verbal.

SCIENCE AND EMPIRICISM

Moreover, these problems lead to problems deeper still. Here one may sense the encroachment of the darkest shadow. Both Comte and Dewey believe that Empiricism is the only true philosophy, because they believe that it alone can provide an account of science which illuminates its history and explains its success. That view presupposes, in its turn, that the methods of science are essentially empirical. Thus the reason why science, unlike religion or metaphysics, can provide real knowledge is that it proceeds by observation and experiment. That also is the reason why science is a comparatively late growth. People in earlier times neglected observation and experiment, basing their views on feeling, received ideas and a priori notions. The trouble is that this view of science is false. In the philosophy of science during the last twenty or thirty years the point has been sufficiently elaborated. We have become familiar with the inadequacies of Empiricism as an account of science. But the inadequacies were evident enough to some of Dewey's contemporaries. Here we may return to Morris Cohen. In his contribution to a symposium on Dewey's philosophy he deals with

the matter in some detail (1940: 209–10). He argues there that the
history of science which supports Dewey's philosophy is apocryphal.
According to that history, the success of modern science is due to its
basis in observation and experiment. The Greeks, by contrast, neglected
experiment and based their science on a priori demonstration. But it is
not true that the Greeks neglected experiment:

> The work of Hippocrates, Archimedes, Hero, Hipparchus and
> Eratosthenes amply indicates the contrary. Even Pythagoras had to
> experiment to discover the laws of musical harmony. It required
> experiment to determine the effects of diet, exercise and climate on
> health and disease. It required refined measurement (which is still
> essential for exact experiment) to decide the choice between rival
> theories of astronomy such as those of epicycles and exocentric
> motion, to determine the procession of the equinoxes, or the actual
> length of a degree of latitude on our earth.

How, then, are we to account for the radical break between modern
and ancient science? The problem is a false one. Contrary to popular
legend, there was no radical break:

> It is a myth to suppose that modern science arose when it suddenly
> occurred to a few men to discard the authority of Aristotle and to
> examine nature for themselves. That was the bright idea of the
> lawyer, courtier, and literary artist, Francis Bacon, and it got him
> nowhere in actual science. Indeed it made him ignore and even
> oppose the most significant scientific achievements of his day, such as
> the Copernican astronomy, the mechanical interpretation of physics,
> the physiologic discoveries of his personal physician, Harvey, and the
> pioneer researches of Gilbert, whose writings were entrusted to him.
> If we read Copernicus' own work we see that he only revived the
> Pythagorean astronomy, that he accepted the method of Ptolemy,
> which is after all still the method of mathematical physics, and that
> his so-called revolution was after all only a simplification of Ptolemy
> by reducing the number of epicycles.
>
> (Cohen 1940: 209–10)

Cohen proceeds to develop the point by reference to the work of
Kepler, Galileo and Newton. None of these men took themselves to be
recording what was revealed to their senses. Their fundamental
assumption was identical with that of Greek science. They presupposed
that the physical world was possessed of intelligible order, imperfectly

revealed to the senses, but amenable to a study which was primarily *theoretical* rather than empirical.

> It is amazing how relatively few mechanical experiments all these men made and how much they were influenced by the idea that the book of nature was written in mathematical terms so that the object of science was to find out this simple underlying mathematical pattern. Anyone who has ever tried to repeat Galileo's experiment of rolling balls on an inclined plane will need no assurance that without prior faith in the simplicity of natural laws Galileo's actual results would have proved nothing at all. For under the conditions of his experiment the necessary degree of accuracy cannot possibly be attained. Even more is this the case with the supposed dropping of two weights from the Tower of Pisa. To prove what it is generally supposed to have proved, it would have been necessary to create a perfect vacuum by eliminating all the air between the tower and the earth. In any medium such as air or water, the resistance to and retardation of a falling body does depend on its mass, as Lucretius clearly pointed out in antiquity and as anyone can observe for himself if not prevented by reliance on the popular anti-Aristotelian mythology. Note that I am not denying the importance of experiment in modern or in ancient science.... But I think that a due regard for the essential role which mathematical or theoretical development plays in experimental work is not only necessary to explain the growth of science, modern or ancient, but also to remove the false dualism between experiment and rational demonstration.
>
> (ibid.)

The Empiricist or Positivist view, which flourished in Western culture for some two centuries, is in fact one of the most remarkable examples of misrepresentation in the whole history of scholarship. The misrepresentation is remarkable not simply because it is in evident conflict with the facts, but because what it portrays is the exact opposite of the truth. Thus the most serious defect in Greek science is not that it evaded but that it was too easily influenced by ordinary observation or experience. For example, Aristotle assumed a plurality in the forms of motion. Gross matter, fire, heavenly bodies have different principles of motion whereby they move towards or away from the earth, or are in circular motion around it. What makes this plausible is that this is precisely how those objects seem to move in ordinary experience. Galileo unified these forms of motion by means of a principle that, in any simple way, does not appear in ordinary experience at all. The disadvantage of the Copernican theory, as compared with the Ptolemaic, is that it seems manifestly in conflict with the evidence of the senses. That was why intelligent people hesitated to accept it, even when they were aware of its enormous theoretical advantages. Galileo, indeed, in his defence of the theory, was accused of undermining science by casting doubt on sense-perception as a criterion of reality. The objection was based on a misunderstanding since sense-perception, when taken in itself, had never been such a criterion. Nevertheless, it was based on a view of the matter which was altogether more plausible than the one adopted by Positivism, according to which it was Galileo who was defending the reality of sense-perception.

Moreover, it is here that we move towards the most important point. Essential to science, both on its ancient and modern form, is the distinction between appearance and reality. The distinction is found amongst the Greeks not because they were averse to considering empirical phenomena but because it seemed to them evident that those phenomena can be rendered intelligible only on the basis of that distinction. Take, for example, a cube. Viewed from various angles, it appears to the senses in different forms. But in none of these forms is it precisely a cube. Its real form, in short, is not found in the ways it appears; rather, its real form is the one which explains how it appears in those ways. One may say, if one wishes, that its real form is grasped *through* the way it appears to the senses; but what is grasped is not equivalent to any of its sensory appearances. *Consequently those appearances have to be interpreted if we are to grasp its real form.* As Cohen implies, we here have a point which is essential to all scientific investigation. Unless 'experience' is to be taken as a superfluous synonym for knowledge itself, then all scientific knowledge presupposes a difference between the world as it is and as it appears in experience. This is a point that occurred to the human mind not through an attempt to evade the real world but precisely through its attempts to understand it. It is the beginning of scientific wisdom to recognise that human experience is not the measure of reality. Now the effect of Dewey's attempt to undermine the distinction between appearance and reality is precisely to render absolute the view of the world which appears in ordinary human experience. That is what becomes the measure of reality. Hence the label which Morris Cohen applies to Dewey's philosophy: Anthropocentric Naturalism. Hence, also, the label applied by Santayana: Dominance of the Foreground. Moreover, we must emphasise that Dewey, in this, is working against the whole drift not simply of ancient but of modern science. Indeed few things are more striking about the development of modern science than the ever-increasing discrepancy it reveals between the world of science and that of ordinary human experience. The discrepancy was evident enough at the beginning of modern science, if we take the Copernican theory to mark that beginning. But the Copernican theory concerned itself, at least, with objects that themselves appeared in ordinary experience. A more radical discrepancy appeared when Galileo treated certain apparent features of the world as relative to the observer, thus distinguishing them from the world itself. This was the so-called distinction between primary and secondary qualities. A discrepancy still more radical appeared with the development of the atomic theory. For the elements which are essential to that theory do not appear in ordinary human experience at all. And with every subsequent development the discrepancy has been rendered not less but more acute.

Now it is against this background that we can best appreciate the views expressed in Dewey's last writings. Those writings, in large part, are attempts to resolve the conflict which lies at the centre of his philosophy. The philosophy rests on Empiricism and on the success of science. But the two are at odds. The philosophy presupposes the success of science but the Empiricism which is also essential to it has proved incapable of explaining that success. Indeed worse: the development of science, in its success, *undermines* the Empiricism which is essential to that philosophy.

At this point, however, one may wonder why Dewey was so wedded to Empiricism. Indeed that is part of a larger problem. Given the evident discrepancy between Empiricism or Positivism and the facts of scientific development, how can one account for the enormous influence it exerted for so long over Western culture? To answer the problem, we need to recall that Positivism is not a doctrine, easily checked against the facts, but a Weltanschauung or apperceptive mass which shapes the way one sees the facts. Thus Positivism did not arise as a doctrine within science, nor yet through a disinterested study of science itself; it arose rather as a replacement for religion and as an explanation for why religion had for so long dominated the human mind. As a replacement for religion, it would not have been effective had it not offered its own mode of deliverance. That is why the most potent of the elements, as we have said, is the moral. For it is this which provides the inspiration. Now there is nothing inspiring about the naturalistic view, when taken in itself. It becomes inspiring, however, when it is portrayed as the view which is natural to the human mind, which any intelligent person would arrive at for himself, were he not subjected to mystification. For then it is easily transformed into a powerful myth, in which the human mind has been alienated from its natural home, has been put under an enchantment but has found in science the instrument to deliver itself from that enchantment and to make for itself on this earth a true home.

A detail in Dewey's earlier account will illustrate the above point. In *Reconstruction in Philosophy* (1920), he contrasts the over-elaboration of metaphysics with the straightforward method of empirical science. 'In dealing with matters of fact, simpler and rougher ways of demonstration may be resorted to. It is enough, so to say, to produce the fact in question and point to it . . . '. Taken in itself, this view is not simply false but absurd. There is not a single theory in science which could be settled in such a manner. For example, how could one settle the conflict between the Ptolemaic and the Copernican theories by producing and pointing to the earth's going around the sun? Indeed there is no empirical phenomenon one could point to on behalf of the Copernican theory which could not have been accounted for on the Ptolemaic. The power of the Copernican theory lies not in this fact or the other but in the sense it makes of enormous range of such facts. Nevertheless, Dewey's contrast is effective enough. On the one hand, we have the slippery or devious methods of the metaphysicians, the enemies of humanity, and, on the other, the simple or straightforward methods of the scientists, who are its friends. The force of the contrast depends on its moral resonance, not on its intellectual substance. In other words, Empiricism is fragile when extracted from the network of Positivism and examined in itself but within the network it has great power because it reinforces the moral element.

Wedded then to Empiricism, Dewey must find the means to resolve its difficulties. We must next consider his attempts to do so.

Chapter 10

Dewey: Radical Empiricism

For the purpose of this study, we may distinguish three ways in which Dewey attempted to resolve the difficulties at the centre of his philosophy.

The first was developed chiefly by Dewey's followers, but it merits our attention since it is based on his ideas. This is the so-called doctrine of Objective Relativism.[1] The doctrine is best understood as a response to the distinction between primary and secondary qualities. Under scientific analysis, as we have mentioned, the colour of an object seems to be explicable without having to attribute that colour to the object itself. Variations in colour, for example, can be explained by variations in the light reflected by the object and received by the observer. In other words, in order to explain the variations in an object's colour we do not have to suppose it has a real colour which thus varies in appearance. By contrast, if we consider the way an object appears to vary in shape, as we walk around it, we find that we do have to suppose it has a real shape which thus varies. Shape is therefore deemed primary and colour secondary. The distinction seems to presuppose that very contrast, between the world as it is and as it appears in ordinary experience, which it is one of the main purposes of Dewey's philosophy to undermine. The doctrine of Objective Relativism attempts to reconcile that distinction, or rather the facts involved in it, with Dewey's philosophy.

In *The Revolt Against Dualism*, A. O. Lovejoy describes the doctrine as follows:

> Those who have formulated its principles concede, or rather insist upon, the relativity of the content of perception (and apparently of other cognition) to a situation in which the perceptual or cognitive act is an essential, and proximately determinative, factor.... The

existence and character of experienced data depends upon the occurrence of percipient events and therefore upon the nature and situation of the organism which has the experience; and it is only 'in relation' to a given organism that the object known possesses the character exhibited by the datum. Nevertheless, all perceptual content is stoutly declared to be 'objective'.

(Lovejoy 1930: 79)

In other words, the doctrine accepts the scientific facts involved in distinguishing between primary and secondary qualities whilst denying that distinction in its usual interpretation. Thus it accepts that an object has a colour only in relation to an observer. It insists, however, that it does have that colour, just in the sense that it has a shape or any other of the primary qualities. In support of this view, it takes a radical line with the distinction between appearance and reality. There is no reality without appearance. All qualities exist in relation to an observer or, as it is sometimes put, within a perspective. The Scientific Positivist, Josef Petzoldt, expresses the view as follows:

There is no absolute standpoint, and there is no exemption from standpoints; there are only and always relative standpoints. . . . I can in reality think of no absolute whatever; I always tacitly place myself upon the scene as the observer who is beholding things in their relation to himself.

(Lovejoy 1930: 81)

In short, there can be no distinction, in the usual interpretation, between primary and secondary qualities since that interpretation presupposes a metaphysical delusion. Secondary qualities derive their status from a contrast with qualities which exist out of relation to an observer. But there can be no such qualities. There is no reality out of such a relation. Consequently there is nothing with which to contrast secondary qualities. They are the only reality.

We may note here the most perfect unanimity between Idealism, Pragmatism in its twentieth-century version, and Positivism. The doctrine is at its most spectacular in dealing with our knowledge of the past. E. A. Burtt writes as follows:

Whatever is found empirically to happen always involves the compresence of an intelligent organism, and (which is more important metaphysically) the way in which it happens is, in the last analysis, the way in which it comes to play the part it does play in the development of the perspectives or centres of experience through which it gains its place in the objective order that we call the world.

(Lovejoy 1930: 124)

From this, there follow interesting conclusions about the past. For example, it follows that 'the world always takes shape from the present outward. It expands into the past as knowledge of the past is needed to satisfy present desires. . . . But it remains within the present all the while, in fact it only generates a vastly larger present.'

Burtt rephrases the above points by saying that 'the order of discovery is the order of reality'. It is not entirely clear, however, precisely what that means. For example, a geologist deals with events which occurred many millions of years before there was anyone to discover their occurrence. How can the order or time in which they were discovered be the order or time in which they occurred? Burtt here distinguishes between abstract time and empirical reality. Thus, 'in abstract time the ages the geologist studies precede the days of his own childhood.' But: 'No past event becomes an empirical reality until it has taken its place in the order of discovery.' Now it is difficult to believe that by the empirical reality of an event Burtt simply means its being discovered. For then he would simply be informing us that the time of the discovery of the event was the time when it was discovered. What he seems to mean is that the time when the event was discovered was the time when it really occurred. The ground for this remarkable view is that one would be metaphysically deluded in supposing the past can have a reality which is independent of how it appears. Since there is no reality independently of some perspective, the past has no reality independently of some perspective, which, of necessity, is in the present.

The doctrine of Objective Relativism is supported by additional considerations, with which we may deal briefly, since by now they are entirely familiar. Thus the doctrine is urged upon us as a means of deliverance from the confusions involved in our philosophical inheritance, these confusions being attributed, chiefly, to such philosophers of the seventeenth century as Locke and Descartes.

Here again the decisive aberration is blamed upon the philosophers of the seventeenth century (in this case chiefly upon Locke). . . . Modern philosophy has been wandering in the wilderness for some three hundred years largely because Locke and his contemporaries, in approaching the problem of knowledge, were dominated by 'the old notion of separate, independent substances, each of which has its own inner constitution and essence', apart from its relations to other things. The objects aimed at by knowledge were conceived as such isolated substances; it was, and by subsequent dualists habitually has been, assumed that 'those characters which the mind attributes to reality must either belong to such reality absolutely or not at all'.

(Lovejoy 1930: 83)[2]

The truth, which delivers us from these confusions, is that substances do not exist out of relation to the human mind and that they really possess the characters attributed but only in relation to the mind that attributes them.

Now Lovejoy, in his classic study, follows the doctrine of Objective Relativism, in copious detail, through all its ramifications. We may extract two of his conclusions. The first is that the philosophers of the seventeenth century, and Locke especially, have been misinterpreted. Thus Locke, so far as he accepted a dualism between mind and matter, is treated as though he denied all relation between the two. He is treated, for example, as though he believed physical substances existed out of all relation to the human mind. This was an assumption habitual with Dewey. He repeatedly treated the advocates of a dualism as though they denied any relation between the elements involved. Having shown that there are relations between the elements involved, he then assumed he had undermined the duality. This seems to be an assumption he inherited from Hegelian Idealism. These Idealists were unable to conceive of relations holding between objects that are distinguishable or separate and they assumed that objects were not distinguishable or separate if they were in any way related. In fact it is only amongst distinguishable or separate objects that relations can hold. It takes at least two objects to make a relation and unless objects are distinguishable or separate, they cannot count as two. But in any case, Locke was evidently not denying that there are relations between physical objects and the human mind. His point was that the *existence* of those objects does not depend on those relations. In that sense, they are independent of the human mind. Moreover, since we know objects only in so far as they enter into relations with ourselves, and since they exist independently of those relations, we have no reason to suppose that our knowledge provides us with an exhaustive understanding of the objects themselves. Locke, in short, was neither a sceptic nor a relativist; his view was entirely Realist.

The second conclusion is that the doctrine continually varies between metaphysical audacity and platitude. To see the point, let us distinguish between the objectivity of a relation and the objectivity of its elements. The latter does not follow from the former. For example, that A appears red to B is obviously an objective fact. It does not follow that the redness is an objective fact in the sense of applying to A *independently* of that relation. By that argument, one could establish the objectivity of hallucinations. For example, it is an objective fact, under certain conditions, that an oasis appears in the desert where none exists. It does not follow that the oasis is an objective fact – that is, that it really exists. Now the Objective Relativist is not, of course, claiming that redness applies to A independently of its relation to B. His claim is that it is an objective fact *within* that relation. But how does an objective fact within a relation differ from being relative? Suppose I claim that the hallucination of an oasis is an objective fact within the conditions that apply to the desert. Surely I claim only that under these conditions the hallucination really occurs, which no one denies.

The process by which an apparently striking statement reduces itself to a platitude may be illustrated by reference to a notorious passage in Dewey's 'The Need for A Recovery of Philosophy' (Bernstein 1960: 44), in which he denies the assumption 'that consciousness is outside of the real object; that it is something different in kind, and therefore has the power of changing "reality" into appearance, of introducing "relativities" into things as they are in themselves – in short, of infecting real things with subjectivity.' He says that 'this assumption makes consciousness supernatural in the literal sense of the word.' He acknowledges that dreams, hallucinations, etc., do not occur save where there are organic centres of experience. 'But to treat them as things which inhere exclusively in the subject, or as posing the problem of a distortion of *the* real object by a knower set over and against the world, or as presenting facts to be explained primarily as cases of contemplative knowledge, is to testify that one has still to learn the lesson of evolution in its application to the affairs in hand.'

Now we may grant that a knower does not stand over and against the whole world but he assuredly stands over and against a great deal of it, the amount of space occupied even by the entire human species being altogether minute when compared with the world as a whole. Moreover, if I look at a distant portion of the desert, I assuredly stand over and against that portion. Now suppose in that portion I see an oasis, which is in fact an hallucination. Some may be inclined to affirm that we have a dualism between the way that portion of the desert appears to me and the way it really is. This, however, Dewey seems to deny. Dreams, hallucinations, etc., he claims are not 'outside of the regular course of events; they are in it and of it. They are not cognitive distortions of real things; they are *more* real things. There is nothing abnormal in their existence ... ' (ibid.). It is conceivable that Dewey is here committed to the remarkable claim that for as long as I hallucinate the oasis, it really does exist in the desert. It is more likely, however, as Lovejoy implies, that he is taking refuge in a platitude. To say that dreams, hallucinations, etc., really exist is only to say that they really occur. Unfortunately, that is common to all the parties. What the opponents of Dewey are seeking to establish is that, so far as I hallucinate, there is a dualism between the way the desert really is and the way it appears to me. To this point, Dewey offers no adequate response.

It is difficult to dissent from Lovejoy's overall view that the doctrine of Objective Relativism is more verbal than substantial and that its opposition to dualism dissolves under close analysis:

It has become the established custom ... sternly to condemn 'dualism' while accepting its essentials; to express the utmost horror of 'bifurcation' and then – the proprieties having thus been duly observed – to proceed cheerfully to bifurcate. ... The recent and current phase of the revolt against dualism is in fact carried on almost exclusively by dualists.

(Lovejoy 1930: 154–5)

The second way in which Dewey attempts to resolve the difficulties in his philosophy depends on his distinction between experience and knowledge. As we have seen, knowledge for Dewey is only one element in experience. Experience in customary behaviour is rather had than known. Knowledge is relative to exploration or inquiry, which arises through the disruption of customary behaviour, as for example when the bright light suddenly appears to the child. The disruption having been explored, customary behaviour is resumed, informed now by the results of the inquiry. The important point, however, is that all this occurs *within* experience. Thus the bright light is a stimulus only so far as it enters *into* the experience of the child. The ensuing exploration has as its object the light as experienced and seeks to inform the child's future experience. Here we have the elements of Dewey's so-called Non-Representationalist view of knowledge or truth. The aim of knowledge is not to correspond to the world, or at any rate, not to a world independent of human experience. Its aim is to anticipate future experience, taking as its material, experience in the present. Thus everything occurs within the circle of experience, which includes the object of knowledge as well as its subject. As evidence for this, Dewey argues that in the course of inquiry there is a change not simply in the subject but also in the object. Thus what is at first a blur of light becomes, in the course of the child's exploration, a source of pain, something to be avoided. As is sometimes said, Dewey here substitutes an instrumental for a correspondence or representationalist view of knowledge or truth. This constitutes what we are calling his second attempt to eliminate the subversive idea that there is a reality beyond human experience.

Now in the above account great play is made with the idea of something's entering *into* or falling *within* experience. What precisely do these phrases mean? In ordinary speech, to say that an object falls within a person's experience is only to say he has experience of it. This carries no implication that the object *exists* within that experience. Indeed in ordinary speech it is not clear what those words mean. What falls within experience might not have done and therefore does not depend on that experience for its existence. But on Dewey's usage there is nothing outside experience. There is, as it were, nowhere else for the object to exist. One may suspect that Dewey is taking a manner of speech in a sense somewhat different from the one found in its common employment. To see the point, consider his view that the bright light counts as a stimulus only so far as it falls *within* the child's experience. As it stands, that is a tautology. For stimulus is a relative term. Something counts as a stimulus only so far as there is someone to be stimulated. We may therefore grant that the existence of the light *qua stimulus* depends on the response of the child. But surely its existence as such does not so depend. Indeed Dewey's own account presupposes that this is not so. Thus the light appears as a *disruption* of the child's prior experience. On the basis of that experience it could not have been anticipated. It comes from outside, and therefore exists independently of that experience. We may note, further, that the alleged change in the object during the course of inquiry is evidently a change in that object *qua stimulus*. It is evidently not a change in the object itself. Thus the light was as much a source of pain at the beginning of the inquiry as it was at the end. The change in its status as a stimulus is wholly explicable by reference not to the light but to the child. At the end of his inquiry he knows more about the light than he did at the beginning. Moreover, the effect of these points is that we find ourselves, once again, with the distinction between appearance and reality. For once it is acknowledged that the object exists independently of the experience into which it falls, it becomes conceivable that certain of its features which fall within experience may be explicable only by attributing to it other features which do not so fall.

For example, compression falls within experience but is not explicable in terms of it. Hence the atomic theory, the details of which explain the phenomenon without themselves falling within experience. It is evident that there are still difficulties involved in Dewey's attempt to reconcile science with Empiricism.

THE LATER WORK

In Dewey's later work, however, we may discern a third attempt to reconcile the two. In this work, he came to accept that there are important differences between the scientific view of the world and that of ordinary experience. What he denied, however, was that the scientific view is the more *fundamental*. He argued, rather, that it is an *abstraction* from the real world. Thus it is experience rather than knowledge which reveals the substance of things and knowledge can deal only with various aspects of what experience reveals. For example, a substance such as water is revealed not by scientific analysis but by common experience. The real water is the substance which appears to the senses, which sparkles, flows, cleanses and refreshes. In chemical analysis, it may be covered by a well-known formula. But the formula is not a description of water at a more fundamental level. Rather it is an abstraction from the real substance, dealing with it only under certain conditions. Its purpose is precisely to serve rather than to subvert ordinary experience. Indeed it is an instrument rather than a description. It enables us the better to deal with water in its conditions and relations; but what it is that has these conditions and relations, the *substance* of water, is given only in experience (Dewey 1925: 193).

As evidence for this view, Dewey pointed out that science has made progress by dealing with matters in its relations rather than in its substance. In this, as we have seen, he was quite correct and it will be useful to remind ourselves of the point. One of the features of the Newtonian system which has puzzled many is that it seems to dissolve qualities into relations. This is evident in the case of the secondary qualities, which are analysed as features not of the object but of its relation to an observer. In ordinary speech, however, it is in terms of these qualities that an object is characterised. In other words, it is characterised in terms of how it appears to sight, touch, etc. But if these qualities are transferred, as it were, to the observer, what now is left in order to characterise the object? At first, the problem may not seem acute, since it is only the secondary qualities which are analysed in that way. The primary qualities are attributed to the object. At a further level of analysis, however, the primary qualities also become relative. A shape, such as a round, will serve as an example. A round object, as apprehended by sight or touch, requires a bound circumference. At the atomic level, however, the object has no such circumference. It is merely a flux of atoms. The bound circumference thus appears as relative, as the effect of the object's being seen or touched. It may be supposed, however, that we still have the atoms, in terms of which the substance of matter may be defined. But what is an atom? In the Newtonian system, it is defined as a point of mass and the mass of a point is defined as its power to attract or repulse other points. In other words, an atom is a centre of attraction and repulsion and an object is a collection of such centres. But attraction and repulsion are relations. What is the substance that upholds them? In short, what is it that attracts and repulses? To this, there is no answer. The substance of matter seems entirely to dissolve.

On Dewey's view, however, the problem does not arise in the first place. It is not surprising that the Newtonian system explains matter in its relations rather than in its substance. It was never intended to do otherwise. It was intended precisely to explain matter not in its substance but in its relations. Moreover, the substance which is missing in the Newtonian system is not in fact missing, for it is already given to us. It is given to us in the sensory qualities of ordinary experience. Thus the substance of water is given to us in its feel, in what we see and touch. This eludes a scientific formula but it is not in fact elusive, for it is given to us immediately. Moreover, this shows that there can never be a genuine conflict between science and ordinary experience, since the substance of what science studies is given precisely by ordinary experience and not by science itself. This constitutes what we are calling Dewey's third attempt to reconcile science with Empiricism.

This attempt, like the others, is not free from difficulties. For example, the atomic theory, even if construed as dealing simply with conditions and relations, seems evidently not to treat those conditions and relations as falling wholly within ordinary experience. Indeed, it seems precisely to attribute to matter a structure which transcends ordinary experience. Dewey's view of the atomic theory is not easy to make precise. In his last years he seemed to entertain the view that, under certain conditions at least, the atoms of the theory might fall within experience. More generally, however, his views seem to have been instrumentalist. In other words, he treated the theory as a device whose point lay in its consequences for ordinary experience. For example, if we treat matter as discontinuous, we can explain and handle more easily a phenomenon of ordinary experience such as compression. The obvious objection to this is that in order to fulfil that purpose, the theory has to be more than a device. Thus, if we simply treat matter *as though* it were discontinuous, we can only treat compression *as though* it were explained. To suppose we have really explained it, we have to suppose that matter is really discontinuous. Moreover, we cannot suppose it is really discontinuous except at a level inaccessible to ordinary experience.

But there is a further problem, which for our purpose is the more significant. For *why* precisely can science deal only with conditions and relations? Why can it not deal with the substance of things? Why, for example, can it not explain sensory qualities? Dewey's reply is that sensory quality is *ineffable*. By its very nature it cannot be explained but can only be given to us. The point is developed in his paper 'Qualitative Thought' (Bernstein 1960: 176–98). 'The world in which we immediately live, that in which we strive, succeed, and are defeated' he says 'is pre-eminently a qualitative world.' He then proceeds to argue that every statement is a discrimination within a qualitative field which cannot itself be expressed in that statement. He gives, as an analogy, the contents of a quart bowl. Whatever these contents may be, they cannot include the bowl itself. To contain the bowl we need another bowl, which in its turn will not include itself. Now similarly any situation is experienced immediately in its pervasive quality. But 'the situation as such is not and cannot be stated or made explicit.' It is like the bowl which contains but is not contained. Thus it will be implicit in, and in a sense will control, whatever is stated but will not be contained in the statement itself. In short, the world as experienced, in its qualitative reality, always goes beyond anything that can be put into words. Dewey denies that this is mystification. The world transcends explicit statement but it is not transcendent; it transcends knowledge but not experience. Quite the contrary; in immediate qualitative experience it is given to us in its full reality.

Dewey develops these points with reference to the traditional account of the subject–predicate proposition. On the traditional account, subject and predicate are made to seem distinct, as though a property were added to a subject already discriminated. But this does not answer to experience. He gives as an example the proposition: 'That thing is sweet.' On the traditional account, it appears as though the property of sweetness were being attributed to an object distinct from it. In fact, we are merely discriminating within, as it were, the qualitative field of sweetness. The discriminations are made, most commonly, for the purpose of location and control. So subject and predicate terms are merely functional. We are locating sweet*ness* for the purpose of sweet*ening*. The copula is really active, implying further effects. Thus *is sweet* really means *will sweeten*, say, coffee, or a batter of milk and eggs. The qualitative field, of course, will normally involve more than sweetness; it may involve, for example, qualities of shape and colour. We may say: 'This white cube is sweet.' But the point is the same. Again there is no subject *as distinct* from its properties. Rather, the subject is a discrimination *within* the qualitative field, a way of taking it for the purpose of location and control. Thus in every proposition there is presupposed a qualitative field, the terms of the proposition being merely functional, performing an operation on a field given only in experience. The word 'given', however, is treacherous. For 'given' can suggest '*to* a mind' or '*to* a subject', and this might suggest that what is given is subjective. But this is not so. 'In truth "given" in this connection signifies only that the quality immediately exists, or is brutely there.' Dewey extends this view to cover not simply the so-called secondary qualities but also those which may be called tertiary or emotive. What immediately exists, or is brutely there, is not simply a quality of sight, or touch, or sound but also a quality that threatens, or amuses, or consoles, or irritates. Thus we are not threatened over and against a situation; it is the situation that threatens; it is pervaded by that very quality.

Increasingly, in his later work, Dewey illustrated his points by reference to works of art. For example, this is how he illustrated the way in which a situation is pervaded by a quality:

> A painting is said to have a quality, or a particular painting to have a Titian or Rembrandt quality. The word thus used most certainly does not refer to any particular line, colour or part of the painting. It modifies all the constituents of the picture and all of their relations. It is not anything that can be expressed in words for it is something that must be *had*. Discourse may, however, point out the qualities, lines and relations by means of which pervasive and unifying quality is achieved.
>
> (Dewey 1938: 70)

As a quality pervades a work of art, so it does a situation in the real world. In both cases, what is said is incidental, has only a functional significance. The pervasive quality, the full reality, can only be experienced. Thus what Dewey attributes to art, in the above passage, is not a peculiarity of art, the product of artifice. Art is a true image of life. In just the same way, any real situation eludes our words and reveals itself only in experience. The increasing use of art in Dewey's later work is very far from an accident. For the burden of his work is that it is within the categories of art rather than those of science that the world most fully reveals itself.

The point will be clarified if we consider for a moment the third chapter of *Experience and Nature* (1925). Dewey there contrasts quality and order:

> Quality is quality, direct, immediate and undefinable. Order is a matter of relation, of definition, dating, placing and describing. It is discovered in reflection, not directly had and denoted as is temporal quality. Temporal order is a matter of science; temporal quality is an immediate trait of every occurrence whether in or out of consciousness.

Science, in short, since it deals only with order, is essentially limited. What eludes it, in a sense, are the elements it orders. For it merely traces relations between substances which are given to it and which it cannot explain. The point is made evident in Dewey's treatment of causality.

> By the nature of the case, causality, however it be defined, consists in the sequential order itself. . . . The view held – or implied – by some 'mechanists', which treats an initial term as if it had an inherent generative force which it somehow emits and bestows upon its successors, is all of a piece with the view held by teleologists which implies that an end brings about its own antecedents.
>
> (Bernstein 1960)

Mechanists and teleologists alike misunderstand causality, for they fail to see that the causal order is merely a sequence. The growth of an oak from an acorn may serve as an instance. The mechanist explains the existence of the oak by reference to the acorn; the teleologist explains the existence of the acorn by reference to the oak. But neither is explained in its *existence*. The oak has features irreducible to those of the acorn and vice versa. There is nothing in the acorn, taken in itself, which would enable one to deduce the existence of the oak and nothing in the oak, taken in itself which would enable one to deduce the existence of the acorn. Indeed every phase in the development of the oak from the acorn has features irreducible to those of any earlier or later phase. Nothing is explained in a causal statement except the order in which the elements fall. To say that the oak grows from the acorn is to indicate a sequence, to show an order in which nature works, but it does not in any other way *explain* that working. Dewey illustrates the point with a variety of examples.

> But in a legitimate account of ends as endings, all directional order resides in the sequential order. This no more occurs for the sake of the end than a mountain exists for the sake of the peak which is its end. A musical phrase has a certain close but the earlier portion does not therefore exist for the sake of the close as if it were something which is done away with when the close is reached. And so a man is not an adult until after he is a boy, but childhood does not exist for the sake of maturity.
>
> (Bernstein 1960)

A lyrical note accompanies certain passages in Dewey's later work and the theme, wherever this occurs, is that the world transcends all our knowledge. The note is especially evident in his paper 'Time and Individuality':

> The mystery of time is thus the mystery of the existence of real individuals. It is a mystery because it is a mystery that anything which exists is just what it is. We are given to forgetting, with our insistence upon causation and upon the necessity of things happening as they do happen, that things exist as just what they qualitatively are. We can account for a change by relating it to other changes, but existences we have to accept for just what they are. Given a butterfly or an earthquake as an event, as a change, we can at least in theory find out and state its connection with other changes. But the individual butterfly or earthquake remains just the unique existence which it is. We forget in explaining an occurrence that it is only the *occurrence* that is explained, not the thing itself. We forget that in explaining the occurrence we are compelled to fall back on the other individual things that have just the unique qualities they do have. Go as far back as we please in accounting for present conditions and we still come upon the mystery of things being just what they are.... Their occurrence, their manifestation, may be accounted for in terms of other occurrences, but their own quality of existence is final and opaque. The mystery is that the world is as it is....
>
> (Bernstein 1960: 224–43)

It will be useful to take the measure of this passage. Existence is a mystery which is final and opaque. But we associate the mysterious with what is awesome and contains the possibility of revelation. For Dewey, the world contains no such possibility of revelation for there is nothing further to reveal. It is just brutely there; indeed it is not so much that it is inexplicable as that it falls outside the category of what can be explained. But what is awesome about being just brutely there and how can there be a mystery where there is nothing to reveal? In short, how is the vision of the world, contained in Dewey's last work, to be distinguished from a vision of ultimate meaninglessness? Dewey's answer is that the world transcends knowledge but not experience and within experience there are moments of consummation. Such moments are revealed, with especial power, in great works of art which, like the world, are gratuitous, having no further purpose, but which nevertheless manifest in themselves intelligible order.

These points are developed, perhaps most fully, in Dewey's last major work, *Art as Experience* (1934). The book advances a view of art which is directly opposed to one of the most influential artistic doctrines of the time. This was the so-called doctrine of Significant Form, advanced by such critics as Clive Bell and Roger Fry. According to this doctrine, the value of art lies in its form rather than in its content, and this affords a pleasure which is *sui generis*. In short, there is a radical difference between the values of life and those of art. Dewey's aim is precisely to show that art and life are continuous. He is at home with his theme and deploys it with skill. We may take an example at random. Fry had argued that the subject matter of a painting is rarely chosen for its intrinsic interest or beauty. He took this to show that the value of art lay not in its subject matter but in its formal properties, such as those of line and colour. Why otherwise, he asked, is an artist more likely to paint Soho than St Paul's? A natural explanation, Dewey replies, is that an authentic artist is likely to avoid material that has already been aesthetically exploited. He then proceeds to show in some detail that Fry's view is incoherent:

> Before an artist can develop his reconstruction of the scene before him in terms of the relations of colours and lines characteristic of his picture, he observes the scene with meanings and values brought to his perception by prior experiences. These are indeed remade, transformed, as his new aesthetic vision takes shape. But they cannot vanish and yet the artist continue to see an object.

(1934: 89)

Central to Dewey's theme is the notion of what he calls '*an* experience'. He introduces the notion, at the beginning of his third chapter, by a contrast with those experiences where we are disturbed and frustrated or those where we proceed simply as a matter of routine.

> In contrast with such experience, we have *an* experience when the material experienced runs its course to fulfilment. Then and then only is it integrated within and demarcated in the general stream of experience from other experiences. A piece of work is finished in a way that satisfies; a problem receives its solution; a game is played through; a situation, whether that of eating a meal, playing a game of chess, carrying on a conversation, writing a book, or taking part in a political campaign, is so rounded out that its close is a consummation and not a cessation. Such an experience is a whole and carries with it its own individualising quality and self-sufficiency. It is *an* experience.
>
> (1934: 35)

Life is not simply a succession of events in random flux. Sometimes we find in the succession a definite beginning and a real end. Moreover, the end is real because it is not simply a cessation but rather a consummation, deriving its meaning from the preceding events and, in its turn, conferring a meaning upon them. Thus a conversation may be like a melody, in which every element is significant, forming an aesthetic whole, having its pervasive quality. Dewey gives many such examples from ordinary life, his point being that even in these examples, however ordinary, we find the aesthetic element, a foreshadowing of that unity amidst difference which is characteristic of great art. His point indeed is that there would be no great art without those foreshadowings. There would be no great moments in art without those moments in life which constitute *an* experience. One is reminded, in reading this chapter, of that first moment of intellectual delight, as much aesthetic as intellectual, when Dewey, as a youth, discovered that amongst the organs of the body there is a real unity.

Moments such as these constitute meaning in life, and art is their cultivation. Moreover, art is not confined to fine art, to the work of poets and painters. There is art in life wherever there is consummation. For there is no consummation where experience is random or merely routine but only where, through the use of imagination and intellect, it is truly mastered.

Dewey's later work has puzzled some of his commentators. They have found it inconsistent with the earlier. Croce, for example, thought that *Art as Experience* was in conflict with all that Dewey had previously written. In fact, however, the later views are a development of the earlier and, indeed, it is only on the basis of the earlier views that the later can properly be understood. To see this, we have only to recall the difficulties which are at the centre of Dewey's philosophy. As we have seen, there is a difficulty for him in the apparent conflict between the development of science and the Empiricism which is supposed to explain it. We have seen, also, that of the two elements it is Empiricism which for him is the more important. Now the difficulties for Empiricism are at their most acute where science is given a Realist interpretation. For example, the atomic theory, on a Realist interpretation, attributes to matter a structure which does not appear at the phenomenal level, the level of experience. Here, we have just that distinction between reality and appearance which Dewey aimed to abolish. The solution is to give science an interpretation which is Anti-Realist. Thus the atomic theory deals only with conditions and relations, not with the substance of things, and its point lies precisely in the consequences at the phenomenal level, the level of experience. Moreover, science, under this analysis, inevitably loses something of its significance. For since it deals only with conditions and relations, not the substance of things, it can hardly be seen as providing the fullest expression of reality. Reality, being revealed only in experience, will find its fullest expression in the re-creation of experience, which is art.

We may note that Dewey, here, was somewhat in advance of the Logical Positivists, who continued to give science the importance it had received in the older forms of Positivism. Dewey, by contrast, anticipated the continental tradition, which has its origin in Nietzsche and includes such thinkers as Heidegger and, in our own day, Foucault and Derrida. According to this tradition, the older Positivists were confused because they gave to science a significance akin to the religious. In other words, they thought that science could reveal a reality which transcends human experience. What science has helped us to see, however, is that there is no such reality. But in that case, having no such reality to reveal, it can hardly be inherently more significant than any number of other human activities. We may note here also the resemblance between Dewey and Nietzsche which we had occasion to mention earlier. As we said, the predominance of biology in the late nineteenth century produced a shift in Scientific Positivism. It became a common view that science does not investigate a reality which underlies the changes in phenomena but merely traces the relations which hold amongst the changes themselves. Now it is evident that if explanation is confined to the relations which hold amongst changing phenomena then those changes, indeed those phenomena, cannot themselves be open to explanation. They cannot be explained; they just *are*. This view, which Nietzsche introduced into the Continental tradition, is precisely the view that Dewey adopted in his later work.

These similarities between Dewey and those in the Continental tradition are not easily explained on the view that philosophy is an expression of personality. Dewey's sweetness of temperament and democratic instincts, for example, are not immediately apparent in, say, Nietzsche. What the two shared was not a common temperament but the same *Weltanschauung*. They were also genuine thinkers and their work is valuable in showing the development of that *Weltanschauung* and the difficulties involved in it. We shall return to these points in the next chapter. But, first, we must place Dewey not in relation to the future but in relation to the past.

In a sense, he has done this for us, for he disowned his philosophical inheritance, believing that it was dominated by confused ideas. As Morris Cohen said, the great scientific discoveries of the sixteenth and seventeenth centuries presupposed a view which we may term Classical Realism. This is the view that the world has an intelligible order which transcends the human mind but to which the human mind is in some measure akin. It has been the characteristic of thinkers, from the nineteenth century onwards, to reject that view. To some extent, that explains the present neglect of philosophers such as Morris Cohen and A. O. Lovejoy. Both of these held a view of the world which might be called Naturalistic but they fell out of fashion because they remained stubbornly Realist. They lived on the wrong side of the line which divides the modern age from the previous history of Western culture. Dewey, by contrast, lived on the right side of the line, in the sense that he was entirely at home in the thought of the modern age. But that is why I wish to speak of two Pragmatisms. For both Peirce and James belonged in spirit to the other side of the line. James, it is true, through his misunderstandings helped to give rise to the later Pragmatism. Nevertheless he as much as Peirce, though not opposed to science, was fundamentally opposed to the scientific *Weltanschauung*.

Having thus distinguished the two Pragmatisms, we must now proceed to consider the later Pragmatism in its most recent manifestations.

Chapter 11

Rorty: the mirror of nature

Dewey's influence on American philosophy was at its greatest during the first two decades of the present century. It declined during the 1930s. This was largely because of the arrival in America of such philosophers as Carnap, Feigl and Reichenbach, who brought with them the doctrines of Logical Positivism. These doctrines were held to be an advance on Pragmatism and for the next few decades they dominated American philosophy. The explanation for their dominance seems to be social rather than philosophical. The newcomers were European intellectuals, who were on familiar terms with some of the leading scientists, who were familiar with the latest scientific discoveries and who were proficient in the techniques of logic and mathematics. This gave them prestige and it was this prestige, rather than their doctrines, which accounts for their success. The doctrines themselves were considerably less sophisticated than those of Dewey. For example, in their earlier days, the Logical Positivists worked with a sharp distinction between theory and sense-experience. Later, it occurred to them that the distinction is not as simple as they had supposed and their views became more sophisticated. As they became more sophisticated, however, they came increasingly to resemble the very Pragmatism they were supposed to have supplanted. Indeed we may trace this process at work within the space of a single text. Thus in *Language, Truth and Logic* (1954), A. J. Ayer begins by stating that the meaning of a hypothesis or theory is determined by the way in which it is verified in sense-experience. But in later chapters we are informed that verification is relative to hypothesis or theory. Thus if a theory is in conflict with sense-experience, we are not bound in logic to reject that theory. We may reject the sense-experience; for example, we may hold that it is delusive. It follows that what sense-experience counts as verification will depend, at least in some measure, on what theories we hold. We now have a position somewhat more complicated than the one we were first offered and it is no longer entirely clear how a theory is to be verified. Ayer's suggestion is that this is to be achieved by an interplay between sense-experience and theory. This means that a theory is likely to be verified or falsified not by a single sense-experience but by an accumulation of such experiences. In short, the test of a theory is likely to be found in the consequences of holding it, in how it fares in the long run. This is a view hardly to be distinguished from Pragmatism. Ayer's view was developed by Quine in his celebrated article 'Two Dogmas of Empiricism' (1953: 20–47). Quine there argued that theory is underdetermined by sense-experience, so that sense-experience cannot, as in classical Logical Positivism, serve as the foundation for theory. Quine's view was seen as an advance on Logical Positivism which was itself an advance on Pragmatism. But this is to make progress by going backwards. The view that sense-experience, when taken in itself, is an inadequate foundation for knowledge, whether practical or theoretical, had been a common-place in American philosophy at least since the 1890s. Dewey – in insisting that sense-experience is to be understood through its role in the whole life of the organism, James – in stressing the idea of the apperceptive mass, Peirce – in emphasising the mass of knowledge which is presupposed in any observation, had all made clear that sense-experience is a source of knowledge only in relation to other knowledge which cannot be analysed in its terms. It is worth noting, also, that James and Dewey especially, in making this clear, had shown the crudity of that stimulus-response psychology to which Quine has given a whole-hearted allegiance.

What we find, then, is that Logical Positivism, having supplanted Pragmatism, proceeded to transform itself into the doctrine it had supplanted. The result is that Pragmatism has reappeared, its influence on American philosophy being now greater than at any time in the past fifty years. Elements of Pragmatism have appeared throughout the works of such leading American philosophers as Quine, Davidson and Putnam (see Murphy 1990). But it is Richard Rorty who, in recent times, has been most prominent in advocating the doctrine. In *Philosophy and the Mirror of Nature* (1990), which is his most substantial work, he named Dewey as one of the three most important philosophers of the century and in subsequent works, such as *Consequences of Pragmatism* (1982), he has continued to advocate a form of Pragmatism which he attributes to Dewey. We must therefore turn to Rorty's work in order to consider Pragmatism in its most recent development.

The theme of *Philosophy and the Mirror of Nature* is elaborated in some detail but it is susceptible to a summary. Philosophy, as hitherto conceived, has assumed that problems arise when one reflects on the foundations of activities which are central to our lives, such as science, morality, art and religion. It has seen as its task the solution of these problems, thus providing a foundation for those activities. In order to achieve this task, it has taken as central the problem of what makes knowledge possible. Providing a foundation for knowledge, it will be in a position, or so it assumes, to provide foundations for those activities into which knowledge enters. Rorty's theme is that this is entirely misconceived. There are problems which may be termed problems about knowledge. But these are precisely the ones that are tackled by such activities as science, morality, etc. There is no specifically philosophical problem about knowledge, the appearance of such a problem being merely an illusion. It follows that philosophy, as traditionally conceived, is itself an illusory activity, providing solutions, essentially confused, to unreal problems. The reader will note that this theme is a familiar one. As it is elaborated, it becomes, he will find, even more familiar. Thus, according to Rorty, illusory problems about knowledge have their chief source in the philosophy of Descartes. Dividing mind from body in a manner which Rorty claims to be unprecedented, Descartes created the so-called problem of knowledge. For there is now a gap between the world and the mind, and the question arises how the mind can know the world. In creating this problem, Descartes was assisted by a powerful image. This is the image of the mirror. The human mind, like a great mirror, reflects or represents the world. But this image, according to Rorty, is treacherous. Once we allow that in seeking knowledge we seek to reflect or represent a world independent of ourselves, we are easily led into the problem of how we can be sure that this world is accurately reflected or represented in our knowledge. We can check one representation only by reference to another and the mind has no access to a world which is independent of its representations. This is precisely the problem which philosophers, since the time of Descartes, have been attempting to solve. But there is a cure for this disease, which is to avoid the search for a solution and to attend rather to the image which gives rise to the problem. In short, we must eschew the idea that the aim of knowing is to mirror or to represent the world. Instead we should adopt a Pragmatist view. It is here that the link with Dewey, already evident, becomes explicit. For by a Pragmatist view, Rorty means a view such as Dewey's which is essentially *Non-Representationalist*. On this view, the aim of knowledge is not to represent the world but to cope with it. Thus, for Dewey there can be no question whether science succeeds or fails in representing a world independent of itself. That is because the world of science is, in a sense, internal to science; it is simply the world with which science already copes, according to those methods for coping which have proved themselves successful.

At this point, however, there arises an apparent difficulty. For what is the measure of our having successfully coped? The history of science reveals a certain incommensurability between the methods, or even concepts, that scientists have adopted at different times and places. If these methods, or concepts, are not intended to represent a world independent of themselves, where is the measure by which one set may be deemed to have coped more successfully than any other? But this difficulty is merely apparent. In these matters, according to Rorty, we are entitled to turn Whiggish. By this he means that we are entitled to use our own standards as the measure by which others are to be judged. That is because where standards are incommensurable, there can be no measure of which are superior, other than our finding which prevail. Now, as it happens, our own standards have in fact prevailed. Consequently, we are entitled to use them in order to judge and to explain the failure of those adopted by others.

I have now summarised some of the main ideas which enter into *Philosophy and the Mirror of Nature* and, to some extent, into *Consequences of Pragmatism*. This summary will make clear that we are dealing with yet another assault on classical Realism. Moreover, as I have here implied, the ingredients are familiar. Philosophy, as traditionally conceived, is entirely confused; the source of this confusion, at least in modern philosophy, is Descartes; philosophy must therefore be transformed and the instrument for this transformation will be a Non-Representationalist view of truth or knowledge. We are dealing, in other words, with Pragmatism in its *second* form. But that in itself, of course, is not to say that these ideas are false. We must therefore consider in some detail how Rorty proceeds to support and to elaborate them.

Philosophy and the Mirror of Nature begins by questioning an assumption commonly made in the philosophy of mind. The assumption is that there is an intuitive or natural distinction between the mental and the physical. Rorty denies this assumption. According to him, the distinction is not intuitive or natural; rather it is the product of philosophical theorising. In short, the philosophy of mind does not seek to elucidate a distinction already in existence; the distinction it examines is one it has made itself. As evidence for this, Rorty traces the history of the distinction and finds that it has its source in a particular philosopher, namely, Descartes. At first sight, this does not seem plausible. The distinction between the mental and the physical may be found at innumerable points not simply in the history of philosophy but in the history of mankind more generally. A belief in disembodied spirits, for example, is found amongst peoples widely separated in time and place. Moreover, if we confine ourselves to the history of philosophy, we find, say, in Plato's *Phaedo*, which was written more than two thousand years ago, a distinction between mind and body which appears remarkably similar to the one drawn by Descartes. According to Rorty, however, there is a radical difference between the one drawn by Descartes and any previously drawn. Moreover, it is the one drawn by Descartes which, ever since, has dominated the philosophy of mind. As evidence for this, Rorty quotes the following passage from Wallace Matson:

> The Greeks did not lack a concept of mind, even of a mind separable from the body. But from Homer to Aristotle, the line between mind and body, when drawn at all, was drawn so as to put the process of sense-perception on the body side. That is one reason why the Greeks had no mind-body problem. Another is that it is difficult, almost impossible, to translate such a sentence as 'What is the relation of sensation to mind (or soul)?' into Greek. The difficulty is in finding a Greek equivalent for 'sensation' in the sense philosophers make it bear. . . . 'Sensation' was introduced into philosophy precisely to make it possible to speak of a conscious state without committing oneself as to the nature or even existence of external stimuli.
>
> (Rorty 1990: 47)

According to Matson, then, the conception of mind and body found amongst the Greeks is radically different from that found in modern philosophy: first, because the Greeks considered sense-perception to be an activity of the body rather of the mind and, second, because they lacked the idea of sensation as a conscious state independent of external objects. Rorty argues that it was Descartes who was responsible for this difference. He extended the term 'thought' to cover all the operations of the mind, including those of sense-experience. This led to the introduction of the term 'idea' to stand for the contents of the mind. The term was used most extensively by Locke, but he was influenced in his usage by Descartes. On Locke's view, objects are known through the ideas in the mind which represent them. The mind inspects the world not directly but by way of those ideas. Here the image of the mirror is in full control. The world is known through inspecting its reflections in the mirror of the mind. This view involves, of course, a radical separation between the mental and the physical. The mental is that which is known immediately or indubitably; the physical is that which is known at a remove, through being reflected by the mental.

Now the obsession with sceptical problems about knowledge, commonly found in modern philosophy, was occasioned by these developments. As evidence for this, Rorty claims that such problems are not found in medieval or in Greek philosophy. Again, one may not find that altogether plausible. Problems about knowledge appear often enough in the dialogues of Plato and in Greek philosophy more generally. Indeed there was a whole school of Greek philosophers, associated with Pyrrho, who are commonly known as the Sceptics. According to Rorty, however, Greek scepticism was concerned not with epistemology but with ethics. Its concern was more with how to live than with problems about knowledge. Before Descartes, there could be no epistemological problem, in the modern sense, because the representationalist view of knowledge, which gives rise to that problem, was invented by Descartes himself. Thus, for a typical medieval or Greek philosopher, the mind in knowledge does not represent but rather *becomes* the object known. Both Aristotle and Aquinas, for example, hold that the mind in knowing an object takes on its form, so that there is an identity between the form of the object and the mind which knows it. Here there is no gap between mind and object, and therefore no space in which scepticism can develop.

Rorty's aim in making these points is not of course simply historical. His aim is to show that philosophical problems about how the mind can know a world independent of it do not rest on any intuitive distinction between the mental and the physical. Rather it is philosophers who have invented that distinction and the problems with which they deal are merely the consequence of the distinction they have invented. It follows that the problems should be removed not by finding their solution but by rejecting the distinction which has given rise to them.

The reader, however, may still have certain misgivings. Can it really be that there is no distinction at all between the mental and the physical? Let us take a simple example. I find out my own height or weight by adopting forms of measurement which are as available to you as to me. Moreover, your use of those forms may be more accurate than mine so that you have better information than I have about my own height or weight. But suppose I am in pain. It seems implausible to suppose that you might have better information of this than I have myself. Indeed it seems hardly intelligible to suppose that I have to find it out or that I can be mistaken about it. Here surely is a difference, which some may find striking. Rorty acknowledges the point. He argues, however, that the difference involved is not between ontological states but is rather a feature of language.

> Following Wittgenstein, we shall treat the fact that there is no such thing as 'a misleading appearance of pain' not as a strange fact about a special ontological genus called the mental, but just as a remark about a language game – the remark that we have the convention of taking people's word for what they are feeling. From this 'language-game' point of view, the fact that a man is feeling whatever he thinks he is feeling has no more ontological significance than the fact that the Constitution is what the Supreme Court thinks it is, or that the ball is foul if the umpire thinks it is.
>
> (Rorty 1990: 32)

It will be useful to make some comments on the above passage. First, even if it were an 'ontological' fact that we cannot be mistaken about being in pain, it need not be a 'strange' one. Perhaps the fact is familiar. Second, even if it were a fact about language that we take people's word for what they are feeling, it need not be 'just' such a fact. Suppose, for the sake of the argument, that there were an ontological or non-linguistic difference between the mental and the physical. There seems no reason why this should not reveal itself in language. Indeed that might be just what we should expect. Third, the analogy between pain and the procedures of a game or a legal system seems not to hold at just the point one would expect it to hold, if it were illuminating. For example, it seems evident that a game is *constituted* by its conventions. Those who play a game need the concept not simply to speak of what they are doing but also to do it. But that is precisely what is *not* true about pain. One does not need the concept to be in pain but only to speak about it. Young children and animals cannot speak about it. But they may certainly be in pain.

So far, then, Rorty's argument may not seem convincing. But he elaborates his point, offering an extended example. We are to imagine that on the other side of our galaxy there are beings who are unacquainted with the difference between the mental and the physical. They use notions such as 'wanting to', 'intending to' and 'believing that' but they apply them also to their pets and even to their robots. Moreover, although they possess all the reactions of people who feel sensations, no word for a sensation occurs in their language. On the other hand, they are blessed with a remarkable knowledge of neurophysiology and frequently refer to their own nervous system, especially in those situations where we refer to our sensations. For example, where we say 'I am in pain', they say 'My C-fibres are stimulated'.

One day there arrives a group of philosophers from earth who fall to discussing whether these beings – whom they term Antipodeans – really have feelings. For example, do they feel pain? Their reactions are the same as ours, which would suggest that they do. On the other hand, they have no word for 'pain' and every attempt to convey to them what we mean by the term proves unavailing. Eventually, the discussion concentrates on a single point. Since one cannot be mistaken about being in pain, the issue of whether they feel pain resolves itself into the issue of whether they have something they cannot be mistaken about. For example, can they be mistaken about whether their C-fibres are stimulated? They reply that they can, which seems to settle the matter. Unfortunately they add that they *cannot* be mistaken about whether their C-fibres *seem* to be stimulated. The question now is what this amounts to. Someone asks whether there is a neural concomitant of 'seeming to have C-fibres stimulated.' It transpires that such a concomitant exists, namely, state T-435. But it transpires, also, that this is the neural concomitant of the *utterance* 'My C-fibres seem to be stimulated.' Moreover, what about state T-435 itself? Can they be mistaken about whether they are in that state? At this point the discussion seems abruptly to terminate. The Antipodeans are prepared to acknowledge that they can be mistaken about whether they are in state T-435 but they show no interest in the question of whether they can be mistaken about seeming to be. This leaves the philosophers in a state of puzzlement.

Now Rorty's aim in framing this example is fairly clear. His aim is to show that the philosophers have no good reason to be puzzled. They are puzzled because they suppose that their dispute has an *ontological* status. In other words, they suppose there is some fact of the matter at stake in the issue of whether the Antipodeans feel pain. The truth is, however, that what is at stake is merely different ways of talking and this may be settled according to one's convenience. Thus it will signify no difference in the behaviour of the Antipodeans whether one says that their C-fibres are stimulated or says that they are in pain. For their behaviour will be exactly the same on both ways of talking. Consequently the only problem is how to talk and that will be settled not by the facts but by what one finds convenient.

One may be certain, however, that not everyone will be persuaded by Rorty's example. Many will argue that the language of the

Antipodeans does not possess an adequate equivalent for the incorrigibility of pain. The nearest equivalent one finds is an inclination to make a certain *utterance*. But – or so they will argue – there is more to being in pain than being inclined to *say* one is in pain. Indeed such people may argue that what Rorty's example provides is a *reductio ad absurdum* of the idea that one can find an equivalent for pain by searching for a neural concomitant. For what one finds, in searching for such a concomitant, is that one has embarked on an infinite regress. As evidence for this, they may point out that an infinite regress is averted in Rorty's example only by an abrupt refusal, on the part of the Antipodeans, to continue the discussion.

Rorty is aware of these difficulties and attempts to remove them by a further discussion. This is complicated, involving references to numerous positions in the contemporary philosophy of mind. For our purposes, we may pass over the details and concentrate on the moral.

The central difficulty is that for many people there seems to be no equivalent in neurophysiology for the incorrigibility of being in pain. Now Rorty eventually concludes that he can acknowledge that point without its affecting his own position. Consider the following argument.

1 Some statements of the form 'I just had a sensation of pain' are true.
2 Sensations of pain are incorrigibly reportable.
3 Neural events are not incorrigibly reportable.
4 Nothing can be both corrigibly and incorrigibly reportable.
5 No sensation of pain is a neural event.

This argument seems valid and its premises true. This suggests that we have to accept its conclusion. That would mean, of course, that Rorty is mistaken. 'I am in pain' is not equivalent to 'My C-fibres are stimulated.' Rorty argues, however, that we do not have to accept the conclusion, for we do not have to accept the fourth premise. We can accept, rather, that something may be both corrigibly and incorrigibly reportable. That may be true, for example, when it is reported from different points of view. Thus, it is easy to see how social practices may differ with regard to the same objects, events or actions, these differences reflecting degrees in the intellectual or spiritual development of the cultures concerned. Similarly, it is easy to see how something may be corrigibly reported (by those who know neurophysiology) and incorrigibly reported (by those who do not). The difference is like that between the expert and the layman, each speaking of the same thing in different vocabularies. Of course, there is here a certain awkwardness, since in this case it is the expert rather than the layman who is the more likely to be mistaken. Still, the idea is clear. Rorty's view is that whether or not there is a neural equivalent for a sensation, we may still treat 'sensation' and 'neural state' as differing not in ontological states but in being different ways of talking about the same thing.

With that view, Rorty concludes his first section. We shall have occasion, later, to discuss in detail some of the issues it raises. Even at this stage, however, it will be useful to make a few comments. The section opened with the claim that there is no intuitive or natural distinction between the mental and the physical. We can now see precisely why that should be so. The reason is that, strictly speaking, there is no such thing as the mental. It is the invention of philosophers, such as Descartes, who have confused a manner of speech with something in the nature of things. The point will be entirely clear if we consider again the difference between 'sensation' and 'neural states'. According to Rorty, these are simply different ways of talking about the same thing. But about *what*, then, are they talking? It is evident, as indeed Rorty acknowledges, that they are both talking about the physical. In short, there is only the physical, and the 'mental' is simply a way of talking about it. The point is evident in a number of ways. For example, consider again the Antipodeans. Here we have beings who have no effective distinction between the first and the third person. Thus they refer to themselves in the language of neurophysiology and comment on what occurs in the manner of a third party. Here, in short, we have beings who have fulfilled the Positivist dream of being wholly describable in the language of physical science. Moreover, Rorty makes clear that, ultimately, this is the truth about all of us. In principle, there is nothing to prevent neurophysiology from explaining and predicting everything we say or do.

It is on the basis of such a claim that Rorty denies there is an ontological difference between the mental and the physical. But we cannot allow him to suppose that he has altogether avoided the ontological himself. For his claim is that nothing exists apart from the physical. That may be true; but it surely smacks of the ontological. There is a further point. I have implied that the type of Pragmatism which Rorty advances is opposed to that of Peirce, being a lightly disguised form of Positivism. The disguise is light, for it often reveals what it covers. Here is an excellent illustration of the point.

In the second section of his book, Rorty develops the view about epistemology which he has stated in his first section. His view, of course, is that epistemology is confused, there being no specifically philosophical problem about knowledge. In his second section, he seeks to reinforce this point by detailed study of epistemology in its contemporary form.

EPISTEMOLOGY

Rorty is generous in acknowledging his intellectual debts, there being few of his views which he does not attribute to one or other of the philosophers who have influenced him. The heroes of his second section are Quine and Sellars. To Quine he is indebted for the view that there is no real distinction between the analytic and the synthetic or the conceptual and the empirical. To Sellars, for his exposing the myth of 'the given'. According to Rorty, these two views, when taken together, will lay waste to the whole of epistemology. The general approach is given on page 178 of *Philosophy and the Mirror of Nature*. The essence of 'the Quine–Sellars approach' is that 'nothing counts as justification unless by reference to what we already accept, and that there is no way to get outside our beliefs and our language so as to find some test other than coherence.'

The 'Quine–Sellars approach' is, of course, identical with what Rorty takes to be Pragmatism. Our beliefs are true not because they correspond to a world independent of themselves but in relation to our other beliefs. We must consider how he develops this view.

According to Rorty, one can think of knowledge in two quite different ways. On the first, one thinks of it as a relation to propositions and thus of justification as a relation between some propositions and others. On the second, one thinks both of knowledge and of justification as privileged relations to the objects those propositions are about. It is a consequence of the first view that justification is potentially infinite. A discussion may be closed when the parties reach agreement. But it can always be re-opened. For the play of reason and argument has no inherent limit. By contrast, the consequence of the second view is that causes are preferred to reasons and compulsion to argument. For it is presupposed that in knowledge one is so gripped by the object known that one is incapable of doubt, seeing no alternative to what one knows. Now it is this second view which forms the basis of epistemology.

The point will be clarified if one turns to the roots of epistemology which, as one might expect, lie in the philosophy of the seventeenth century. In Locke, for example, one finds the idea that knowledge is essentially a relation between the mind and an object, in which the object leaves its impression on the mind. This leads easily to a confusion between explanation and justification. Explanation concerns *the way* a belief occurs to the mind, justification concerns the validation of that belief. The processes are distinct but Locke runs them together. Thus, for him, a belief is validated by *the way* it enters the mind. Rorty traces a source of confusion also in an inheritance from the Greeks. The Greeks had distinguished sharply between knowledge given to the intellect and knowledge given to the senses, the latter being contingent, the former, as in mathematics, being necessary. Moreover, they treated mathematics, which has the mark of necessity, as the paradigm of what knowledge should be. This of course reinforces the idea that knowledge is compulsive, leaving the mind incapable of doubt. In short, it reinforces the *second* way of considering knowledge. Here then we find the sources of epistemology, which is the search for *Privileged Representation* – the search, in other words, for that in the mind which *guarantees* knowledge.

But it is here that we find, also, the precise relevance of Quine and Sellars. Quine in 'Two Dogmas of Empiricism' (1953: 20–47) demolished the distinction between the necessary and the contingent. He showed that differences in certainty amongst our beliefs are never absolute but reflect only the degree to which we give them our adherence. Thus we should, it is true, be more reluctant to abandon our mathematical or logical beliefs than our scientific ones. But that is a matter of degree. There are no beliefs, even in mathematics or logic, which cannot be revised. Sellars, in his turn, demolished the idea that anything is absolutely given to the mind, by making clear the difference between explanation and justification. Rorty quotes the following passage:

> In characterising an episode or a state as that of *knowing*, we are not giving an empirical description of that episode or state; we are placing it in the logical space of reasons, of justifying and being able to justify what one says.
>
> (1990: 141)

It follows that the *way* a belief occurs to the mind is irrelevant. It acquires its status as knowledge not through an empirical relation to the world but through a logical relation to other beliefs. Taken together, Quine and Sellars have demolished epistemology. For they have shown that the interplay of beliefs within a language requires no foundation in the world. The justification of belief is, as Rorty puts it, *conversational*. In other words, it occurs within the conversation of which it is a part. The conversation, itself, requires no foundation, and epistemology, which seeks to provide it, is therefore irrelevant.

It will be useful to make some comments on this analysis. Sellars's distinction between justification and explanation requires a sharp, some might think over-sharp, distinction between reason and fact. Thus, in the passage just quoted, he distinguishes sharply between what falls under an empirical description (the *way* a belief occurs) and what falls within the logical space of reasons (whether it is *justified*). The trouble is that this distinction is just what Quine denies. According to Quine this is not itself a logical distinction but merely a difference in the *way* we hold our beliefs. Thus, for him, we are more reluctant to abandon our beliefs about logic than to abandon our other beliefs. But that is the only difference. In short, the only difference is *psychological*. Sellars' very point is that it is a matter of psychology how a belief occurs but *not* whether it is justified. The latter belongs to the logical space of reasons. For Quine this difference is simply a matter of degree. He and Sellars, so far from marching arm and arm, are evidently in conflict.

One may wonder at this point whether Quine's view is essential to Rorty's account. Rorty takes him to have shown that the truths of logic or mathematics are not privileged representations. In other words, they are not infallible truths about the world. But in order to show this, it is not necessary to deny the distinction between logic and fact. At the time when Quine wrote his paper, the philosophers who were most prominent in defending that distinction were the Logical Positivists. None of the Logical Positivists believed that the truths of logic or mathematics were infallible truths about the world. Indeed their very point in distinguishing such truths from those of fact was to show that they do *not* represent the world, whether infallibly or otherwise. They are truths not about the world but about our *methods* for representing it. Some may consider that they made this distinction too sharp. But it seems a matter of common sense that one must make some such distinction. For example, there must be a difference between what a statement means and whether it is true, since in order to discover whether it is true, one must first know what it means. One might suggest therefore that Rorty should abandon Quine and fall back on Sellars.

Unfortunately, there is a difficulty, also, in Sellars's account. It is true, of course, that one may distinguish between explanation and justification, since they imply different interests. For example, even if one knows that a person's belief is false, one may still be interested in how he acquired it. Further, indeed for that reason, an interest in whether a person's belief is true cannot be satisfied by just *any* account of how he acquired it. But it plainly does not follow that how a person acquired a belief is *never* relevant to one's interest in whether it is true.

All that follows is that a person's belief is not likely to be true *however* he acquires it. What that suggests, however, is that it *may* matter how a person acquires a belief. Now that is what Sellars denies. How a person acquires a belief is *never* relevant to whether it is true. He assumes that since explanation and justification imply different interests, they can never be satisfied by the same process.

Now to see the fallacy in that view, one has only to reflect on how often a belief is in fact justified by the way it is acquired. For example, if I claim that it is raining, I may prove that I am entitled to that belief by revealing I have been outside to look at the weather. I have here justified my belief by reference not to another belief but to the way I have acquired it. Indeed, precisely what I claim is that, given the way I have acquired it, I am entitled to that belief *without* having to justify it by reference to another belief.

Now this, it may be said, is to succumb to the myth of the given. It is to imply that the world is given infallibly in sense-perception, independently of belief. But nothing of the sort is implied. It is evident that observation requires a background of belief. The point is, however, that this background is a necessary not a sufficient condition for observation. Thus my present beliefs are consistent with my finding, when I look out of the window, that it is raining. But they are equally consistent with my finding that it is not raining. This means they are not sufficient in themselves to determine which is true. I have to look. Moreover, whatever I find when I look will be consistent with what I believed previously. Nor does it follow that sense-perception is therefore infallible. We may note here a tendency on the part of Rorty to assume that he has exhausted the field by whatever alternatives he presents to us. Thus if we do not accept that knowledge is equivalent to justified belief, we are bound to hold that it is acquired in a manner entirely compulsive and infallible. But if I claim I am entitled to my belief, because I have looked, what I claim is not that I am infallible but simply that I am correct.

Let us contrast the above view with Rorty's view that knowledge is equivalent to justified belief. This view, as Rorty acknowledges, entails an infinite regress. If one attempts to justify a belief by reference to another then that other has to be justified by reference to another and so on *ad infinitum*. Rorty thinks this regress benign, for he thinks that the regress will be broken when we end our conversation and that we can always reopen the conversation if we wish. But we shall have to reopen it, if we wish to justify our belief, and even then we shall not succeed, because the chain is endless. In short, the regress is not benign but vicious. If belief A can be justified only by reference to belief B and that only by reference to C, and so on *ad infinitum*, then belief A will never get justified. It is not so much that the justification never ends as that it never gets started. For the truth is that along this road there is no justification. We are engaged in a conversation which has no point except to keep itself going.

CONTEMPORARY PHILOSOPHY

Philosophy and the Mirror of Nature is divided into three sections, of which the first two are critical, seeking to reveal the confusion in traditional philosophy. We must now complete our exposition of the critical sections by considering Rorty's treatment of two issues in contemporary philosophy. The first concerns the relation of epistemology to the philosophy of psychology; the second, its relation to the philosophy of language.

At first sight, the philosophy of psychology, in its contemporary form, seems not to be a field which requires the exercise of Rorty's critical abilities. For most of its practitioners have concentrated their efforts on attacking Cartesian dualism. Ryle led the assault in the 1940s and it has proceeded, with some force, ever since. A common view, mentioned by Rorty, is that there is no middle ground between empirical descriptions of behaviour on the one hand and neurophysiology on the other. Here, of all places, there seems little room for the idea of the mind as 'an inner space'. There has, it is true, been some revival, very recently, of the idea of 'the inner' through the work of Jerry Fodor, of which Rorty is critical. But, for the most part, he is content to exercise a moderating influence on views to which, in other respects, he is sympathetic.

We shall see more clearly what this involves, if we return for a moment to the view that there is no middle ground between neurophysiology and empirical descriptions of behaviour. The tendency of this view is to eliminate psychology altogether. Rorty believes that this goes too far. His view is that once we remove epistemological confusion from psychology, we shall find that it has a useful role to play. Now we remove epistemological confusion from psychology when we recognise that the mental has no ontological status. At first sight, this seems also to eliminate psychology. But Rorty thinks otherwise. He acknowledges that psychology can in principle be replaced by neurophysiology. For he thinks that neurophysiology can in principle provide a complete explanation of human behaviour. But that is possible only in principle; at the moment, it is not possible in practice and perhaps it never will be.

This means that we can take a *pragmatic* view of psychology. In other words, for as long as it is convenient, we can continue to use mental language.

The philosophy of language provides a striking contrast with the philosophy of psychology. Here epistemological confusion is in almost full possession of the field. One source of such confusion is a view especially associated with Michael Dummett. This is the view that epistemological issues can be reformulated as issues in the theory of meaning. Rorty spends little time on this view because he believes it is merely a variation of the view, held by the Logical Positivists, that the analysis of language will provide a foundation for the whole of philosophy. This view was undermined – or so Rorty believes – when Quine demolished the distinction between meaning and fact.

There is, however, a second source of confusion. This is found in a revival within the philosophy of language of full-blooded metaphysical Realism. This arises out of a problem in the philosophy of science. Philosophers such as Kuhn and Feyerabend have argued that when there is a conflict between fundamental theories, there is bound to be a difficulty in specifying facts which are neutral between them. That is because what counts as a fact will depend on which theory one holds. In short, reference to the facts is relative to one's basic theories, beliefs or conceptual scheme. Within what Kuhn calls 'normal' science there will be an agreement in basic theories and therefore agreement in referring to the facts. But when science is in an 'abnormal' state, when there are revolutionary changes, there will be a conflict between basic theories and therefore no agreement about which facts will verify the theories involved. As we shall see, this difference between the 'normal' and the 'abnormal' is of considerable importance in the development of Rorty's views. The point for the moment, however, is that the views of Kuhn and Feyerabend suggest that reference is relative to a conceptual scheme or set of theories or beliefs.

Now before he turned to a form of Pragmatism, Hilary Putnam led an assault on this view. He argued that what science requires is a theory which makes reference independent of the beliefs and intentions of the scientists. Otherwise, he argued, truth itself will be relativised. The 'truth' of a theory will be relative to what, according to our more basic theories or beliefs, warrants our assent. Consequently, there will be no difference between truth and warranted assertion. But what science seeks to achieve is truth about the world, which is independent of our theories or beliefs. Even an assertion warranted by those theories or beliefs may still turn out to be false. Putnam therefore framed the so-called causal theory of reference. On this view, which was adopted also by Kripke, the reference of a term depends on its causal relation with the world, which is independent (or largely independent) of the beliefs or intentions involved in using that term.

Rorty's criticism falls into two parts. First, he rejects Putnam's claim that we must distinguish between 'true' and 'warranted assertion'. He acknowledges that the two are not identical in meaning. He argues, however, that they amount to the same thing. He here works a variation on an earlier argument. Two ways of talking need not be exactly equivalent in order to be ways of talking about the same thing. He argues therefore that a philosopher, such as Dewey, who identified the two would not be worried by Putnam's criticism.

The trouble with this is that truth and warranted assertion are evidently *not* the same thing. One may go wrong because one has not conformed to the accepted procedures; but one may do so, also, because there is something wrong with the accepted procedures, to which one has conformed. In the latter case, unlike in the former, one's assertion is warranted. But in neither case is it true. Moreover, the whole of scientific progress depends on the reality of that difference. It is because the scientist may go wrong in either of those ways that he cannot be content simply to revise his assertions in the light of accepted procedures. He must also be prepared to revise accepted procedures in the light of what happens to his assertions. For however they are warranted they may still turn out to be false. It is on the interplay between these forms of revision that scientific progress depends.

Rorty's second criticism is that the causal theory of names rests on an ambiguity in the term 'reference'. Here he seems to me correct. Rorty distinguishes several senses of the term but for our purpose it will be sufficient to distinguish two. Thus reference may be either intentional or accidental. For example, we can say that when people first spoke of the 'morning' star and the 'evening' star they referred to different stars. For this is what they intended when they spoke and that is how they took one another when they did so. In short, there is a sense of 'reference' which is roughly equivalent to what people talk about when they use a term and this is determined by how they intend to use it.

But, of course, we may also say that when those people spoke of the morning star and the evening star, they referred not to two stars (or planets) but only to one. Here we are no longer using 'reference' in the first sense, for it is evident that they did not intend to refer to a single star. Rather they did so by accident. 'Reference' in this sense is most commonly used to explain or to correct mistakes in intentional reference. For example when we say those people were really referring to one star, we imply that they would not have formed the intention they did, had they not mistaken one star for two.

Now when the causal theorists speak of reference, they are not using the term in the first sense nor yet, quite, in the second. The impression they create is that whilst those people were intending to speak of two stars, their words, without their knowing it, were guided or directed to one. In short, their reference was guided, as in the first sense, whilst being non-intentional, as in the second. It seems evident, however, that they have simply confused the two senses. The truth is that, so far as it is guided or directed, reference is intentional and, so far as it is non-intentional, it is not guided or directed but is accidental.

Rorty, then, is correct in his criticism. What one might wonder, however, is why Putnam was so anxious to deny that reference is relative to intention or belief. As Rorty acknowledges, it is plainly fallacious to infer that if our *reference* to an object is relative to our beliefs, the object itself *exists* only relative to those beliefs. But if objects exist independently of our beliefs, where, for a Realist, is the problem? Perhaps there would be a problem if, when beliefs conflict, we can refer to the facts only by means of those conflicting beliefs. But as has been pointed out, by many people, Kuhn and Feyerabend seem to move illicitly between two quite different views. The first is that any reference to the facts presupposes *some* belief. The second is that where beliefs are in conflict any reference to the facts presupposes just those elements in the beliefs which are conflicting.

Those, however, are issues to which we shall return. We must now turn to Rorty's more positive views and especially to his views about what future there is for philosophy once it has been removed in its traditional form.

Chapter 12

Rorty: hermeneutics and irony

Rorty opens the third section of *Philosophy and the Mirror of Nature* by contrasting epistemology and hermeneutics. His aim is to show that hermeneutics provides a better model than epistemology for a new philosophy. He is anxious to make clear, however, that he does not envisage hermeneutics as replacing epistemology by taking over its tasks. Rather it provides a quite different attitude to knowledge or understanding. Thus on the epistemological model, we obtain knowledge by deducing conclusions from central principles. The aim is to obtain conclusions which are binding on all people. This is a model which, according to Rorty, involves confrontation and constraint. Presumably he means that the aim is to confront people with conclusions they are bound to accept. It is possible, however, to give up this desire for confrontation and constraint. Consider, by contrast, what is involved in understanding a strange culture. Here we have no principles of knowledge already given to us. So far as they exist, we must find them. In doing so, we are involved in the so-called hermeneutic circle. Thus we cannot understand the parts of a strange culture until we get some sense of the whole and we cannot get a sense of the whole until we have some understanding of the parts. Here we have a different model of understanding, which is not *confrontational* but *conversational*. It is more like getting acquainted with a person than like following a demonstration. 'In both cases we play back and forth between guesses about how to characterise particular statements or other events, and guesses about the point of the whole situation, until gradually we feel at ease with what was hitherto strange' (Rorty 1990: 319).

There may be some, however, who wonder whether the epistemological model can be entirely incorrect. For, on some occasions, we surely do argue from common principles and reach conclusions which people feel bound to accept. Rorty acknowledges the point. The epistemological stance is at fault only when it aims to take full possession of the field. To explain the point, Rorty distinguishes between 'normal' and 'abnormal' discourse. The distinction is taken from Kuhn. Discourse is 'normal' where people share principles or criteria and on their basis arrive at common views. Where discourse is in that respect normal, one may be satisfied with the epistemological model. But discourse is not always in that respect normal. For example, where cultures differ, the respective standards will overlap at certain points and diverge at others, so that discourse between the two cultures cannot throughout be governed by common standards. Even within the same culture there may be divergences in principles or criteria between different generations or people who live different types of life. Even within the same type of life, the principles which prevail may cease to do so, as novel situations make it difficult to see how they are still to be applied. In all these cases, it is the hermeneutic, rather than the epistemological model, which prevails.

But what, one may wonder, has this to do with philosophy? Rorty's view is that it is precisely where the hermeneutic model prevails that the philosopher should find his role. He is the one who can mediate between incommensurable statements, criteria or principles. Or again, even where common principles prevail, he is the one who can suggest other possibilities. In short, he is the one who operates where there are possibilities of abnormal discourse.

One may still find this somewhat vague. For example, what is the precise subject or set of problems with which philosophy, in its new phase, is supposed to deal? The vagueness is not accidental. Rather, it is in the nature of the case. The whole point is that the new philosopher will not deal with any specific subject or set of problems. As envisaged by Rorty, he is to be the 'informed dilettante, the polypragmatic, Socratic intermediary between various discourses. In his salon, so to speak, hermetic thinkers are charmed out of their self-enclosed practices. Disagreements between disciplines and discourses are compromised or transcended in the course of the conversation' (1990: 317). In short, having eschewed confrontation and constraint, the philosopher is free to flit from one subject to another.

In support of this view, Rorty argues that the distinction between normal and abnormal discourse can be applied independently of subject. At first one might suppose that there are some subjects – the humanities – which are more suited to the hermeneutic model and others – the sciences – more suited to the epistemological. But this is mistaken. Every subject, at different times, may go through both a normal and an abnormal phase. For example, one can easily imagine a period in painting or literature when criteria are shared alike by artists, critics and public and where there is unanimity in artistic taste. The eighteenth century, perhaps, is an example. But also one can imagine a period where there is no agreement over *scientific* criteria. There was such a period during the fifteenth and sixteenth centuries when the Ptolemaic and the Copernican theories both seemed to cover the facts and there was no agreement over which was correct.

One may still feel, however, that there are some permanent differences between the sciences and the humanities. For example, surely the scientist, unlike the artist, is a *discoverer* not a *creator*. His aim is not to create the truth but to find it. He is governed by what exists objectively, independently of himself. But that is a model of the scientist which applies only in a period of *normal* science, when there are firm criteria for what counts as a discovery. In such a period, one may even speak of the scientist as 'representing the world' or of his theories as 'corresponding to the facts'. But that is because, relative to the period, there are agreed standards or criteria for what is to count as doing so. In a period of *abnormal* science, however, there are no such standards or criteria. In such a period, the scientist, or at any rate the great scientist, is essentially a *creator*. He creates the standards for what in the future will *count* as 'corresponding to the facts' or 'representing the world'.

But surely, one may be inclined to say, a great scientist, such as Galileo, influenced future standards because his theories were true, because they did correspond to the facts. This, however, is naive. The standards by which we judge that Galileo's theories correspond to the facts are those we have been persuaded to adopt by precisely those theories. Since Galileo has won, we now view the world through Galilean, as distinct from Ptolemaic, spectacles. Consequently, to say that Galileo's theories correspond to the facts is merely to indicate that he has created our standards; it is to indicate, in short, that he has won.

It will be useful to consider in more detail how Rorty establishes this last point. In his celebrated battle with the church, Galileo was criticised by Cardinal Bellarmine on the grounds that his views were in conflict with the Scriptures. According to Rorty, we would now view Bellarmine's criticism as irrational or irrelevant, since it is based on theological rather than on scientific ground. But he then raises the question of what is to constitute scientific ground. Bellarmine thought his criticism was relevant. Was he in conflict even at the time with scientific standards? But many of Bellarmine's contemporaries would have agreed that his criticism was relevant. Rorty then goes on to argue that the standards with which Bellarmine is in conflict are those which have arisen *since* his time, as a result of our accepting Galileo's views:

> Obviously, the conclusion I wish to draw is that the 'grid' which emerged in the later seventeenth and eighteenth centuries was not there to be appealed to in the early seventeenth century, at the time that Galileo was on trial.... The notion of what it was to be 'scientific' was in the process of being formed. If one endorses the values... common to Galileo and Kant, then indeed Bellarmine was being 'unscientific'. But, of course, almost all of us... are happy to endorse them. We are the heirs of three hundred years of rhetoric about the importance of distinguishing sharply between science and religion, science and politics, science and art, science and philosophy, and so on. This rhetoric has formed the culture of Europe. It made us what we are today.
>
> (1990: 330)

The passage may raise a difficulty. If Rorty himself endorses Galilean standards, or post-seventeenth century values, and this is what he implies, then surely he does believe that Bellarmine's criticism was irrelevant, not just now but even at the time. The difficulty disappears once one appreciates what Rorty means by endorsing a view. He means that he is happy to go along with it. Thus when he says that he endorses post-seventeenth century values, he does not mean that he thinks Bellarmine was 'objectively wrong', in the sense of being, even at the time, in conflict with what was true. Indeed that is precisely what he does *not* mean. Nothing is 'objectively wrong' except relative to some standard and there is no further standard by which one can show post-seventeenth century values to be superior to those of Bellarmine. What one can say is that post-seventeenth century values have prevailed and that one is happy to go along with this. That is what Rorty means when he says that he endorses those values.

Nevertheless, certain difficulties remain. According to the values which Rorty endorses one should make a sharp distinction between, say, science and politics or science and art. That is part of the rhetoric which has formed the culture of Europe and has made us what we are today. But Rorty, himself, has been busy undermining that very distinction. Indeed, on the very next page, he tells us that there is no difference in kind between the Galileo–Bellarmine issue and the issue between Kerensky and Lenin or between the Royal Academy and Bloomsbury. Here we have what might be termed the Rorty Dilemma. There is a persistent tendency for his philosophy to undermine his values. For example, his account of how post-seventeenth values have prevailed, which is intended to be neutral, has the effect of making those values seem less persuasive. The reason for this is obvious. Rorty has abolished objective truth except as relative to standards which cannot themselves be objectively true. Now, as it happens, the surest way to persuade a person to accept a belief is to convince him that it is objectively true. He is much less likely to be persuaded to accept a belief by being told that it is the product of three hundred years of rhetoric. Here we have a problem that ought to puzzle Rorty. His view is that since metaphysics is meaningless, one can remove the metaphysical 'foundation' from any set of values whilst leaving the values intact. Unfortunately, whenever he does so he seems to affect the values. One must add immediately that this does puzzle Rorty. He is aware of the difficulties I have raised and makes a detailed attempt to meet them in his third book, *Contingency, Irony and Solidarity* (1989). We shall turn later to what he says.

For the moment, let us complete the argument. We have seen that the future of philosophy lies in adopting the hermeneutic, as distinct from the epistemological, model. The hermeneutic model flourishes where there are no standards for objective truth. Consequently the aim of philosophy will not be to find the truth but rather to *edify*. One edifies when one ceases to confront and starts to participate, when one seeks not to end a conversation but to keep it going, by turning it to a new side or by throwing in a fresh idea. All this, of course, stands in the sharpest contrast with the activities of the traditional philosophers or epistemologists, who treated philosophy as a normal science and whose aim was to find the truth rather than to edify. Rorty's aim, by contrast, is to edify as distinct from finding the truth.

> Here, finally, I come around to the suggestion with which I ended the last section – that the point of edifying philosophy is to keep the conversation going rather than to find objective truth. Such truth, in this view I am advocating, is the normal result of normal discourse.
>
> (1990: 377)

It will be useful to make some comments on the above views. We may begin with Rorty's account of the issue between Galileo and Bellarmine. On Rorty's view, we should now treat Bellarmine's criticism as irrational, because he criticised Galileo not on scientific but on theological ground. In fact, however, Bellarmine referred only to those parts of theology which, in his view, overlapped with science. In his day, it was commonly held that the Scriptures provided an accurate, indeed authoritative, account of the structure and history of the world. In short, it was commonly held that they carried authority at certain points - not just in religion but also in science. Now we may certainly think that Bellarmine was mistaken in criticising Galileo on the basis of the Scriptures. But it is hard to see how he was irrational. For he based his criticism on what was generally held to be scientifically authoritative. His would serve as a paradigm case of warranted assertion. In other words, he based his assertion on the best evidence he knew. It is worth adding, because it is contrary to legend, that Bellarmine did not dismiss Galileo's views as simply false. As Rorty acknowledges, he attempted to reconcile Galileo's views with the Scriptures. Thus, he suggested that those views might be taken not as statements of ultimate truth but as devices for organising and predicting empirical data. Had they been presented in that form, he would have accepted them.

Moreover, we must consider why we no longer accept Bellarmine's standards. According to Rorty, we reject those standards because we have accepted Galileo's. But that does not explain why people came to accept Galileo's in the first place. The obvious reason is that they believed there were inconsistencies, at the relevant points, between Galileo's views and the Scriptures. This meant they had to decide between them, not in order to keep the conversation going, but because they could not both be true. Consequently, so far as they were interested in the truth, they were bound to decide between them. Moreover, that seems to explain why people came to accept Galileo's views. They accepted those views because they believed it was they rather than the Scriptures which, at the relevant points, were nearer the truth. There is nothing in this to suggest that the change from the earlier to the later view consisted in a non-rational switch between entirely incompatible values. This seems, rather, to be an illusion, produced by omitting the details in the change and emphasising only the differences in the values involved.

There is a second point. Rorty, throughout, makes the objectivity of truth depend on the objectivity of standards. Thus there is objective truth only in normal science, because only in normal science are there objective standards. Now standards are objective when they are a matter of common agreement as distinct from individual will. But it seems evident that objective truth is not a matter of common agreement. The mark of an objective truth is that it would be true *whether or not people agreed with it*. Thus the primitive feeling of objective truth is the feeling that goes with 'This is not my invention'. I feel that nothing can explain my belief which does not include the occurrence of what is believed. The feeling, in short, is that one is related not to common agreement but to the *world*. Often enough, for example, one has a belief, perhaps about the past, one could never prove to the satisfaction of other people. Nevertheless, one may be certain, beyond all doubt, that the belief is objectively true. It is idle, incidentally, to say that this is just a feeling. Suppose it is 'just' a feeling. Still it is one that is unintelligible without the notion of objective truth and the point is that this cannot be explained as conformity to common agreement.

In Rorty's account, by contrast, there is nothing to make a belief objectively true *except* its conformity to common agreement. This has several consequences. First, one cannot ask of standards which are objective, in the sense of commonly agreed, whether they are themselves objectively true. On reflection, this is not just false, but plainly so. For example, as we have just seen, the Scriptures served for many generations as a standard of truth, not simply in religion, but also in other matters. Their authority was doubted, however, when people began to discover that they contained inconsistencies. That is because those people began to doubt whether the scriptures were themselves objectively true. But Rorty's point is made to seem initially plausible, because he has tacitly defined objective truth in terms of common agreement. Second, objective truth can never play a part in explaining the change from one standard to another. That is because truth is irrelevant *before* one adopts the new standard and becomes relevant *afterwards* only because the standard now determines what is true. Third, Rorty is enabled to attribute objective truth to any subject or activity which exhibits a sufficient degree of agreement. For example, if an artistic fashion becomes sufficiently entrenched, whatever conforms to it becomes objectively true. By contrast, a scientific issue ceases to be a matter of objective truth the moment there is a lack of agreement about how to settle it. It will be useful to elaborate the implausibility of this view. It is amongst trivial whims and likings that one can most easily find human agreement. Thus the human species is united in being averse to eating mud or excrement. Other species are not so fussy. It seems absurd, nevertheless, to take this agreement in human reaction as signifying an entirely objective property in mud or excrement. By contrast, there are many issues of objective fact where it is impossible to secure agreement, even in principle. Very often, for example, we have no idea how to settle our disagreement over whether another person was in pain or was simply feigning. It seems absurd, nevertheless, to hold that it is an entirely subjective matter whether another person is in pain.

None of this implies that there is no connection at all between agreement and objective truth. Thus if we differ in whims or likings, there is usually little I can do about it. By contrast, if my belief is objectively true, it is no peculiarity of mine and I may therefore hope that you also will be convinced of its truth. But that in itself shows that the two are not the same. It is because my belief is objectively true, which is one thing, that I hope to secure agreement, which is another. Moreover, although there are circumstances where my belief's being objectively true will give me an advantage in securing agreement, there are innumerable other circumstances where it will give me no advantage at all. There will be many where it puts me at a disadvantage. For example, my belief's being objectively true is precisely what you might fear, in which case the more persuasive my arguments, the less you will be inclined to listen to them. Moreover, we must remember that reasoning in any subject rests on fundamental judgements which are not themselves acquired by reasoning but only by training and experience. Now it often happens that those who are interested in a subject are more numerous than those who have acquired the necessary training or experience. That is why, as Socrates pointed out, a doctor may be less persuasive than a sophist on the subject of medicine. In short, it is often easier to secure agreement than to establish the truth. For in order to secure agreement, you have only to say what people are inclined to believe, whereas to establish the truth you may have to tell them that they are wrong, which is not conducive to agreement.

CONTINGENCY AND VALUE

I have said that Rorty is aware of some of these difficulties and that he makes an attempt to resolve them in his third book, *Contingency, Irony and Solidarity* (1989). It will therefore be useful to look in some detail at this book in order to see how he does so.

As we have just seen, Rorty treats as illusory the idea that there is an objective truth which is not relative to some set of standards. The distinction, he says, is a metaphysical one. Sometimes in this connection he speaks of 'a difference which *makes* no difference'. By this he means one that has no practical consequences, existing only in the minds of the metaphysicians. As such, the difference is illusory. The trouble is that some of these differences do seem to make a difference. For example, not simply in science but also in morals, some people feel that we do need the notion of objective truth. They are dissatisfied with the idea that our values have nothing behind them but the play of chance and blind causation, feeling that this idea does make a difference, not simply in philosophy but also in practice. It is this problem that Rorty deals with in his book. Taking as an example his own values, which are liberal ones, he explores their relation to his philosophy.

He begins by giving a sketch of his philosophy, with which for the most part we are now familiar. It is worth noting, however, that in this book Rorty places himself even more conspicuously in that line of development, beginning with Comte, which we traced when we were discussing Dewey. He informs us, for example, that we Westerners have passed through a religious phase and are now coming to the end of a metaphysical one. He is anxious to emphasise, along with Dewey and Nietzsche, that the metaphysical phase includes some versions of Positivism – for many Positivists treated science in metaphysical or even quasi-religious terms. Thus they retained the idea that the world has an intelligible structure which science represents in ever increasing detail. In fact, the world has no intelligible structure. All is flux; all meaning is temporary, arising from our own activities, which are themselves the product of chance or the play of circumstance. On this point, however, Rorty is somewhat inconsistent, combining a determinist view with a voluntarist one. Thus he affirms, on the one hand, that our activities are the product of chance or blind causation and, on the other, that it is we who make our values. For example, there is no tendency to solidarity in human nature; indeed Rorty denies that human beings have a common nature. Nevertheless, he exhorts us to create that solidarity.

The point for the moment, however, is that we are emerging from the metaphysical phase. Rorty takes the French Revolution as the symbol of this emergence. This was the time when people realised that social and political institutions are not inherent in the nature of things but can be replaced almost overnight. This idea has its parallel in the artistic field, where it became recognised that the aim of art is not to represent or imitate; rather it is what Rorty calls 'the artist's self-creation'. The idea that the artist has the power to create himself appears frequently in Rorty's book. But it is a very puzzling one. The idea seems to be that since human beings have no metaphysical nature, they are free to make of themselves what they wish, and are enabled to do so by the power of language and of art in general. But in order to make themselves what they wish, human beings would need to be free, not simply of all metaphysical constraints, but also of all natural ones. The tension is here acute between Rorty's determinist and voluntarist views. We become free through seeing that we are submerged in the flux of things.

The general idea, however, is clear. Freeing ourselves from

metaphysical notions, we see ourselves not as representers or imitators but as creators. This idea has extended itself even into science. For we now see that the aim in science is not to *find* but to *make* the truth. Truth, as Rorty puts it, is not 'out there'. He explains himself as follows:

> We need to make a distinction between the claim that the world is out there and the claim that truth is out there. To say that the world is out there, that it is not our creation, is to say, with common sense, that most things in space and time are the effect of causes which do not include human mental states. To say that truth is not out there is simply to say that where there are no sentences there is no truth, that sentences are elements of human languages, and that human languages are human creations.

(Rorty 1989: 5)

We have already noted Rorty's tendency to present alternatives as if they exhausted all the ones available. In the present case, if we do not hold that truth is a feature of the physical world, quite independent of the human mind, we are obliged to hold that it is a feature of the sentence we have ourselves created. But why should we not hold that it consists in a relation between the two? If 'truth' is being applied both to a sentence and its object, as distinct from the object alone, then obviously it cannot be independent of the sentence. But, by the same token, it cannot apply to the sentence alone. As we have said, language enables us, for any given sentence, to create its contradictory by a simple act of negation. The trouble is that we do not know which is true and language will not enable us to settle the matter. For we can settle it by reference to other sentences only if we know which of them are true and then the same problem arises.

Rorty now summarises the tendencies he has been discussing:

> I can sum up by redescribing what, in my view, the revolutionaries and poets of two centuries ago were getting at. What was glimpsed at the end of the eighteenth century was that anything could be made to look good or bad, important or unimportant, useful or useless, by being redescribed. What Hegel describes as the process of spirit gradually becoming conscious of its intrinsic nature is better described as the process of European linguistic practices changing at a faster and faster rate. The phenomenon Hegel describes is that of more people offering more radical redescriptions of more things than ever before, of young people going through half a dozen spiritual gestalt-switches before reaching adulthood. What the

Romantics expressed as the claim that imagination, rather than reason, is the central human faculty was the realisation that a talent for speaking differently, rather than for arguing well, is the chief instrument of cultural change. What political utopians since the French Revolution have sensed is not that an enduring, substantial human nature has been suppressed or repressed by 'unnatural' or 'irrational' social institutions but rather that changing languages and other social practices may produce human beings of a sort that had never before existed. The German idealists, the French revolutionaries and the Romantic poets had in common a dim sense that human beings whose language changed so that they no longer spoke of themselves as responsible to nonhuman powers would thereby become a new kind of human beings.

(1989: 7)

Now at this point, as Rorty recognises, there may arise a certain question. The view of the world, which is involved in these tendencies, is it in fact true? For example, the view that human beings have no enduring nature seems itself advanced as a general truth about human beings. But is it in fact a truth? Again, is it true that a talent for speaking differently is the chief instrument of cultural change or that through a change of language we may become a new kind of human beings? To some, these views may seem a species of Romantic delusion.

These questions, however, are beside the point, for they reflect the *old way of thinking*, the very way of thinking which has been redescribed or revolutionarised. Rorty acknowledges there is a difficulty in how this is to be put:

The difficulty faced by a philosopher...who thinks of himself as auxiliary to the poet rather than to the physicist...is to avoid hinting that this suggestion gets something right, that my sort of philosophy corresponds to the way things really are.

(1989: 8)

There is a temptation, in short, to fall back on outmoded forms of philosophical thought. But this temptation is to be resisted, for what is before us is a new method of philosophy, which addresses itself not to what is true but to how we should talk. Rorty explains it as follows:

The method is to redescribe lots and lots of things in new ways, until you have created a pattern of linguistic behaviour which will tempt the rising generation to adopt it, thereby causing them to look for appropriate new forms of non-linguistic behaviour, for example, the adoption of new scientific equipment or new social institutions. This sort of philosophy...works holistically and pragmatically. It says things like 'try thinking of it this way' – or more specifically, 'try to ignore the apparently futile traditional questions by substituting the following new and possibly interesting questions'. It does not pretend to have a better candidate for doing the same old things which we did when we spoke in the old way. Rather, it suggests that we might want to stop doing those things and do something else. But it does not argue for this suggestion on the basis of antecedent criteria common to the old and the new language games. For in so far as the new language really is new, there will be no such criteria.

(ibid.: 9)

But now we approach the central problem. What is the relation of philosophy, thus conceived, to Rorty's own values which, as we have said, are liberal ones? He defines a liberal as one who believes that cruelty is the worst thing one can do. It is evident, however, that he also values democratic processes, regular elections, rights before the law, a free press, and so on. Now there are other, opposing, values. Fascism is an obvious example. In any dispute between a fascist and a liberal there can be no appeal to independent standards. Liberal values are defined by liberal standards; fascist values are defined by fascist ones. These standards are incommensurable. Consequently, any dispute between a fascist and a liberal can proceed only by redescription. Each party redescribes his opponent's position, with the aim of winning him over to his own side. Now suppose the fascist wins. Rorty is converted. From his present point of view he would regret this; but he would no longer have his present point of view and presumably would be glad that he had changed. Is there nothing more to be said?

We may take another example. In his second chapter, Rorty illustrates artistic self-creation by reference to Nietzsche's distinction between the will to truth and the will to self-overcoming. The difference between the two is that the former treats redemption as making contact with something larger and more enduring than oneself, whereas the latter treats it as recreating oneself by one's own power. Thus the genius has the power to provide a narrative of his past in terms which the past itself never knew. He has thereby mastered his past by recreating it in language. In Nietzsche's terms, he has recreated all 'it was' into a 'thus I willed it'.

But suppose I provide a different narrative of Nietzsche's life and conclude 'Thus he did not will it.' Has he or has he not achieved redemption? Which is the better or the more correct narrative? Or rather, what do these words mean? Presumably, which is 'the better' or 'the more correct' narrative will depend on which is the more persuasive. But which is the more persuasive, like everything else, will depend on contingent circumstances. Alter the circumstances, perhaps only slightly, and what was persuasive becomes unpersuasive, it being what was unpersuasive which now persuades. In short, according to the flux of circumstance, good becomes evil and evil becomes good. At this point, everything begins to shimmer and we lose our sense of good and evil. This occurs, of course, only if we accept Rorty's philosophy. But then Rorty's philosophy, it seems, does affect our values. Indeed it seems to dissolve them.

Now it is evident, not only that Rorty is aware of these difficulties, but also that they worry him for, in responding to them, he shifts his ground, occupying a number of positions, not all of which are consistent with one another. It will be useful to put these responses in some order, ending with the one which seems to represent his final position.

He argues, first, that scepticism about value arises only if we expect our values to correspond to something independent of them. But since this idea is illusory, is devoid of substance, there is nothing to be sceptical about. The trouble with this argument is that it is liable to turn against him. Since people do feel sceptical when told that their values correspond to nothing independent of them, they may conclude that the idea does have some substance to it.

He argues, second, that if people were to accept that their values have no metaphysical foundation, this would have no effect on their practice. As evidence for this, he refers to earlier predictions about religious values. It was often claimed, for example, that values would be affected if people ceased to believe in God. These predictions, he claims, have not been confirmed. But in claiming this he seems to place himself in a difficult position. For unlike the older Positivists, he himself seems anxious to confirm many of those predictions. For example, his views serve to confirm that when people lose their belief in God, they cease eventually to believe in absolute value and even in objective truth. He claims, it is true, that these changes do not matter, but one may be certain that people in earlier times would have taken this as an additional confirmation of their predictions.

He argues, third, very plausibly, that people do not arrive at their values through philosophical reasoning. It is not on the basis of philosophy that one comes to love truth or to hate cruelty. He then implies that since people do not base their values on a philosophical foundation, they cannot be worried when they hear that no such foundation exists. This argument, however, is plainly fallacious. When they hear that there is no such foundation, they may for the first time think about the matter. As Dewey pointed out, it is only in the course of their activities, not at the beginning, that people reflect on the foundations of what they believe or do. Earlier, they did not feel the lack of such a foundation but that was because, not having thought about the matter, they could not feel the need. It does not follow, now that they do think about the matter, that they cannot feel the need for such a foundation and in consequence regret that it does not exist.

Finally, we come to what seems to be Rorty's settled position. This is stated most conveniently in his fourth chapter, which is entitled 'Private Irony and Liberal Hope'. He begins the chapter by defining what he calls a final vocabulary. This is the vocabulary in which one formulates one's fundamental values. This is final because there is no appeal beyond it. He then introduces the notion of an 'ironist':

> I shall define an 'ironist' as someone who fulfils three conditions: (1) She has radical and continuing doubts about the final vocabulary she currently uses, because she has been impressed by other vocabularies...; (2) she realises that argument phrased in her present vocabulary can neither underwrite nor dissolve those doubts; (3) insofar as she philosophises about her situation, she does not think that her vocabulary is closer to reality than others, that it is in touch with a power not herself.
>
> (1989: 73)

Rorty says of such people that they are 'never quite able to take themselves seriously because they are always aware that the terms in which they describe themselves are subject to change, always aware of the contingency and fragility of their final vocabularies, and thus of their selves' (ibid.).

Now this response, we may note, is quite different from the first one we mentioned, since Rorty here acknowledges that his philosophy will make a person somewhat sceptical not only about other values but also about his own. One may find this hardly consistent with his overall position. If metaphysical foundations are entirely unsubstantial how can their absence induce, in the clear sighted, even a momentary scepticism? This, however, appears to be the case. As Rorty makes clear, it is only the ordinary unthinking person who in these matters is confident; the clear sighted are sceptical or, as he puts it, ironic. This being Rorty's position, how does he cope with it?

He does so by a division between spheres. Liberalism is a doctrine of the public sphere, to which philosophy is irrelevant. The liberal *qua* liberal neither has nor requires a philosophy. So far as he has a use for philosophy, it will be in the private sphere. In this sphere, protected by the liberal state, the individual can experiment with different perspectives, in a play of philosophical redescription, thereby recreating himself in the pursuit of self-mastery or private perfection. In short, he is a philosopher in private and a liberal in public.

There are several difficulties in this view. For example, the liberal is the same man in both spheres and one of the things he will be ironic about in private is precisely his liberalism. However he acts in public, he cannot avoid whilst in private from being ironic about his public values. The difficulty is to see how he can leave his irony behind when he passes through his front door. How, in short, can he prevent his private thought from affecting his public actions? Those who are committed to their values do not view them somewhat at a distance and in an ironic light; they feel, rather, that these values are part of their very being. Rorty's liberal, by contrast, is a person essentially divided, having to suppress in public what he thinks in private. Such suppression can work, but only at the cost of persistent effort. This means that a liberal who accepts Rorty's philosophy is to that extent put at a disadvantage.

Now Rorty says remarkably little about how this disadvantage is to be overcome. What are the countervailing motives which may prompt the ironic liberal into committed action? Rorty mentions only the inspirational power of literature. The liberal, he argues, may derive from literature the sustenance that he cannot find in philosophy:

So our doubts about our own characters or our own culture can be resolved or assuaged only by enlarging our acquaintance. The easiest way of doing that is to read books, and so ironists spend more of their time placing books than in placing real live people. Ironists are afraid that they will get stuck in the vocabulary in which they were brought up if they only know the people in their own neighbourhood, so they try to get acquainted with strange people (Alcibiades, Julian Sorel), strange families (the Karamazovs, the Casaubons), and strange communities (the Teutonic Knights, the Nuer, the Mandarins of the Sung).

(1989: 80)

Similarly, he claims that liberal energies may be stimulated by the imaginative insight into the sufferings of others that literature provides. It is difficult to find these suggestions impressive. Rorty seems evidently to be working against the main line of causation. Someone, in real life, who enters into the sufferings of others may thereby be enabled, easily enough, to do so in literature, but someone who enters into the sufferings of others in literature is not thereby so easily enabled to do so in life. For example, those who enter into real suffering feel committed to do something about it. But those who do so in literature have only to *imagine* they would do something about it. That is why literary sympathy so easily evaporates when the reader puts down his book. This is not to deny that literature can have an effect on life; but the effect normally takes the form of reinforcing already existing tendencies. In other words, the main line of causation runs from society to literature rather than the other way around. The quality of a literature depends on the quality of the surrounding culture, there being no example in history of a society, otherwise rotten, which has been transformed by the quality of its literature.

Moreover, the problem of what is to motivate the liberal ironist becomes especially acute when one considers the difficulties that confront him. As we have seen, Rorty believes that there is no common human nature and therefore no inherent tendency amongst human beings towards solidarity. Nevertheless, it is the task of the liberal to *create* that solidarity. But how is this to be done and what is to motivate the liberal in making the effort? A little reflection on the circumstances in which solidarity arises will reveal that it is inextricably intertwined, on innumerable occasions, with cruelty and hate. That is because nothing is more calculated to bring people together than their finding that they have a common enemy. Hatred for the other side is a fruitful source of solidarity amongst ourselves. Now Rorty would see it as our task to extend the solidarity we have amongst ourselves so that it includes the people on the other side. But how am I to do this, when my extending my sympathy to the other side will be seen by my fellows as an act of treachery tending to weaken the solidarity we have amongst ourselves? Someone in those circumstances who nevertheless extended his sympathy would require a degree of dedication and courage hardly to be fostered by an ironic attitude to human values.

Moreover, the problem is as acute in the private as in the public sphere. Indeed Rorty's view that a human being in this sphere may recreate himself seems to ignore the very nature of good and evil. For example, if I recognise in myself a moral deficiency, I recognise a deficiency in *myself*. This may be contrasted with my recognising a deficiency I have in some skill or accomplishment. Suppose, to take a trivial example, that I recognise my swing in golf is in some way deficient. Still, if I change my stance and keep practising I can reasonably hope to overcome it. That presupposes, of course, that I want to do so, that I approach my task with undivided will. Now if I recognise in myself a moral deficiency, precisely what I recognise is that my will is not undivided. For example, suppose that I recognise in myself certain malicious tendencies. It is not that although I do not want to hurt other people, I find through some deficiency that I often happen to do so. What I recognise is that I *do* want to hurt other people. It is not that I am a human being with a deficiency; I am a deficient human being.

Now, it is by no means clear what is meant by the ability to recreate oneself but it suggests an ability to be found only amongst those whose faults are so incidental to themselves that they stand on the very verge of perfection. In that case, however, what Rorty says is of no use to the rest of us; the problem for the rest of us is how to get into that condition.

It is evident that Rorty's philosophy does nothing to foster and much to hinder the liberal in his values. Moreover, the effect will be the same whatever one's values, so long as one accepts Rorty's philosophy. In other words, Rorty's philosophy is not fruitful, productive of good consequences. It fails the Pragmatic test. It is idle to say that all the same it may be true. For Rorty's philosophy stands or falls precisely by that test, there being no 'truth' which is outside the play of consequences. In short, Rorty's philosophy is not true, even when judged by his own standards.

Chapter 13

Rorty: the history of philosophy

For our purpose, the interest in Rorty's work lies in its representative quality. It is an expression of those Positivist views which have been dominant in Western philosophy for the better part of two centuries and which, in the hands of their successors, have transformed the work of Peirce and James. It has the merit of taking those views to what some will consider their logical conclusion. In this chapter, we must consider some remaining elements in these views and then assess their impact on Pragmatism.

Amongst the most distinctive elements in Positivism is its view of philosophy. As we have seen, it holds that philosophy, as traditionally conceived, rests on basic confusions and, with regard to modern philosophy, it usually finds the source of these confusions in philosophers of the seventeenth century, such as Descartes and Locke. Usually, also, its view of philosophy is *historicist*. In other words, it denies that the problems of philosophy are independent of time and place, reflecting permanent features of the human condition. Human beings under different conditions exhibit very different features and the problems of philosophy vary according to those conditions.

All these elements are present in the first section of Rorty's *Philosophy and the Mirror of Nature* (1990). Thus his view is historicist. The problems of modern philosophy are radically distinct from those of any previous era. They have their source in a confused doctrine of ideas introduced by Descartes, that doctrine being based on an unprecedented distinction between mind and body. Rorty holds, indeed, that the distinction between the mental and the physical is wholly the product of philosophy, there being no natural or intuitive difference between the two.

This last view is not entirely plausible. For example, students in philosophy grasp the distinction between the mental and the physical without having first to consider the views of any particular philosopher.

It may be said that this is because they have been introduced to the distinction by their teacher. But that applies to every distinction. Every distinction has to be introduced by some kind of teacher. What makes a distinction natural, one would have thought, is that people, having been introduced to it on the basis of some examples, go on and supply others, working independently and yet in agreement with one another. In that respect, the distinction between the mental and the physical seems to be as natural as any other. In my experience, it is only those who doubt the distinction who need first to have read the views of some particular philosopher. In this, there is a parallel with the distinction between the analytic and the synthetic or the conceptual and the factual. This distinction also is supposed to be the product of false philosophical theorising. Yet here again, it is only those who doubt it who need to have absorbed some philosophical theory. In my experience, for example, the only people who doubt it are those who have first read Quine or one of his followers.

There is undoubtedly some truth, however, in Rorty's other views. For example, the doctrine of ideas, especially as employed by Locke, seems to contain a serious confusion. Thus, at least on some occasions, Locke treats sensory experience, or an idea in the mind, as though it were itself the object of perception, from which we infer the existence of objects external to us. It follows that objects external to us are never themselves directly perceived. As Reid pointed out, if 'ideas' stands for sensory experiences, they are not *what* we perceive but that *whereby* we perceive other things. We must note, however, that this seems to have been a confusion into which Locke fell, rather than a doctrine which he specifically advanced. It requires very little charity to suppose that Locke intended the word 'idea' as a device for referring to the powers of the mind and would have been bemused to discover that he had advanced a theory about the nature of those powers. The confusion, all the same, remains serious. The question for our purpose, however, is whether it is sufficiently serious to justify our drawing a line across philosophy, characterising what falls on one side of the line as radically different from what falls on the other. It will be necessary to consider the matter in some detail.

According to Rorty, the doctrine of ideas rests on Descartes' unprecedented distinction between mind and body. Now a distinction between mind and body may be found at almost any point in the history of philosophy. Rorty's view, however, is that Descartes drew the distinction in such a way that he made knowledge of the world seem problematic. This occurred because he attributed sensory activity to the mind rather than to the body. Moreover, it is this which makes his distinction so different from any drawn previously. As evidence for this, Rorty quotes Wallace Matson. According to Matson (1966), the Greeks attributed sensory activity to the body rather than to the mind. Indeed, according to Matson, the Greeks had no word for 'sensation', where it signifies a process in the mind rather than in the body. That is why they had no mind-body problem. I take him to mean that the Greeks could have no problem about how the mind knows physical objects because they are known through sensory activity and for the Greeks this is not a process distinct from the physical but itself a physical process.

We may note that Matson is all-encompassing in his use of 'the Greeks'. The impression he conveys is that in these matters every Greek thinker held the same view as every other. In fact, he seems principally to be thinking of Aristotle, a particular Greek thinker who on many topics held views strikingly different from those of other Greek thinkers. What is true is that when Aristotle discusses sensation, it is sometimes difficult to know whether or not he is referring simply to the physiological processes involved in the exercise of the sense organs. But, as a matter of fact, the same is true of both Descartes and Locke. Rorty (1990: 145) quotes a passage from Reid which makes exactly that point. What is certainly not true is that Aristotle attributed sensory knowledge simply to the body, though he held, as do most thinkers, that bodily activities are involved in obtaining that knowledge. Indeed that is precisely why in these matters it is so difficult to keep bodily and mental processes apart.

It will be useful, if only briefly, to consider Aristotle's account of sensory knowledge. He distinguished three levels in the soul: the vegetative, the sensitive and the intellectual. These distinctions became traditional, being adopted by Aquinas and the Scholastics. At none of these levels can the workings of the soul be explained in purely bodily terms. Rather, bodily activities require the soul, and specifically the vegetative level, for their workings. *A fortiori*, the sensitive level cannot be explained in bodily terms, for it is on a level above that of the vegetative. It is here that one finds the source of sensory knowledge. The sense organs, in their exercise, leave behind a residue in the form of a phantasm or image. This image is a representation of the object perceived. But it is a particular image of a particular object. In other words, it does not possess the generality of conceptual knowledge. This is obtained by the intellect, through a process of abstraction. This process is somewhat complicated and can hardly be made intelligible without taking into account Aristotle's realist view of the forms or universals. Unlike Plato, Aristotle held that the forms or universals are entirely inherent in objects. Consequently, the intellect can obtain conceptual knowledge by taking the form of the object represented by the phantasm or image. It is important to note, however, that this is possible only because there is an aspect of the physical object which is not physical. Aristotle's account depends directly on the metaphysical view that objects are impregnated with thought or with intelligible forms which are already akin to the human mind and which the human mind can therefore assume.

It is possible that the modern reader will find this metaphysical view obscure or unconvincing and may wish to remove it from Aristotle's overall account. In which case, he will find himself with an account which is indistinguishable from Locke's. The exercise of the sense organs gives rise to images in the mind, from which the intellect by a process of abstraction obtains its concepts. Indeed there is nothing in Locke which is not already contained in Aristotle. The difference is that Aristotle's account depends also on the metaphysical view we have mentioned. That difference is real enough. But it is difficult to believe that the modern reader, who considers the two accounts, will not find the resemblances between them at least as striking as the differences.

Moreover, Matson's views rest on a false assumption. The assumption is that 'the Greeks' raised no problems about the relation between mind and matter. One may find these problems in any number of Greek philosophers. For example, in *De Anima*, Aristotle discusses the problem of whether the soul is so intimately related to the body that it cannot survive its destruction. He concludes that it is intimately related only at the vegetative and sensitive levels. It is not so related at the intellectual and may therefore survive the destruction of the body. The same problem is central to the whole of Plato's *Phaedo*. Indeed, in that dialogue, problems about mind and body are considered from a number of different angles. For example, the dialogue contains one of the most celebrated discussions of the relation between causes and reasons. Socrates argues that the explanation for his remaining in prison cannot be given simply in terms of physical causes but only at a level above the physiological, by referring to his reasons for remaining there.

It is important to note that in these various discussions one may discern a variety of positions. In short, there is no view on these matters which can be attributed to 'the Greeks'. Different Greeks held different views. Plato, for example, is usually taken to be defending an extreme dualism, in which soul and body consist of distinct substances. Over and against this position, one may place the views of the materialists.

Democritus, for example, argued that perception can be explained as an influx of atoms passing from one object to another. It seems evident that Aristotle was attempting to hold a position midway between these extremes. His view is similar to the so-called double aspect theory. In other words, he held that soul and body differ not as distinct substances but as different aspects of the one person. Thus he insists that the soul is not lodged in the body as, say, a pilot is lodged in his vessel.

We may note a further point. It is not simply that Greek philosophers, in those matters, held a variety of views; the views they held seem to be exhaustive of the field. Thus in the many discussions of these matters that occur in modern philosophy, it would be difficult to find a single view that could not be construed as a variation on one of the views held some two thousand years ago by those Greek philosophers.

The Rorty–Matson view contains a further assumption. This is the assumption that the Greeks, having no mind–body problem, were unacquainted with sceptical problems about how the mind can know the world. Now, as we have said, problems about knowledge were rife in Greek philosophy and there was a whole school, usually called the Sceptics, who explicitly advanced various versions of extreme scepticism. Rorty argues, however, that this scepticism is radically different from the modern kind, which is wholly attributable to the influence of Descartes. This presupposes that Descartes' work constitutes a sharp break with that of his predecessors, such as that of the medieval philosophers, raising problems which to them would not have seemed problems at all. As Rorty puts the point:

> When Cartesianism burst upon a startled world in the seventeenth century, it was not because a new view was being offered about long-debated questions concerning the relation between theory and evidence. It was rather because questions were being taken seriously which ... the scholastics had been too sensible to ask.
>
> (Rorty 1989:222)

It will be useful to consider a directly opposed view. In *The History of Scepticism from Erasmus to Descartes* (1960), Richard Popkin argues that a commonly accepted view of Descartes is mistaken. This is the view which sees him 'as the scientific enemy of scholasticism and orthodoxy'. Popkin wishes to replace this view with:

> a more conservative interpretation of Descartes as a man who tried to reinstate the medieval outlook in the face of Renaissance novelty,

and a thinker who sought to discover a philosophy adequate for the Christian world in the light of the scientific revolution of the 17th Century.

(ibid.: 174)

In support of this, Popkin considers in some detail the background to Descartes' work. One of its most striking features is the prevalence of scepticism. The cause of this lay in the bitter disputes between the Catholics and the Protestants. The parties differed not simply in their particular views but also in what they took to be authoritative. The Catholics took the church as their authority; the Protestants took the Scriptures. But there was no further authority by which it could be determined which of these authorities was the superior. Here we have a problem that was central in Greek scepticism. The Greek sceptics argued that knowledge is impossible, since in order to know the world, one needs some criterion; but it is impossible to know which criterion is correct unless one already has knowledge of the world. Moreover, arguments of this form served to increase the current scepticism. For the arguments of the Greek sceptics had been widely circulated and were well known. Popkin sees Descartes' work as a response to this situation. In other words, so far from giving rise to scepticism hitherto unknown, it was an attempt to cope with a scepticism already prevalent. Moreover, this was not a scepticism distinct from that of the Greeks but, rather, was one and the same scepticism.

As evidence for Popkin's view, one can show that the sceptical arguments which appear in Descartes were familiar not simply at the time of the Greeks but also at many other times. We can illustrate the point by reference to the Islamic philosopher Al Ghazali, who was born in 1058. In his autobiography (see Montgomery Watt 1963: 47–9), he describes the scepticism he passed through as a result of his philosophical studies. It began when he reflected that men become Jews, Christians or Muslims through the influence of their parents and teachers. He then wondered how beliefs acquired in this way could themselves be tested for truth.

I said to myself, I am seeking knowledge of what things really are, so I must know what knowledge is. I saw that certain knowledge must exclude all doubt and the possibility of error, indeed even the supposition of this....

When I examined my knowledge, I found that none of it was certain except matters of sense-perception and necessary truths. It further occurred to me, however, that my present trust in sense-perception and necessary truths was perhaps no better founded than my previous truths.

(ibid.)

Ghazali then proceeds to supply arguments, of a familiar kind, to show that the senses are fallible. For example, the senses in themselves would suggest that the sun is the size of a coin, but astronomical proofs show that it is larger than the earth.

I said to myself, 'Since my trust in sense-perception has proved vain, perhaps all that is to be relied on are rational propositions and first principles such as that ten is more than three.... Then sense-perception said, 'Do you not expect that your trust in rational propositions will fare like your trust in sense-perceptions? You used to trust in me, but Judge Reason came and showed I was false. Perhaps beyond rational apprehension there will be another judge; when he appears he will show that reason is false. The fact that this supra-rational apprehension has not appeared yet, does not show that it is impossible.'

(ibid.)

It will be noted that the supra-rational judge is the counterpart in Ghazali's philosophy of the malignant demon in Descartes'. Ghazali proceeds as follows:

While my self was hesitating about the reply to this, sense-perception increased its difficulties by a reference to dreams, and said, 'In dreams you imagine things, and you believe they are real and genuine so long as you are in the dream-state; but when you wake, you know that what you have been imagining has no basis in reality. How are you sure of the real existence of all that you believe in your waking state through sense or reason? It is true in relation to your present state; but another state may come upon you whose relation to your present waking state is like the relation of that state to the dream state....

When these thoughts occurred to me, I tried to find a remedy for them, but it was not easy. They could not be disproved, for a proof has to be based on first principles, and here it was the truth of first principles that was in question. The illness proved a difficult one. It lasted almost two months. During this time I was a sceptic in fact, though not in outward expression.

(Montgomery Watt 1963)

It will be noted that Ghazali's investigation is identical with Descartes', not simply in the overall structure but also in the arguments used and even in some of the examples used to illustrate them. Someone who encountered these passages, without knowing their context, would surely assume that they were copied from Descartes. In fact they were written some five hundred years before Descartes was born. Nor, so far as I am aware, is there any evidence that Descartes copied Ghazali. It seems that people who live in different times and places may nevertheless have similar thoughts.[1]

In any case, there can be little difficulty in explaining why Descartes and Ghazali use the same arguments since they are drawn from the stock of sceptical arguments found in Greek philosophy. The point could be illustrated in copious detail, but it will suffice to be brief. We may take as an example the argument from dreaming. Ghazali's use of the argument seems to be based on a passage in the so-called fourth mode of Sextus Empiricus.

> When we are awake, we view things differently from the way we do when asleep, and when asleep differently from the way we do when awake; so the existence or non-existence of the objects becomes not absolute but relative – relative to being asleep or awake.
>
> (Annas and Barnes 1985: 79)

There is also a celebrated, though somewhat different, use of the argument in Plato's *Theaetetus*. Sceptical arguments based on the fallibility of the senses are innumerable. To take an argument at random, Sextus points out that paintings seem, to the sight, to have recesses and projections, but not to the touch. So the senses are in conflict. We may note that the image of the mirror, so far from being a prerogative of the moderns, appears very frequently amongst the Greek philosophers. For example, in his first mode, Sextus argues that the way external objects appear to ourselves cannot be the way they appear to the animals since the animals are constructed differently from ourselves. The effect must therefore be like that of reflections in different mirrors, which vary not according to the nature of the external object but according to the way mirrors are constructed. Thus one and the same object will appear minute in a concave mirror and elongated in a convex one. Indeed the image of the mirror appears in the New Testament. In a celebrated passage, St Paul says that we know reality only indirectly and in part, so that we view it as through its puzzling reflections in a mirror.

A close study of the evidence suggests that the history of philosophy advanced by Rorty is almost entirely mythical. Thus Descartes was not introducing startling novelties but rather continuing an argument that has proceeded throughout the centuries. What is striking, indeed, is how often these problems appear, how relatively impervious they are to changing circumstances. The most likely explanation seems to be that they reflect permanent features in the human condition.

We may illustrate the point further if we consider the second main feature of Rorty's views, which is their Anti-Realism. As we have seen, the Greek sceptics raised the so-called problem of the criterion. To know the world, we need a criterion; but to find the right criterion we need to know the world. One way to avoid this problem is to treat criteria as not representational. In other words, they do not correspond to the world and cannot themselves be true or false. Rather, truth or falsity is relative to such criteria. Moreover, this is a view which was adopted by some Greek philosophers, namely, the Sophists. Thus Protagoras's maxim 'man is the measure of all things' is plausibly interpreted to mean that truth and falsity are relative to the criteria of human practices. It may be argued that the problem of the criterion still arises, since the criteria of human practices are often in conflict. So how does one know which are the superior ones? The answer is that this will be determined by which criteria prevail and those will prevail which are most persuasively presented. That is why the Sophists specialised in teaching the art of persuasion. That art is a device for securing agreement, and agreement at this level is the only substitute for objective truth. Now this view, already contained in Greek philosophy, is precisely Rorty's.

Let us consider what is fallacious about the sceptical problem. For Rorty, it lies in the view that criteria are intended to reflect an independent world. But the real fallacy is in the view that one cannot know the world unless one has a criterion. It is easy to show that this view is incoherent. Thus one cannot exercise a criterion unless one can recognise a situation which satisfies it. But how can one recognise this? Either one can do so without needing a criterion or one needs a further criterion to recognise when one is satisfied. But the latter assumption leads to an infinite regress. Consequently, it cannot be true that one needs a criterion to know the world, for such knowledge is already presupposed in the very exercise of a criterion.

The above argument is taken from the philosophy of the later Wittgenstein. The point is of some significance, since Rorty makes use of that philosophy in defending his own views. Indeed he takes Wittgenstein, along with Dewey and Heidegger, to be one of the three greatest philosophers of the century. It will be useful to consider why he thinks so, for this will provide further evidence of how he interprets the history of philosophy and will throw further light on his own central views.

According to Rorty, Wittgenstein is one of the three most important philosophers of the century because he has shown how to move from a view of language as representation to a non-representationalist view of language. Thus, in the *Tractatus*, he treated language as the medium by which we represent the world. Language, thus construed as a medium, comes between ourselves and the world, which lies, as it were, on the other side of language. It is the merit of the later work, however, to show the confusion in this idea. Thus in the *Investigations* language is treated not as a means of representing the world but as a means of coping with it. We are to ask of a word not what it stands for but how it is used. The analogy here is with a tool rather than with a medium. The meaning of a word, as of a tool, depends on its use or function rather than on what it represents.

Now we must begin by noting that Wittgenstein nowhere denies that we represent the world in our use of language. Indeed that we do so is the whole presupposition of his investigation, as much in the later as in the earlier work. Thus in the later work he is not seeking to defend a non-representationalist as distinct from a representationalist view of language. Rather he presupposes, as in the earlier work, that we do represent the world in language and seeks to elucidate what this involves. Thus it is spurious to make a contrast, as Rorty does, between representation on the one hand and use or function on the other. For Wittgenstein employs the notion of use or function precisely in order to elucidate how we represent the world, there being no contradiction in supposing that representing the world is amongst the various uses or functions of language.

These points will be clarified if we bring out some of the essential differences between the earlier and the later work. In the *Tractatus*, Wittgenstein assumed that we can use language to represent a state of affairs only if this representation has logical form. Moreover, logical form is prior to the use of language being inherent in the world itself. In other words, in any particular representation, there is presupposed a more general connection between language and the world, which shows itself in the intelligible use of language, in our being able to represent a particular state of affairs. Later he came to recognise that the idea of a connection between language and the world, so far from being explanatory, needs itself to be elucidated. Moreover, when we consider the matter, we find that there are *various* connections between language and the world and that these arise only because human beings in various ways are already in contact with the world through their activities. It is these activities which are basic to the investigation, for it is they which are elucidatory. Thus the connection between language and the world is elucidated by the relations between language and those activities. The connection is then made, for those activities are already related to the world. The point is evident in the development of the child. The only child who acquires a language is one who is already active in the world, who, in however primitive a form, already exhibits powers of discrimination or knowledge. Thus it is not through language that the child is related to the world; one might say that language is related to the world through the child. In other words, language is a development, an outgrowth, of the child's relations to the world, permitting of course still further relations, which the child could not otherwise have acquired. It will be noted how closely akin these views are to those of Peirce.

Now it seems equally misleading to call this account of language either representationalist or non-representationalist. Wittgenstein, it is true, is not claiming that the world is on the other side of language, which comes between the world and ourselves. His point is that if we were not already related to the world, there would be no language. But to call his account non-representationalist would suggest that he holds the opposing view, namely, that the world is not on the other side but on this one, thereby perpetuating the delusion that it must be on one side or the other. Moreover, it would suggest that Wittgenstein *denies* language can represent an independent world, when in fact he is elucidating how it does so. It does so through its *use* in our lives, through its *function* in our activities, through the ways, in short, that it enters into our relations with the world.

The above points have been well expressed by the literary critic M. H. Abrams. It is worth quoting his words not simply for their own sake but because they would serve to express the views of either Wittgenstein or of Classical Pragmatism and therefore exhibit the connection between the two. Abrams had been criticised by Hillis Miller, an exponent of Deconstructionism, for holding that a literary or philosophical text has an unequivocal meaning 'corresponding' to the various entities it 'represents' in 'a more or less straightforward mirroring'. Abrams replied as follows:

I don't know how I gave Miller the impression that my 'theory of language is implicitly mimetic', a 'straightforward mirror' of the reality it reflects, except on the assumption he seems to me to share with Derrida, and which seems to me obviously mistaken, that all views of language which are not in the deconstructive mode are mimetic views. My view of language, as it happens, is by and large functional and pragmatic: language, whether spoken or written, is the use of a great variety of speech-acts to accomplish a great diversity of human purposes; only one of these many purposes is to assert something about a state of affairs; and such a linguistic assertion does not mirror, but serves to direct attention to related aspects of that state of affairs.

(Abrams 1988: 266)

NINETEEN-EIGHTY-FOUR

We must now come to a final estimate of Rorty's views. In doing so, we may put them to a test which has been suggested by Peter van Inwagen. In his *Metaphysics*, he mentions Orwell's *Nineteen-Eighty-Four* as the greatest of all attacks on anti-Realism (Van Inwagen 1993: 69). The novel contains, at its climax, a philosophical discussion between the Realist Winston Smith and the anti-Realist O'Brien. Van Inwagen suggests that the following question should be addressed to an anti-Realist: How does your position differ from O'Brien's?

The test is a fair one since Rorty discusses Orwell's book, in some detail, in *Contingency, Irony and Solidarity* (1989: 169–88). It will be worth considering what he says.

According to Rorty, Orwell is an artist whose aim is essentially practical. Thus his aim in *Nineteen-Eighty-Four* (1949) is to redescribe the Soviet Union. By this Rorty means that Orwell sought to give a persuasive account of the Soviet Union, which differed from the account accepted at the time by liberals in the West. In this, he was brilliantly successful, for he broke the hold of 'Bolshevik propaganda' on the liberal imagination. This aim, however, is very largely achieved in the first two-thirds of the novel. In the last third we are offered something different. Here Orwell is concerned not with current politics, but with how an intellectual might conceive of himself in a world where liberalism has no possible future. Thus, in this section it is a particular intellectual – O'Brien – who becomes the dominant character. In short, Orwell had 'two jobs' – 'redescribing Russia and inventing O'Brien'.

Now Rorty's concern is rather with the second job than with the first. He says, however, that the success of the first is not due, as is commonly thought, to Orwell's having revealed to the liberal mind certain awkward facts or moral truths. To accept this is to subscribe to the Realist or 'windowpane' view of literature. It is to suppose, in short, that a book, like a windowpane, allows us to look through it straight at reality. But Orwell's success is an altogether different matter. 'It is a matter of playing off scenarios against contrasting scenarios, projects against alternative projects, descriptions against redescriptions'. Such redescriptions, he argues (Rorty 1989: 174), are not like windowpanes. 'On the contrary, they are the sort of thing which only writers with very special talents, writing at just the right moment in just the right way are able to bring off.'

We may note, once again, how readily Rorty assumes that the alternatives he offers are exhaustive. As an explanation for Orwell's success we have to choose between his having revealed certain facts or moral truths and his special ability as a writer. Yet it seems obvious that his success may depend on both. Thus, the explanation for his success may lie in his special ability as a writer to express certain facts and moral truths which otherwise we should have been inclined to overlook or to evade.

As I have said, however, Rorty's main concern is with the final section. In what does its success consist? It consists, first, in Orwell's showing that the distinctive evil which is found in O'Brien is a real possibility and, second, in his showing that there are no metaphysical forces to prevent our going O'Brien's way. In short, 'there is nothing deep inside each of us, no common human nature, no built-in human solidarity, to use as a moral reference point' (Rorty 1989: 177).

As evidence for this latter interpretation, Rorty quotes two passages from Orwell. The first is taken from a column he wrote in 1944:

> The fallacy is to believe that under a dictatorial government you can be free *inside*. . . . The greatest mistake is to imagine that the human being is an autonomous individual. The secret freedom which you can supposedly enjoy under a despotic government is nonsense, because your thoughts are never entirely your own. Philosophers, writers, artists, even scientists, not only need encouragement and an audience, they need constant stimulation from other people. . . . Take away freedom of speech, and the creative faculties dry up.

The second is taken from *Nineteen-Eighty-Four* itself:

> [Winston's] heart sank as he thought of the enormous power arrayed against him, the ease with which any Party intellectual would

overthrow him in debate....And yet he was in the right!...The obvious, the silly, and the true had got to be defended. Truisms are true, hold on to that! The solid world exists, its laws do not change. Stones are hard, water is wet, objects unsupported fall towards the earth's centre. With the feeling that he was speaking to O'Brien, and also that he was setting forth an important axiom, [Winston] wrote: 'Freedom is the freedom to say that two plus two make four. If that is granted, all else follows.'

Rorty's comment on those passages is that they endorse his own view, according to which human values depend on contingent circumstances and neither have nor require metaphysical support. Thus it does not matter whether it is objectively true that two plus two is four; all that matters is that one has the freedom to say so.

> I suggest that the two passages can both be seen as saying that it does not matter whether 'two plus two is four' is true, much less whether this truth is 'subjective' or 'corresponds to external reality'. All that matters is that if you do believe it, you can say it without getting hurt. In other words, what matters is your ability to talk to other people about what seems to you true, not what is in fact true. If we take care of freedom, truth can take care of itself. If we are ironic enough about our final vocabularies, and curious enough about everyone else's, we do not have to worry about whether we are in direct contact with moral reality or whether we are blinded by ideology, or whether we are being weakly 'relativistic'.
>
> (Rorty 1989: 176–7)

Now that is a remarkable interpretation of those passages. It will be useful to reconsider them. In the passage from *Nineteen-Eighty-Four*, Winston Smith knows that the powers of persuasion belong wholly to the Party. Even though he were in the right, he could not prove it. Indeed the Party could easily convince everyone that he was in the wrong. Nevertheless some things are true whether or not people believe them. Here there is a limit to persuasion, and therefore to the power of the party. In this we have a condition for freedom. But in that case – so the argument might run – why is it so necessary to defend those things? Whatever the Party says, we still have the freedom to believe them. It is the other quotation which provides the answer to that argument. Although there are some things which are true whether or not people believe them, the Party has the power to destroy one's belief in such things. It has the power, in short, to destroy *the sense of objective truth*. Here is the central theme, indeed the central horror, of *Nineteen-Eighty-Four*. The book is by no means divisible into distinct sections, for it is this horror which pervades the whole and provides its unifying theme. Moreover, we must note that the apprehension of this horror is itself a mark of objective truth, a sign of its reality; and it is its power to evoke that apprehension which makes *Nineteen-Eighty-Four* a great philosophical novel, the greatest of all attacks on anti-Realism.

Rorty, by contrast, holds that the evil with which Orwell is specifically concerned is that of cruelty. This is embodied in the figure of O'Brien. Moreover, O'Brien's cruelty takes a specific form in that he seeks to inflict not so much physical suffering as humiliation. It is Orwell's treatment of humiliation which, for Rorty, constitutes his second great achievement in the final section. To appreciate this achievement, we need to recognise that the essence of humiliation is not to make a person scream in agony 'but to use that agony in such a way that when the agony is over she cannot reconstitute herself'. That is the point of O'Brien's making Winston affirm that two and two are five and his making him betray Julia, whom he loves. His aim is to get Winston into a condition where he cannot 'reconstitute himself'. Rorty emphasises that truth and falsity have nothing to do with this process. 'Truth and falsity drop out'. Thus O'Brien might have broken Winston by getting him to believe what was in fact true. It might have been, for example, that Julia was really a secret agent for the Party. In getting Winston to believe this, O'Brien would still have humiliated him, for he would have made him incapable of 'weaving a coherent web of belief and desire'. The effect of this is to undermine the self, which is the essence of humiliation. Rorty explains what he means as follows:

> Getting somebody to deny a belief for no reason is a first step towards making her incapable of having a self because she becomes incapable of weaving a coherent web of belief and desire. It makes her irrational in a quite precise sense. She is unable to give a reason for her belief that fits together with her other beliefs. She becomes irrational not in the sense that she has lost contact with reality but in the sense that she can no longer rationalise – no longer justify herself to herself.

> (1989: 178)

Now there is an obvious difficulty with this analysis. Winston does reconstitute himself. He does so by accepting the beliefs of the Party and coming to love Big Brother. To many this is the most horrifying part of the book. What makes it horrifying is not that Winston has failed to justify himself to himself, but that he succeeds in doing so by losing all contact with reality.

We can summarise Rorty's account by saying that for him the issue of objective truth does not arise in *Nineteen-Eighty-Four*. The book is wholly concerned with exposing political evils and with enforcing the liberal view that cruelty is the worst thing one can do to a person. This view of course is not peculiar to Rorty. When *Nineteen-Eighty-Four* first appeared its significance was widely assumed to lie in its implicit criticism of the Soviet system. This interpretation seems to me to illustrate the truth that a partial account of a book can often be more misleading than one which is completely false. It is obvious that Orwell was critical of the Soviet system. But the view that his criticism exhausts the aim of the book leads easily to the view that the evils that Orwell criticised have their origin in the Soviet Union and this, in its turn, to the view that those evils are found only over there and not over here. That, however, is the opposite of what Orwell intended. His aim was to show that the Soviet system merely exhibited in an acute form evils which are found everywhere. It is well known, for example, that Orwell was influenced in writing his book by James Burnham's *Managerial Revolution* (1945). It is one of the main theses in Burnham's book that the growth of managerial power is found throughout the industrialised nations, being found as readily in the capitalist system as in the communist. Moreover, the state which Orwell portrays differs in a number of ways from the one in the Soviet Union. For example, the Party exerts its control only over its members, who are a minority of the population. The proles, or working class, are left in comparative freedom.

> Heavy physical work, the care of home and children, petty quarrels with neighbours, films, football, beer, and above all, gambling filled up the horizons of their minds... There was a vast amount of criminality in London, a whole world-within-a-world of thieves, bandits, prostitutes, drug-peddlers and racketeers of every description; but since it all happened among the proles themselves, it was of no importance.... The sexual puritanism of the Party was not imposed upon them. Promiscuity went unpunished, divorce was permitted. For that matter, even religious worship would have been permitted if the proles had shown any sign of needing or wanting it.
>
> (Orwell 1949: 74–5)

These are conditions one more readily associates with a free-market system than with totalitarian Socialism. Nevertheless the corruption of power has certain effects which are common to the proles as well as to members of the Party. For example, they have no sense of the past. Winston goes amongst them, hoping to find someone who remembers the time before the Party came into power. He does find one old man who lived at that time and has certain memories. But they are fragmentary, have no connection with one another and make no overall sense.

The theme of *Nineteen-Eighty-Four* is the effect of power in controlling the mind, in corrupting language and in destroying the sense of objective truth. As such, its theme is timeless. It is identical, for example, with that of Plato's *Gorgias*. In both works, we see how the sense of objective truth is impaired, through the effect of power in eliminating the difference between truth and persuasiveness. Moreover, the implication of both is that those who diminish the sense of objective truth help to remove the conditions, not simply for truth, but also for freedom. For they help to deliver us over to those who find in the exercise of power their only value.

Now O'Brien is just such a person. It will be useful to consider his views as they appear in the discussion with Winston. Winston, of course, believes that there is objective truth, which sets a limit to the power of the party. O'Brien draws his attention to one of the Party's slogans: 'Whoever controls the past controls the future; whoever controls the present controls the past.' He then asks Winston whether he believes the past has real existence. Winston says he does.

> O'Brien smiled faintly. 'You are no metaphysician, Winston' he said. 'Until this moment you had never considered what is meant by existence. I will put it more precisely. Does the past exist concretely, in space? Is there somewhere or other a place, a world of solid objects, where the past is still happening?'
> 'No.'
> 'Then where does the past exist, if at all?'
> 'In records. It is written down.'
> 'In records. And...?'
> 'In the mind. In human memories.'
> 'In memory. Very well, then. We, the Party, control all records, and we control all memories. Then we control the past, do we not?'
>
> (ibid.: 260)

O'Brien's point may be rephrased. There is no past, as it were, 'out there', against which to measure memories and records. For the past, by definition, no longer exists and whether it *has* existed will depend on those memories or records. It follows that the truth about the past will be internal to those memories or records, a matter of how they cohere rather than of what they represent. The point is the same as Rorty's. But what if there are different and incompatible ways of making the memories or records cohere? Which story, then, is the true one? Rorty's view is that it will depend on which story prevails. That also is O'Brien's view. It follows that the truth about the past will be whatever the Party says it is. For it is the Party which has the power to make its story prevail.

O'Brien then explains how the Party differs from other persecutors. The others have killed their heretics, turning them into martyrs and therefore perpetuating the heresy. The Party, by contrast, reconstitutes its enemies. It waits until they have recreated themselves in its image:

> We are not content with negative obedience, nor even the most abject submission. When finally you surrender to us, it must be of your own free will. We do not destroy the heretic because he resists us: so long as he resists us we never destroy him. We convert him, we capture his inner mind, we reshape him. We burn all evil and illusion out of him; we bring him over to our side, not in appearance, but genuinely, heart and soul.
>
> (ibid.: 267)

But what is the aim of the Party? To what end does it seek power?

> The Party seeks power entirely for its own sake. We are not interested in the good of others; we are interested solely in power. Not wealth or luxury or long life or happiness: only power, pure power. (ibid.)

It is of course a familiar view that the will to power is the source of all value. But O'Brien differs from those others, such as Nietzsche, who have held this view, because the will which he takes as the source of value is that of the Party not his own. In defence of his view, he argues, not unreasonably, that his own will cannot prevail. For, one day, he will die. But there is no reason why the Party should ever die.

In short, man is the measure of all things and the measure of all other men is the Party. One may grasp the consistency of the position. But the position itself, is it not crazy? How can the Party be the measure of reality? The whole universe exists independently, not simply of the Party but also of man.

'Before man' [says O'Brien] 'there was nothing. After man, if he could come to an end, there would be nothing. Outside man there is nothing.'

'But the whole universe is outside us. Look at the stars! Some of them are a million light-years away. They are out of our reach for ever?'

'What are the stars?' said O'Brien indifferently. 'They are bits of fire a few kilometres away. We could reach them if we wanted to. Or we could blast them out. The earth is the centre of the universe. The sun and stars go around it.'

Winston made another convulsive movement. This time he did not say anything. O'Brien continued as though answering a spoken objection:

'For certain purposes, of course, that is not true. When we navigate the ocean, or when we predict an eclipse, we often find it convenient to assume that the earth goes round the sun and that the stars are millions upon millions of kilometres away. But what of it? Do you suppose it is beyond us to produce a dual system of astronomy?'

(ibid.: 278)

The position seems consistent. As Rorty argues, the aim of science is not to represent a world independent of itself. Truth in science is relative to its standards. It follows that what is true in science may be false in some other system, such as politics, where the standards are different. There is no reality, independent of both systems, which could serve as a measure of either.

We have returned to where we started. Truth is not 'out there'; it is relative to human practice. Grant that point and everything else follows.

We are applying the test suggested by Van Inwagen: How does your position differ from O'Brien's? In the case of Rorty, the answer seems to be that in his philosophy he does not differ at all. He and O'Brien differ in their politics but in their philosophy they are indistinguishable.

Summary and conclusion

As Peirce remarked, we may discern in any succession of events the interplay of continuity and discontinuity. The point is well illustrated by the history of Pragmatism itself. The ideas of Peirce, being the product of genius, have their fruitful implications and admit of indefinite development. That is the line of continuity. But it is not along this line that Pragmatism has developed. The element of discontinuity, the contingencies of history, have had their effect. Thus, Peirce's ideas became influential not through their inherent logic but through the misunderstandings of James. It was a matter of chance, not of logic. The development of Pragmatism from Peirce to Rorty exhibits a movement between two sets of ideas which are directly opposed to each other. The former may be taken as a paradigm of Realism; the latter of Anti-Realism. The two have nothing in common except that they are called by the same name. It is evidently not through any continuity in the ideas that this development can be explained. It is a phenomenon of history, subject to its contingencies. Amongst the most prominent of these contingencies is the body of ideas which happened to be dominant in the period. This body of ideas was itself the product of contingency, being united rather by association than by logic. As we have seen, there is no logical connection between Empiricism and the success of science. Yet together they formed the central element in that body of ideas. Having become dominant, the body tended to absorb into itself any other ideas which appeared in its vicinity. It is through this process that Peirce's ideas, during the course of a century, have been turned into their opposite.

The study of history has as its supreme merit that it makes apparent these contingencies, so that one is the better prepared to follow the line of truth, as distinct from that of fashion. Looking through some journal, half a century old, in search of an article by a famous figure, one comes across half a dozen unknown or half-remembered names. Glancing, at first idly, through what they have written, one often finds one's attention held. Sometimes one continues to read not simply with interest but with fascination. The latest theory, one discovers, is not as new as one thought. Indeed one sometimes discovers not simply the latest theory but also its refutation. Returning to the famous figure, one wonders why it is he, rather than the other person, who is now remembered. The point is well illustrated, once again, by the history of Pragmatism. Why, for example, is Morris Cohen no longer read? In the 1920s and '30s, he was one of the most famous American philosophers and he was perhaps the first to appreciate Peirce at his real worth. The answer is that he lost his reputation in the 1940s, after the arrival in America of the Logical Positivists. The arrival of the Logical Positivists is to be explained by the political crisis in Europe during the late 1930s. Cohen's loss of reputation, in short, is to be explained by reference to historical contingency not by reference to the truth.

But there are elements also of continuity. These we may find in James's two masterpieces and in the philosophical psychology of Dewey. At the centre of this work is Peirce's idea that the relation between mind and body is mediated through the functioning of the organism as a whole. This idea is developed so as to avoid the extremes of Rationalism on the one hand and Materialism on the other. Rationalism attributes to the mind powers which go beyond its natural conditions, treating the mind as though it stood over and against the world; Materialism eliminates the distinctive powers of the mind by assimilating it to its natural conditions. For both James and Dewey, the mind cannot be extracted from the conditions which give rise to it but neither can it be assimilated to them. Without stimuli from the surrounding world, the mind cannot function but it responds to those stimuli according to its distinctive powers.

Moreover, both thinkers are at one with Peirce in denying that the workings of the mind can be explained by mechanical causation. As Dewey argued, even in its simplest responses the mind is purposive, so that the effect any stimulus has on the mind will depend in part on how the mind takes that stimulus. Yet, again, the mind though *distinctive* in nature is not *discontinuous* with it. Thus it is an error to suppose – in the manner of Descartes – that the mind can wholly reconstitute its own beliefs and arrive at the truth entirely through its own powers. The mind acquires knowledge only because it is already related to the world in innumerable ways that are not of its own making, this being evident once the knowing subject is viewed not in abstraction but in his practical context.

Here we have a body of work entirely consistent with that of Peirce, forming, together with it, what may be termed Classical Pragmatism. Yet at the same time, James and Dewey were framing a general philosophy incompatible with that work. We have noted the point especially in our account of Dewey. His psychology is repeatedly in conflict with the scientism which is at the centre of his philosophy. In his psychology, he is opposed to the *Weltanschauung* of his age; in his philosophy, he is in conformity with it. Thus, both he and James, in their psychology, make sense of the mind by showing how its distinctive powers arise within the order of nature. The idea of purpose, which is at the centre of this psychology is irreducible, as Peirce showed, to empirical sequence. Their psychology is unintelligible unless it presupposes that the mind partakes of an order which transcends it. Yet James, in his philosophy, reduces all order to empirical sequence and Dewey holds that there can be nothing in reality which transcends the categories of the human mind.

This philosophy may be termed the second pragmatism. It was cultivated by Dewey and achieved a full flowering in the work of Rorty. My argument has been that it is not a new philosophy but is a variation on Positivism, a form of extreme Empiricism. It is in conflict with the first Pragmatism, not at incidental points, but in its essentials.

Notes

1 PEIRCE: HIS BACKGROUND AND HIS ACCOUNT OF INQUIRY

1 See Peirce's review of Frazer's 'The Works of George Berkeley' in Houser and Kluesel (eds) (1992(I): 86). It is a convention amongst commentators to quote Peirce by reference to his *Collected Papers*, supplying the relevant volume and section and mentioning no other details. This is a device more convenient to the writer than to the reader, who is not likely to have easy access to the eight volumes of Peirce's *Collected Papers*. This has been pointed out by I. Scheffler and I have followed him in attempting to vary my references.

2 For a similar assessment of Edwards and Peirce compare Murray G. Murphey (1993: vi).

3 Murray G. Murphey's arguments for this dating seem to me persuasive (see Murphey 1993: 301).

4 The philosophers of this school have been badly misrepresented during the past century. The leading members of the school, Reid and Hamilton, both seem to have influenced Peirce. Indeed he sometimes referred to his own philosophy as Critical Commonsensism. His relation to the school deserves more detailed study than it has received.

5 The articles are as follows: 'Questions concerning certain faculties claimed for man'; 'Some consequences of four incapacities'; 'The fixation of belief'; 'How to make our ideas clear' (see Volume V of *The Collected Papers* edited by Charles Hartshorne and Paul Weiss; also Buchler (ed.) (1950) *The Philosophy of Peirce*).

6 More strictly, the mind is passive in receiving *simple* ideas. As my colleague, I. C. Tipton, has pointed out, the mind for Locke is active in forming *complex* ones.

7 'A person may, it is true, in the course of his studies find reason to doubt what he began by believing; but in that case he doubts because he has a positive reason for it and not on account of the Cartesian maxim' (see Peirce, 'Some Consequences of Four Incapacities' in Buchler (ed.) 1950: 229).

8 For Peirce's criticism of intuition, in the Rationalist sense, see his 'Questions concerning certain faculties claimed for man' in *The Collected Papers* (1935).

2 PEIRCE: THE THEORY OF SIGNS

1 This, as we shall see, is a point that had a great influence on later Pragmatists, such as Dewey and G. H. Mead.
2 There is a brilliant discussion of these issues in the work of the French philosopher and scientist A. A. Cournot – see *An Essay on the Foundations of Our Knowledge* (Cournot 1956). There are striking resemblances between Cournot's work and Peirce's. They were contemporaries but, so far as I am aware, arrived at their views independently of one another.
3 See *The Collected Papers* (Peirce 1935: 121). It is important to note that 'practical conduct' in this quotation *includes* intellectual practice and is not intended to contrast with it.
4 As we shall see, Peirce in his earlier work fell into this error. It is worth noting that Wittgenstein fell back into the error even in his later work. In his argument against a private language, for example, he refers at a crucial point to criteria where he should have referred to a practice. For a criticism of him on this point see A. J. Ayer's *The Idea of a Private Language* (1954).

3 PEIRCE: PRAGMATISM AND WILLIAM JAMES

1 'The true', to put it very briefly, is only the expedient in the way of our thinking, just as 'the right' is only the expedient in the way of our behaving. Expedient in almost any fashion; and expedient in the long run and on the whole of course . . . '. See 'Pragmatism' in *Pragmatism in Focus* (James 1992: 109): this contains the whole text of James's lectures together with critical articles by various authors.

5 JAMES: BACKGROUND AND THE PRINCIPLES OF PSYCHOLOGY

1 As we shall see, these are points which were emphasised by later pragmatists

10 DEWEY: RADICAL EMPIRICISM

1 The label was invented by A. E. Murphy.
2 Lovejoy is quoting Dewey and A. E. Murphy, respectively.

13 RORTY: THE HISTORY OF PHILOSOPHY

1 It may be worth mentioning that Ghazali also anticipated many of the essential points in Hume's famous analysis of causation.

Bibliography

Abrams, M. H. (1988) 'The deconstructive angel' in D. Lodge (ed.) *Modern Criticism and Theory*, London: Longman.

Annas, J. and Barnes, J. (1985) *The Modes of Scepticism*, Cambridge: Cambridge University Press.

Ayer, A. J. (1954) *The Idea of a Private Language*, London: Aristotelian Society.

—— (1936) *Language, Truth and Logic*, London: Gollancz.

Barzun, J. (1983) *A Stroll with William James*, Chicago: Chicago University Press.

Bernstein R. J. (ed.) (1960) *On Experience, Nature and Freedom*, New York: Bobbs-Merrill.

Boutroux, E. (1912) *Science and Religion in Contemporary Philosophy*, London: Longman.

Brent, J. (1993) *Charles Sanders Peirce*, Indiana: Indiana University Press.

Buchler, J. (ed.) (1950) *The Philosophy of Peirce*, London: Routledge & Kegan Paul.

Burnham, J. (1945) *The Managerial Revolution*, London: Putnam.

Cohen, M. (1931) *Reason and Nature*, London: Kegan Paul.

—— (1940) 'Some difficulties in Dewey's anthropocentric naturalism', *Philosophical Review* 49: 209–10.

Comte, A. (1974) *The Essential Comte*, S. Andreski (ed.) London: Croom Helm.

Cournot, A. A. (1956) *An Essay on the Foundations of Knowledge*, trans. M. H. Moore, New York: Liberal Arts Press.

Dewey, J. (1896) 'The reflex arc concept in psychology' in *Contributions to Philosophy* (vol. I, no. 1), Chicago: Chicago University Press.

—— (1897) *My Pedagogic Creed*, New York: Kellog.

—— (1910) *How We Think*, Boston: Heath.

—— (1916) *Democracy and Education*, New York: Macmillan.

—— (1917) 'The need for a recovery of philosophy', in R. J. Bernstein (ed.) *On Experience, Nature and Freedom*, New York: Bobbs-Merrill.

—— (1920) *Reconstruction in Philosophy*, New York: Holt.

—— (1925) *Experience and Nature*, Chicago: Open Court.

—— (1934) *Art as Experience*, New York: Minton Balch.

—— (1938) *Logic: The Theory of Inquiry*, New York: Holt.

—— (1960) *On Experience, Nature and Freedom*, R. J. Bernstein (ed.) New York: Bobbs-Merrill.

Feuerbach, L. (1853) *The Essence of Christianity*, trans. M. Evans, London: Chapman.

Flower, E. and Murphey, M. (1977) *A History of Philosophy in America*, New York: Capricorn Books.

Gallie, W. B. (1952) *PeIrce and Pragmatism*, Harmondsworth: Penguin.

Hamilton, W. (1858–60) *Lectures on Metaphysics and Logic* (4 vols), Edinburgh: Longman.

Hauser N. and Keleusal C. (eds) (1992) *The Essential Peirce*, Indiana: Indiana University Press.

Hofstadter, R. (1963) *Anti-Intellectualism in American Life*, New York: Knopf.

Hook, S. (1961) *The Quest for Being*, New York: St Martin's Press.

Hookway, C. (1985) *Peirce*, London: Routledge & Kegan Paul.

James, W. (1904) *The Principles of Psychology* (2 vols), New York: Longmans.

—— (1912) *Essays in Radical Empiricism*, New York: Longmans.

—— (1918) 'The will to believe' in *Selected Papers on Philosophy*, London: Everyman.

—— (1961) *The Varieties of Religious Experience*, Glasgow: Fontana.

—— (1992) *Pragmatism in Focus*, D. Olin (ed.) London: Routledge.

Lao Tzu (1985) *Tao Te Ching*, trans. R. Willhelm, Harmondsworth: Arkana.

Lovejoy, A. O. (1930) *The Revolt against Dualism*, Illinois: Open Court.

Mead, G. H. (1934) *Mind, Self and Society*, C. W. Morris (ed.) Cambridge MA: Harvard University Press.

Murphey, M. (1993) *The Development of Peirce's Philosophy*, Indianapolis: Hackett.

Murphy, J. P. (1990) *Pragmatism from Peirce to Davidson*, Boulder: Worldview Press.

Orwell, G. (1949) *Nineteen-Eighty-Four*, Harmondsworth: Penguin 1989.

Peirce, C. S. (1878) 'How to make our ideas clear' in *The Collected papers* Charles Hartshorne and Paul Weiss (eds) Cambridge MA: Harvard University Press.

—— (1935) *The Collected Works* (8 vols), Charles Hartshorne and Paul Weiss (eds) Cambridge MA: Harvard University Press.

Perry, R. B. (1958) *In the Spirit of William James*, Indiana: Indiana University Press.

Popkin, R. (1960) *The History of Scepticism from Erasmus to Descartes*, Assen: Von Gorcum.

Pratt, J. B. (1992) 'Truth and its verification' in *Pragmatism in Focus*, D. Olin (ed.) London: Routledge.

Putnam, H. (1995a) *Pragmatism*, Oxford: Blackwell.

—— (1995b) *Words and Life*, Cambridge MA: Harvard University Press.

Quine, W. V. (1953) *From A Logical Point of View*, Cambridge MA: Harvard University Press.

Reichenbach, H. (1951) *The Rise of Scientific Philosophy*, California: University of California Press.

Rorty, R. (1982) *Consequences of Pragmatism*, Sussex: Harvester Press.

—— (1989) *Contingency, Irony and Solidarity*, Cambridge: Cambridge University Press.

—— (1990) *Philosophy and the Mirror of Nature*, Oxford: Blackwell.

Santayana, G. (1913) *Winds of Doctrine*, London: Dent.

Scheffler, I. (1974) *Four Pragmatists*, London: Routledge & Kegan Paul.

Schiller, F. C. S. (1924) *Problems of Belief*, London: Hodder and Stoughton.

Skorupsky, J. (1993) *English Language Philosophy*, 1750–1945, Oxford: OUP.

Smith, N. K. (1924) *Prolegomena to an Idealist Theory of Knowledge*, London: Macmillan.

Van Inwagen, P. (1993) *Metaphysics*, Oxford: Blackwell.

Watt, W. Montgomery (1963) *Muslim Intellectual: A Study of Al-Ghazzali*, Edinburgh: Edinburgh University Press.

White, M. (1949) *Social Thought in America: The Revolt Against Formalism*, Boston: Beacon.

Wittgenstein, L. (1958) *Philosophical Investigations*, trans. G. E. M. Anscombe, Oxford: Blackwell.

—— (1961) *Tractatus Logico-Philosophicus*, trans. D. F. Pears and B. F. McGuiness, London: Routledge & Kegan Paul.

Index

empirical method 85–6
Empiricism 43, 229, 231; Dewey 126,
    149, 150, 151 (science and
    Empiricism 152–7, 165–74); James
    43, 44, 47, 80–1, 128–9; knowledge
    13, 14, 21, 146, 149; law 29–31;
    mind 79, 128–9; Quine and
    dogmas of 51–2; Radical *see*
    Radical Empiricism; sensation and
    emotion 80–1; sense experience 8;
    thought 77; tough philosophers 44
ends and means 131–3, 137
epiphenomenalism 71–2
epistemology 184–9; and
    hermeneutics 193–200; and
    philosophy of language 190–2; and
    philosophy of psychology 189–90;
    see also knowledge
Eucharist, Catholic doctrine of 37,
    38–9
everyday knowledge 99–100
evolution of the species 61, 128
examples 103–4
existence 53, 63–4; Dewey 169,
    170–1; qualia and 57–8
experience: art as 171–2; Dewey
    149–52, 155–6, 163–5, 171–2;
    James's Radical Empiricism 85,
    86–7; knowledge and 12, 13,
    163–5; psychologist's fallacy 77;
    reality and 41–2, 155–6; religious
    108–9; sensory and order 7–9;
    theory, verification and 175–6
experiment 153–4
explanation 185–6, 187

facial neuralgia 4
fact: logic and 187; objective and
    appearance of objects 19–21;
    reference to facts 190–2; value and
    105–6, 134–5
faith: doubt and 95–6, 109; and gift of
    healing 117–18; and verification
    92–3; *see also* beliefs, religion
Fallibilism 16–21, 39
fascism 204
Feigl, Herbert 175
Feuerbach, Ludwig 145
Feyerabend, Paul 190, 192

fideism, principle of 46
final vocabulary 206
Flower, E. 43, 126
Fodor, Jerry 189
forced options 92–3
forms/universals 212–13
Foucault, Michel 173
freedom 222–3, 225
Frege, Gottlob 24
French Revolution 201, 203
Freud, Sigmund 113
Fry, Roger 171

Galilei, Galileo 154, 156; Bellarmine's
    criticism 195–6, 197–8; and
    Copernican theory 92, 155;
    experiment 153–4
Gallie, W.B. 24, 29, 32, 59, 62, 65;
    sign relation 25
Gardiner, Colonel 115–16
generality: ideas 74–5; Peirce
    (cosmology 60–1, 63; First category
    55–6; law 30–1; theory of signs
    26–7, 28, 30–1)
genetic fallacy 105–6
genuine options 92–3
geometry 137
Gestalt psychology 76
Ghazali, Abu Mohammed Al 215–17
God 89, 205; arguments for existence
    of 67–9, 121–3; Edwards 6; James
    94, 108–9, 121–3; Peirce 6–7, 54,
    64, 67–9
Greek thought 217; knowledge 149,
    186; mind-body distinction 179,
    212–14; origins of philosophy 147;
    problem of the criterion 215, 218;
    Sceptics 180, 214, 215, 218;
    science and Empiricism 153, 154,
    155

habit 27; law and 29–35; meaning
    and 13, 32–3, 48
haecceity 12
hallucinations 162–3
Hamilton, William 55–6, 57, 232
healing, gift of 117–18
healthy minded (once-born) religious
    temperament 109–10